DAVID HOFFMAN

LIFE, LETTERS AND LECTURES

AT THE UNIVERSITY OF MARYLAND

1821-1837

DAVID HOFFMAN

LIFE, LETTERS AND LECTURES

AT THE UNIVERSITY OF MARYLAND

1821-1837

EDITED BY
BILL SLEEMAN

Assistant Director for Technical Services
Thurgood Marshall Law Library
The University of Maryland School of Law

THE LAWBOOK EXCHANGE, LTD.
Clark, New Jersey

Copyright © 2011 by Bill Sleeman

ISBN 9781584779834 (hardcover)
ISBN 9781616190897 (paperback)

THE LAWBOOK EXCHANGE, LTD.
33 Terminal Avenue
Clark, New Jersey 07066-1321

*Please see our website for a selection of our other publications
and fine facsimile reprints of classic works of legal history:*
www.lawbookexchange.com

Library of Congress Cataloging-in-Publication Data

David Hoffman : life, letters and lectures at the University of Maryland
1821-1837 / edited by Bill Sleeman.
 p. cm.
 Includes bibliographical references.
 ISBN 978-1-58477-983-4 (hardcover : alk. paper) --
ISBN 978-1-61619-089-7 (pbk. : alk. paper)
 1. Hoffman, David, 1784-1854. 2. Hoffman, David, 1784-1854--
Sources. 3. Hoffman, David, 1784-1854. Course of legal study. 4.
Lawyers--Maryland--Baltimore--Biography. 5. Law--Study and teaching--
United States--History--19th century. I. Sleeman, William.
 KF368.H582D38 2010
 340.092--dc22
 [B]
                            2010030620

Printed in the United States of America on acid-free paper

Contents

Introduction	vii

Part I

David Hoffman: A Biographical Sketch	13
David Hoffman Time Line	53

Part II

Introductory Lectures title page, 1837	59
Syllabus of a Course of Lectures on Law Proposed to be Delivered in the University of Maryland, 1821	61
A Lecture, Introductory to a Course of Lectures Now Delivering in the University of Maryland, 1823	157
An Address to Students of Law in the United States, 1824	233
A Lecture, Being the Second of a Series of Lectures, Introductory to a Course of Lectures Now Delivering in the University of Maryland, 1825	249
A Lecture, Being the Third of a Series of Lectures, Introductory to a Course of Lectures Now Delivering in the University of Maryland, 1826	299
To the Trustees of the University of Maryland in Relation to the Law Chair, 1826	361
A Lecture, Being the Ninth of a Series of Lectures, Introductory to a Course of Lectures Now Delivering in the University of Maryland, 1832	397
Advertisement, October, 1837	439

Part III

What Books Did David Hoffman Own and Read?	445
Auction Catalogue	451

INTRODUCTION

In 1817 Baltimore lawyer David Hoffman presented to local publisher John Coale the elaborate synthesis of Anglo-American legal scholarship that he had been developing. It was his hope that the work - *A Course of Legal Study*[1] - would serve as the key document in creating a new American system of legal education. Hoffman's massive compilation of readings and analysis would do this in part by integrating legal thought, philosophy and scientific method into a program that would be taught through his Law Institute at the recently established University of Maryland.[2] Although never employed in its entirety, even at the University of Maryland, Hoffman's *Course of Legal Study* quickly became one of the most celebrated outlines of formal legal instruction in the United States.[3]

Hoffman's emphasis on detailed study was not unique for its time; the application of a systematic methodology to both formal and private study had already become common in the early 19th century.[4] In point of fact, Hoffman, as suggested by Steve Sheppard in his *History of Legal Education in the United States,* was not unique at all but rather typical of his era and the desire to systematize law and knowledge.[5] What *was* original about the work was his intention to create a system for studying the law and liberal arts as interrelated subjects. This goal is illustrated in the introduction to his 1825 lecture where Hoffman urges his listeners to consider the relationship of "metaphysicks, ethicks and natural law…and how intimately akin they are to the proper studies of the accomplished lawyer."[6] Hoffman's experience as a practitioner had left him with the sense that most of his fellows at the bar, as well as American legislators, lacked both the education and the opportunities necessary to be successful members of the legal community.[7] Like many legal critics in the early 19th century Hoffman believed that it was only through proper guided and methodical training that lawyers and politicians could obtain the skills needed to help them rise above what he saw as the pragmatic needs of day-to-day practice.[8]

His 1817 course and his lectures were designed to answer this shortcoming by offering both practitioners and students alike the chance to acquire a deeper understanding of law, law making and natural philosophy. His method of study would "reclaim the time and labour thus often and unprofitably expended" by law students who chose other methods of approaching the subject, and would lead by its application to a more organized and more scholarly system of law in the United States.[9]

Simultaneous with Hoffman's efforts to attract students to the University of Maryland he also began to publish for public consumption his lectures and addresses on the law. The facsimiles reproduced in this work capture the depth of Hoffman's efforts, his passion and, as the fuller biography demonstrates, his frustrations in trying to create a truly academic orientated community of legal practitioners in a nation that was still developing its own identity.

In 1837 Hoffman compiled these various circulars and lectures as well as several letters and advertisements into a single published volume which is reproduced in Part II.[10] This volume is extremely rare and only one copy, located in the Law Library of the Library of Congress, has been noted by Morris Cohen in his *Bibliography of Early American Law*.[11] This 1837 volume appears to be an effort by Hoffman, as he explains in the Advertisement (which serves as the volume's introduction), to influence the Trustees and to call into question the wisdom of their decision to, as Hoffman claims, break up the law professorship. Here we see Hoffman as he really was, a combative lawyer who at times was both brilliant and self-righteous. In this 1837 compilation he included copies of his letters to the Trustees of the University of Maryland, letters that highlight his disagreements and frustration with both the Trustees and many of his medical school colleagues who sided with the Trustees.

The several lectures reproduced here, which Hoffman included in 1837 to buttress his contention that he had been treated unfairly, were originally published over a span of almost ten years. We do not know exactly how the lectures were first presented although in his 1837 advertisement Hoffman suggests that they may have been delivered to law students and the general community as part of his Institute, perhaps either as a way to raise funds through the purchase of lecture tickets or to raise awareness of his Institute in the larger legal community. The "third introductory lecture" (1826) lends some support to the latter idea as Hoffman claims therein that in his "prelections" he will limit his topics to those introductory to his Law Institute.[12] One puzzling aspect of the lectures is the absence of a fourth through eighth lecture. Were these ever delivered? There is no mention of these in Cohen's *Bibliography* or in any of the other standard bibliographic tools. Given Hoffman's desire to prove his case via this 1837 compilation it is probably safe to assume that had copies of the other lectures existed he most certainly would have included them. It is also interesting to note that none of the lectures reproduced here – although introductory to his Law Institute - appear to directly follow the syllabus of either his 1817 or 1836 *Course of Legal Study*.[13]

The author would like to thank Professors Andy King and Garrett Power of the University of Maryland School of Law and Rich Behles, Historical Librarian, Health Sciences and Human Services Library, The University of Maryland, Baltimore for their careful reading of earlier drafts and their many helpful suggestions. The author also thanks Pamela Bluh, Associate Director for Technical Services, Thurgood Marshall Law Library for her support throughout this project. Finally, thanks to Professor Warren M. Billings for his early interest and encouragement of this project. Errors of fact and analysis are the sole responsibility of the author.

Bill Sleeman
Baltimore
September, 2010

Endnotes

1. David Hoffman, *A Course of Legal Study; Respectfully Addressed to the Students of Law in the United States* (Baltimore: Published by Coale and Maxwell, 1817). Thurgood Marshall Law Library, Special Collections, The University of Maryland School of Law.
2. Ibid., xi - xii.
3. Thomas L. Shaffer, "David Hoffman's Law School Lectures, 1822 - 1833," *Journal of Legal Education*, 32 (1982)," 127.
4. Paul D. Carrington, "The Revolutionary Idea of University Legal Education," *William & Mary Law Review*, 31 (1990): 527. See also: *An Introductory Lecture on the Study of Law: Delivered in the Chapel of Transylvania University, Lexington, Kentucky in 1821* by William Barry for a very similar presentation.
5. Steve Sheppard, *The History of Legal Education in the United States: Commentaries and Primary Sources* (Pasadena, CA.; Hackensack, NJ.: Salem Press, Inc., 1999). v.1, p. 8.
6. Hoffman, *A Lecture being the second of a series of lectures introductory to a course of lectures now delivering in the University of Maryland* (Baltimore: John Toy, 1825), 2.
7. Charles M. Cook, *The American Codification Movement: A Study of Antebellum Legal Reform* (Westport: Greenwood Press,1981), 61.
8. Ibid.
9. Hoffman, *Course of Study*, xv.
10. Unlike the original volume, we have arranged the contents in chronological order here. Also, the resignation letter originally reproduced in the composite volume is now on p. 19.
11. David Hoffman. *Introductory Lectures, and a syllabus of a course of lectures, delivered in the University of Maryland. New re-published in reference to the recent resignation of the medical and law professorships in that institution.* Baltimore, John D. Toy, printer, 1876. [Law Library, The Library of Congress].
12. David Hoffman. *A Lecture, being the third of a series of lectures, introductory to a course of lectures now delivering in the University of Maryland. Published at request of the Faculty of Law*. Baltimore, Printed by J.D. Toy, 1826. [Thurgood Marshall Law Library, The University of Maryland School of Law].
13. Hoffman. *A Course of Legal Study*, 1817 and Hoffman, *A Course of Legal Study*, 1836.

Part One

DAVID HOFFMAN
A Biographical Sketch

Introduction

David Hoffman (1784-1854) has been cast as America's first legal ethicist,[1] as the founder of America's first original method of legal instruction,[2] as a social critic[3] and as a land speculator.[4] His academic interests and publishing efforts ran from legal scholarship[5] to religious history.[6] While each of these aspects of his career is interesting in its own right, little effort has been made to look at Hoffman's life and career as a whole.[7] Despite his talents Hoffman's career was hampered by his difficult personality that often put him at odds with those who were best in a position to help him. This led to frustration on Hoffman's part and bemused tolerance for his peculiarities on the part of his colleagues and friends. Nevertheless his influence on legal education remains strong. This biography will review in individual sections the many facets of Hoffman's life and career in an effort to provide a more complete picture than has previously existed.

Early Years

Not a great deal is known about Hoffman's youth. His father, Peter Hoffman, was a successful merchant who, when not expanding the family mill works, was active in Baltimore and Maryland politics.[8] As the youngest son in a family of twelve children of one of Baltimore's merchant elite, (another brother, Peter, was one of the founders of the Baltimore and Ohio Railroad), David Hoffman grew up in a world that was filled with educational opportunities beyond those available to other young men and an expectation on the part of his family that he would use his education and position to improve his community.[9]

David Hoffman received his college education at St. John's College in Annapolis where he completed the traditional classics based studies in 1802. He left before taking his degree, claiming that the method of education was insufficient for his needs.[10] After leaving St. John's, Hoffman set about obtaining his legal instruction. Although Hoffman makes no mention of where he gained his American legal training it is probable that he "read" the law in a local practitioner's office and then was presented before the Maryland bar after a period of apprentice-like training. This was the most common method of acquiring legal training in early nineteenth century America but was one that offered little intellectual stimulation, a fact lamented by many of his contemporaries.[11] This lack of an intellectual content to his own legal education may have contributed to Hoffman's desire to create a new method of legal education.[12] Some time after completing his apprenticeship Hoffman left Baltimore for London where he planned to study law more thoroughly.[13] Hoffman's desire to learn and to teach would continue throughout his life and eventually he would be granted honorary degrees for his contributions to legal education from both Oxford University and the University of Gottingen in Germany.[14]

A Course of Legal Study - 1817 and beyond

In 1817 Hoffman presented to Baltimore publisher John Coale the lengthy synthesis of Anglo-American legal scholarship that had been occupying his life outside the courtroom. This *Course of Legal Study*[15] quickly became one of the most celebrated outlines of formal legal instruction in the United States.[16] The program was developed with the goal of instituting what Hoffman hoped would be an integrated study of legal thought, philosophy and scientific method to be employed at the recently established University of Maryland (1812).[17]

Hoffman's emphasis on detailed study was not unique for its time; the application of a systematic methodology to both formal

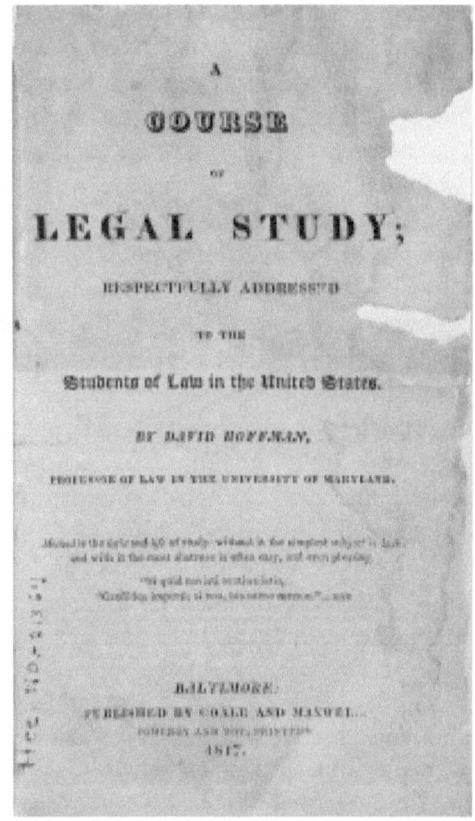

A Course of Legal Study, 1817
(Thurgood Marshall Law Library, Special Collections, The University of Maryland School of Law)

and private intellectual endeavors had already become common in the early 19th century.[18] What was truly original however was his effort to create a system for studying the law and liberal arts as interrelated subjects. This goal is illustrated in the introduction to his 1825 lecture wherein Hoffman urges his listeners to consider the relationship of "metaphysicks, ethicks and natural law…and how intimately akin they are to the proper studies of the accomplished lawyer."[19] Hoffman's professional experience had left him with the sense that most of his fellows at the bar, as well as American legislators, lacked the educational opportunities necessary to be successful members of the legal community.[20] His 1817 course and subsequent efforts were designed to answer this need by offering both practitioners and students alike the chance to acquire a deeper understanding of law, law-making and natural philosophy. The method would, he wrote, "reclaim the time and labour thus often and unprofitably expended" by law students who chose other methods of approaching the subject, and would lead by its application to a more organized and more scholarly system of law in the United States.[21]

Like many legal critics in the early 19th century Hoffman believed that it was only through proper philosophical training that lawyers would obtain the skills needed to help them rise above the pragmatic needs of day-to-day practice.[22] Even so, Hoffman realized that his thirteen "titles" and four "auxiliary subjects" would demand a great investment of time and commitment from students and he attempted to make the demands of his course more palatable by reminding his potential audience, which doubtlessly included practitioners, that their efforts would produce not only a better lawyer but better personal habits:

> Notwithstanding the seemingly great extent of this course, (and certainly we cannot flatter the student with the hope of mastering it with the degree and kind of attention which is usually bestowed on it) let him not be discouraged. What necessarily proves difficult to the desultory and immethodical reader, who comes to his books in the intervals of idleness or dissipation only, and resumes with reluctance what is willingly abandoned on the first call of pleasure, or the first apology of relaxation, may, by a temporary exertion of method and attention, be converted first into a habit, and eventually into a pleasure. [23]

Sticking to the course of study despite the hardships it presented was paramount, in Hoffman's view, if the student were to succeed. However, the student should not be so possessed of a "zeal for study" that he would be caused "to neglect the interests of the few clients they may have."[24] Financial concerns were never far from Hoffman's mind during this period and would remain a concern throughout his career.

Turning to Title Eleven of Hoffman's 1817 work which deals with the laws of the United States provides a ready example of what Hoffman saw as the essential components of American law. In this portion he included as readings sections of the *Federalist*, John Adam's *Defence of the Constitutions of the Government of the United States*, and *Marbury v. Madison*.[25] While his selections are tilted towards political jurisprudence, they clearly reflect the ideals to which Hoffman thought lawyers and legislators ought to be trained in and to which they should aspire.

The University of Maryland

In 1817, three years after securing his appointment as a Professor of Law, Hoffman undertook to have his methodology for teaching law introduced at the University of Maryland.[26] The University, which had been chartered in 1812, was essentially a private corporation controlled by the medical faculty. Though the enabling legislation called for the creation of a law program, a theology school and a college of arts and sciences support for these programs depended upon the interest of the medical department. Despite the General Assembly's willingness to pass legislation authorizing a lottery to raise money for a law program at the University, events moved slowly.[27] During most of the University's early years Hoffman was the only member of the law faculty to devote his full attention and time to the institution. It was not until 1822 and the death of Judge Walter Dorsey, who had been the head of a competing, private law program in Baltimore City, that Hoffman's goal of expanding his Law Institute at the University was realized.[28]

Once Hoffman began his series of lectures at the University of Maryland, almost eight years after he had first approached the faculty, things did not go as he had hoped.[29] The changing environment at the University did not prove to be to the liking of the ever mercurial scholar, who often seemed to be at odds with someone in the university community - either faculty or trustees. The faculty minutes of 1821 provide one example of this. Hoffman, who was then serving as Secretary of the Faculty, called an emergency meeting of all medical and law faculty to discuss the methodology being used to teach in the College of Arts and Sciences. Hoffman had learned that someone was not teaching by lecture but relying instead on readings and discussion! This was, in Hoffman's view, a direct violation of the University's charter. Intriguingly, Hoffman's position was at odds with the complaints he later raised in 1826 in a letter to the Trustees wherein he argued strongly for the need for more than just lectures to be included in legal education.[30] After lengthy debate, the issue of instruction methods was tabled until the faculty committee that had been charged two years earlier with creating by-laws for the university produced a final product - this committee, as most of the faculty was aware, had long been chaired by Hoffman.[31]

Here one gets a glimpse into Hoffman's sometimes self-righteousness approach to dealing with people and situations that did not meet his standards of behavior. To Hoffman, his view was the only one that mattered. Had Hoffman taken the time to discuss his concern with some of his colleagues he might have discovered that the issue was not as great a concern to them as he thought it was, although that is no indication that he would not still have called the meeting. Still, had Hoffman taken a more politic approach he might have avoided a divisive argument with the highly regarded leader of the medical faculty, John Beale Davidge, and have avoided having the work of the "Ordinances Committee" that Hoffman served on questioned about their lack of progress in creating by-laws for the University.[32]

During the late 1820s and through the 1830s some medical faculty members pursued the idea of transferring the University from a private corporation to state control.[33] As word of this effort got out, both Hoffman, whose Institute was now established and underway at the University, and Dr. Nathaniel Potter of the Medical School spoke out in opposition to the plan.[34] By 1835, perhaps in part as a result of this struggle over control, Hoffman had announced his intention to close the Law Institute and leave the University.[35] Hoffman's ties to the University were strong however and his name would appear in circulars for the University's law program for

Baltimore, April 21, 1836

GENTLEMEN:

Having patiently waited for some reply to my repeated communications respecting the embarrasing situation in which you have placed the Law Professorship, and the numerous acts indicative of the most marked hostility to me as Professor,—and finding my usefulness entirely destroyed by those proceedings, and that my just requests have not only been withheld from me, but that *all action* has ceased in respect to me, and the Law Faculty, I have come to the conclusion that I can no longer retain the Professorship, and must submit to the wishes of the Trustees—or a portion of them, however prostrative of my individual rights and those of the Faculty; I therefore beg leave to resign into your hands and do hereby resign my said Professorship of Law.

In regard to my large and just pecuniary claims on the University, secured to me by law, and by every principle of sound morals and of justice between that institution and its earliest and fastest friend (which it is not assuming too much to declare that I have been) I pray leave to say that I have prepared an address to the legislature of Maryland in respect to these claims, and principally as to the violation through me, of the legal and vested rights of the Law Faculty, under the hope that, although now wholly separated from the institution, my claims may be justly settled, and the rights of my successors in the chair of law, be effectually secured from further encroachments.

I am, gentlemen, your obd't,

DAVID HOFFMAN.

To the TRUSTEES OF THE
UNIVERSITY OF MARYLAND.

☞ No notice was ever taken of the foregoing letter of resignation, nor had the writer any means of knowing whether it had been received, until the recent appointment of a new professor was published in our papers, more than *fourteen months* after!! Which appointment, as I have understood, has *not been accepted*, or *if* accepted, has been since resigned!

DAVID HOFFMAN.

BALTIMORE, *September*, 1837.

Letters to the Trustees, The University of Maryland, 1836, 1837
(Law Library, The Library of Congress)

several more years.[36] In 1839 he was persuaded to serve on a faculty committee that was charged with drafting a response to the State's efforts to take over the University.[37]

The final cause of Hoffman's decision to leave the University of Maryland remains a mystery.[38] Based on his published *Letter to the Trustees* we do know that at least part of his final decision to break with the University was his struggle with the University Trustees and medical faculty over control of the University of Maryland and their interference in how his Institute was conducted. Moreover, his financial situation at this point in his life was doubtlessly troubling - Hoffman claimed to have spent $20,000 dollars of his own money on the program, an extraordinary sum – if accurate – and one that would have been impossible to recoup from teaching and lecture fees alone.[39]

As the Maryland General Assembly changed the requirements for attorneys to be admitted to practice in the state, interest in his lengthy and expensive course of study dwindled.[40] This declining enrollment, in a program that seems to have never been very large to begin with, coupled with his already precarious financial situation most certainly played a role in his decision.

Finally, legislation passed in 1833 by the General Assembly made it more difficult for attorneys in Maryland to collect outstanding fees from their clients.[41] For Hoffman this included the University, which according to his *Letter to the Trustees*, owed him fees for legal work performed on behalf of the school; fees that the Trustees, according to Hoffman, refused to even acknowledge.[42]

Hoffman's decision to depart is made even more troubling by the fact that the Trustees, shortly after his announcement, filed a law suit for the return of furnishings, library books and other materials that Hoffman was entrusted to purchase for the University.[43] These items, allegedly, were not accounted for at the time of his departure. Although the case was eventually dropped by the Trustees, Hoffman's apparent decision to take the material with him reinforces the image of him as impetuous and difficult.[44] Hoffman may have purchased the material using his own funds or on personal credit, as other faculty in the medical school had done the same, yet unlike his fellows on the medical faculty Hoffman decided either not to seek, or not to wait, for reimbursement from the General Assembly of Maryland.[45]

While his plan for legal education did not succeed at the University of Maryland Hoffman never abandoned his efforts to improve the intellectual environment of the legal community. He continued to write and publish his legal education theories, revising his 1817 work in 1836, expanding it into two volumes and even offering an edition published in London for British students.

Looking at the 1836 edition it is possible to gauge the growth of Hoffman's interests. Now included were "Mr. Story's Commentaries on the Constitution of the United States" while many of the individual constitutional readings by James Wilson (who Hoffman profusely praised in 1817) were moved to the second group of readings in the chapter. New cases that Hoffman added included many of the same cases studied in today's first year Constitutional Law classes: *Martin v. Hunter's Lessee* (1816), *McCulloch v. State of Maryland* (1819), *Dartmouth College v. Woodward* (1819) and *Cherokee Nation v. State of Georgia* (1836). Perhaps reflecting a change of heart on Hoffman's part he also added *Fletcher v. Peck* to his list of important cases. Although it was available to him at the time, having been decided in 1810, it was not included in the 1817 edition.[46] It is possible that this last case, which played a key part in the decision in *Dartmouth College*, was added by Hoffman after his own legal battles with the University Trustees over the takeover of the University of Maryland.

Hoffman's educational goals for his Institute attracted many of the leading figures of the Maryland bar and at one time or another his faculty included Robert Goodloe Harper, Nicholas Brice, Upton Heath and, briefly, future Chief Justice of the United States Supreme Court, Roger B. Taney.[47] Students who would go on to proclaim the value of Hoffman's method included Maryland Judge George Dobbin[48] and Brantz Mayer the future philanthropist, historian and founder of the Maryland Historical Society.[49] Others such as author, journalist and occasional lawyer John Neal would claim that they

> # COURSE OF LEGAL STUDY,
> ADDRESSED TO
> STUDENTS AND THE PROFESSION GENERALLY.
>
> *Second edition—Re-written and much enlarged in two volumes, paged through* pp. 876.
>
> The work is now under the sole agency, *in Baltimore*, of
> BAYLY & BURNS, *No.* 132 *Baltimore street*.
>
> RECOMMENDATIONS OF THE FIRST EDITION.
>
> This work is recommended in the strongest terms by CHIEF JUSTICE MARSHALL, *Mr. Justice Story, Chancellor Kent, Judge Spencer, De Witt Clinton, Professor Stearnes, Chief Justice Tilghman, Mr. Justice Washington, Mr. Justice Story,* the *Hon. Daniel Webster*, and by more than 200 eminent lawyers of this and other countries. It has been elaborately reviewed by the *North American Review,* the *Analectic Magazine,* and by many other periodicals. The British and Continental Reviews speak of it in the highest terms, and the entire edition was exhausted in eighteen months.
>
> JUDGE DUVALL considers it 'a most valuable acquisition to the *practitioner*, and to the student it is *inestimable*.'
>
> JUDGE STORY says 'It is truly delightful to me also to perceive that the author does not confine the student to the mere walks of the Common law; but he has drawn him to the noble studies of the Admiralty, Maritime and Civil Law. The work is an honour to our country, and if its precepts are steadily pursued by the profession, I think it will not be rashness to declare that the next age will exhibit an American bar not excelled by any in Europe. No present could be more acceptable than a work which enables young men to see the paths of legal science, and points out so many excellent instructions to guide and cheer them on their journey.'
>
> The *North American Review* of 34 pages, concludes with saying 'In quitting the work we have not the slightest hesitation to declare that it contains by far the most perfect system for the study of the law that has ever been offered to the public. We cordially recommend it to all lawyers as a model for the direction of all students who may be committed to their charge; and we hazard nothing in asserting that if its precepts are steadily pursued, high as the profession now stands in our country, it will attain a higher elevation, an elevation which shall command the reverence of Europe, and reflect back light and glory upon the land and the law of our forefathers.'
>
> CHANCELLOR KENT says 'Whoever follows its directions will be a well read and accomplished lawyer. Many of the departments of the science to which the student is pointed suits my taste exactly.'
>
> DE WITT CLINTON says 'The design is judicious and the execution most felicitous. It contains a mass of information and learning seldom equalled, and is an invaluable guide to legal knowledge.'
>
> RECOMMENDATIONS OF THE SECOND EDITION.
>
> The Foreign Reviews of England, France, and Germany have favourably noticed this work.

Course of Legal Study – testimonials, 1836, p. 1

studied Hoffman's outline as soon as it became available but make no mention of actually attending Hoffman's Institute.[50] No doubt Neal, like many others, took advantage of Hoffman's decision to make his outline available for sale outside of the Law Institute,

Course of Legal Study – testimonials, 1836, p.2

thereby contributing to the contrarian situation of spreading Hoffman's fame while decreasing attendance at his Institute.

After leaving the University of Maryland, and between occasional visits to England, Hoffman briefly moved to Philadelphia

Faculty list, 1820
(The University of Maryland, Baltimore, Health Sciences and Human Services Library, Special Collections)

where he published his *Hints on the Professional Deportment of Lawyers, With Some Counsel to Law Students* (1846). This work, which was enthustically received by the legal community, was one of the first American efforts to codify a lawyers professional conduct both generally and with specific reference to his duties to his clients and helped to cement Hoffman's role as one of the founders of an American theory of legal ethics.[51] While in Philadelphia Hoffman also proposed to begin anew his efforts to teach law using a now greatly expanded version of his original method. Interestingly, Hoffman proposed to operate the school not as a university effort but as a privately-run program, an environment where he would be able to retain control of the entire undertaking.[52]

Legal Career

At the time he undertook his first teaching appointment at the University of Maryland Hoffman was already a respected member of the Baltimore bar.[53] He was active before the United States District Court and the U.S. Supreme Court, handling a variety of cases, although his work seems to have focused primarily on admiralty, estates, collections and insurance issues.[54]

One of the earliest federal cases with which Hoffman can be clearly identified was a criminal case; the defense of three Maryland men - John Alexander, Lewis Hare, and Joseph Thompson Hare who were convicted of robbing the mail and sentenced to death. Hoffman's team included one of the leading Baltimore lawyers of the period - General William Winder. They faced considerable legal talent in the form of William Wirt, the Attorney General of the United States and Reverdy Johnson who, along with Elias Glenn, U.S. District Attorney; and Thomas Kell, represented the United States.

Among the several issues the case examined was whether the Court could proceed to trial against the defendants when the defendants, upon the advice of counsel, refused to enter a plea. Since an affirmative decision would expand the role of judges when dealing with a crime against the United States the case briefly became a *cause celebre* among those who opposed expansion of the judiciary's power. The case, which ultimately went against the defendants, was heard by Supreme Court Justice Duvall – in his role as Circuit Judge - and District Judge Houston.[55]

In 1832 Hoffman appeared before the Supreme Court as the lead attorney in an intriguing case from the Court's early period - *James Sheppard and Others* v. *Lemuel Taylor and Others*.[56] The case involved a suit by a group of sailors who had shipped out on the *Warren* for what was to have been a typical merchant voyage to Canton. Once underway the ship instead proceeded to the coast of Chile to trade with the rebels involved in a revolt against Spain. The ship was seized by the Spanish Navy and the crew imprisoned. Over the course of the next four years various crew members were released by the Spanish authorities. Meanwhile, the ship owners had declared bankruptcy and the *Warren* had passed to a group of creditors, including Lemuel Taylor. The original group of sailors began an action for payment of their wages against the creditors of the *Warren*, who were the only people in a position to pay the wages, but who maintained that they were not responsible for the crew's back pay.[57]

Hoffman along with his friend and associate, Charles F. Mayer, represented the surviving sailors and presented an argument that, in typical Hoffman style, relied on numerous cases both British and American. His counterparts before the Court, William Wirt and Roger B. Taney, likely counting on their known skills as speakers, seemed to have relied on considerably fewer authorities.[58] While Hoffman and Mayer prevailed that day an appeal by Taylor would have the case back before the Supreme Court the following year.[59] Hoffman, who thought the case was "endless," and probably was as frustrated as the sailors of the *Warren*, wrote to his friend Joseph Story in 1832 to seek some guidance in actually collecting the award from the ship's creditors:

> The Bank of the US and Mr. Oliver will pay but the obstinate Quaker President of the U B[60] will not, as I believe, without execution, hoping to find some difficulty in making a corporation pay, as they think the only process is by attachment for contempt, and they say the creditors cannot be attached – Surly [sic] there must be some process in our Courts on the nature of Fieri Facias- I have looked over the books and can get no light, but have found a note somewhat after the fashion of a Fi Fa! Can you give me some advice as the case is now forever out of your jurisdiction?[61]

An examination of the various reporters published in Maryland between 1812 and 1854, along with a search of the Westlaw© database, revealed only seven reported Maryland cases (listed below) in which Hoffman is clearly identified as one of the participating attorneys.[62] One of these, *Kalkman v. Causten*, 2 Gill and Johnson 365 (1830), dealt with a historically interesting case of the ship *Temperance* owned by Kalkman and sunk at the entrance to Baltimore harbor in defense of Fort McHenry and Baltimore in 1814. Causten was hired by Kalkman to represent him (along with other ship owners) in Washington to seek the passage of legislation authorizing payment for the ship owners' losses. During the process of this effort Kalkman declared bankruptcy. Elias Glenn then became Kalkman's trustee and authorized the payment of Causten, if he was successful in Washington, to be paid from the money set aside by Congress. Causten was successful but was unable to obtain payment either from the Treasury Department or from Glenn, acting on behalf of Kalkman. For Hoffman, who represented Causten, the case involved a familiar situation - namely who should be responsible for paying an attorney his fee when the client becomes insolvent? Other questions raised in the case included what instructions should have been given to the jury in the lower court (the then sixth judicial circuit of Harford and Baltimore Counties) and when exactly had Kalkman and Causten committed to the contract.

In looking at Kalkman along with Hoffman's other known reported cases it is possible to get a general sense of the types of legal work that he handled:

> • *Hunt v. Edwards*, 4 Harris and Johnson 283 (1817). H. represented the appellant. The case dealt with who is responsible for paying a promissory note and what evidence is acceptable as proof that the note had been endorsed.
>
> • *Harris v. Earle's Executors*, 4 Harris and Johnson 274 (1817). H. represented the Appellees. What constitutes performance in an agreement to assign part of a judgment from one party to another, third party?

• *Sloan* v. *Wilson*, 4 Harris and Johnson 322 (1818). H. represented the Appellee. The case, among other things, dealt with who could be held responsible for paying the note of a debtor and if, the letter presented to the court as evidence of an agreement to pay the note of the debtor was sufficient to serve as an agreement.

• *Owings* v. *Baltimore and Reister's-Town Turnpike Road*, 5 Harris and Johnson 84 (1820). H. represented the appellant. Case considered if, in the meaning of the statute incorporating the turnpike, Owings lived on a tract attached to the road and thus had only to pay a toll once in any 24 hour period or if the tract was far enough removed that Owings was obligated to pay each time he traveled the road.

• *Ringgold* v. *Ringgold*, 1 Harris and Gill 11 (1826). H. represented the appelles (in part). A complicated estate case that dealt with several questions: who is responsible for paying debts of the deceased; which set of directions when the deceased died intestate are to be followed; what constitutes evidence in response to a bill.

• *State, to use of Mayor, etc, and City Council of Baltmore et al.* v. *Boyd*, 2 Gill and Johnson 365 (1830). H represented the appellant. Although initially a debt action several issues were raised before the Court but after demurrers and withdrawals the only issue remaining dealt was to determine the meaning and intent of the "limitations" in the Acts of Limitations.

At the state level Hoffman was also part of another important case that would eventually make its way to the U.S. Supreme Court, *Barron* v. *Baltimore*.[63] Hoffman along with his nephew Peter Hoffman Cruse and long time associate Charles Mayer represented John Craig and John Barron in their initial action against the Mayor and the City of Baltimore.[64] Hoffman maintained that the City of Baltimore, by re-grading streets and alleys, had caused silt to flow into the harbor above and adjacent to the wharves owned by Barron and Craig, and therefore deprived Barron and Craig of the use of their property. Therefore, they were, Hoffman reasoned, entitled to compensation.[65] The Maryland Court of Appeals decided for the City and on appeal in 1833 the United States Supreme Court affirmed the decision. By the time the case was heard by the Supreme Court, Hoffman was engaged in his own struggle with the University and the Trustees and in making his plans to sail to England and likely was not available to appear before the court in *Barron*.[66]

In 1845 Hoffman again teamed with Mayer this time in an effort to persuade the U.S. Congress to pay the descendants of Richard S. Hackley for land in East Florida that had allegedly been appropriated by the government under the *Armed Occupation Act of 1842*.[67] The claim was subject to some dispute as the transfer of lands from Spain to Richard S. Hackley may have been in conflict with the terms of the *Adam-Onis Treaty* since the transfer took place after the deadline discussed in the treaty.[68] In fact, Richard Hackley and his heirs had been contesting the status of his lands in Florida since about 1820 and his protests had been continually rejected by Congress.[69] It is unclear who actually wrote this second protest, Hoffman or Mayer, but it is likely that the strident tone exhibited throughout is Hoffman's. Although much shorter than other similar petitions by Hoffman, perhaps this was Mayer's influence, the overall style of the Hackley protest mirrors an earlier and unsuccessful petition to Congress prepared by Hoffman in 1828 on behalf of Peter Guistier.[70]

In addition to his law practice Hoffman was a regular contributor to the fledgling legal journals in America offering opinions on the practice of law and analyzing cases.[71] Always interested in law reform, Hoffman supported the codification movement and urged the adoption of detailed state codes as a means of establishing a unique American system of law.[72] In 1834 Hoffman was appointed to serve as the Director of the Digest of the Laws of Maryland as part of an early effort to codify Maryland law. However, there is no indication that he ever began this work. In 1836 the Maryland General Assembly repealed the resolution creating the Director position and withdrew the Governor's right to pay anyone serving in the position. Hoffman's response to this is lost but it is not too great a speculation that, given his penchant for writing exactly what he thought, the letter received by the Maryland Senate in 1836 did not mince any words.[73] Finally, his surviving letters to Justice Story,

Henry Wheaton, James Causten and fellow Marylander Virgil Maxcy all attest to Hoffman's continued relationship with his colleagues in the legal community even after he moved on to other projects.[74]

It is interesting though to note that Hoffman is conspicuously absent from the biography of one his Baltimore legal contemporaries, John H.B. Latrobe. Latrobe and Hoffman were briefly members of the same social club and doubtlessly their paths must have crossed at some point. The absence of Hoffman from the Latrobe work probably has more to do with their respective political leanings than any personal animosity. This seems particularly likely considering the strong attachment Hoffman held to the correctness of his political views.[75]

Politics

Along with his legal and teaching career David Hoffman was also an active participant in both Baltimore and national politics, first as a Federalist and later as a member of the Whig party. In 1812, As a member of the Federalist Party, Hoffman, Revolutionary war hero "Light Horse" Henry Lee, local publisher (and future Maryland Congressman) Alexander Contee Hanson and several others were involved in a pitched street battle with those who supported President Madison's declaration of war.[76] Hoffman and Hanson both attended St. John's College during the same period and it is probable that Hoffman became involved in Hanson's venture as much out of his devotion to the Federalist cause as he did out of his association, and shared personality traits, with Hanson. It is clear from a reading Hanson's own account of the riots that he and Hoffman both shared a temperament that could drive them on to disaster as they focused solely on the "rightness" of their cause.[77]

While it has been maintained that Hoffman was "too self-righteous" for politics he did in fact enjoy an active, albeit low profile, influence that might have grown into more had he taken a more circumspect approach.[78] Hoffman's lack of skill in

Journal of the
Executive Proceedings of the United States Senate

[Aug. 16, 1841.] EXECUTIVE JOURNAL. 419

SATURDAY, AUGUST 14, 1841.

The following messages were received from the President of the United States, by Mr. Tyler, his secretary:

To the Senate of the United States:

I nominate to the Senate David Hoffman, of Maryland, to be a commissioner, under the act of Congress, to carry into effect the convention with the Mexican Republic of the 11th of April, 1839, in the place of John Rowan, resigned.

JOHN TYLER.

422 EXECUTIVE JOURNAL. [Aug. 24, 1841.

To the Senate of the United States:

I nominate to the Senate H. M. Breckinridge, of Pennsylvania, to be a commissioner under the act of Congress to carry into effect the convention with the Mexican Republic, of the 11th of April, 1839, in the place of David Hoffman, who has declined accepting the appointment.

JOHN TYLER.

WASHINGTON, *August 23d, 1841.*

Journal of the Executive Proceedings of the United States Senate, 1841
(Thurgood Marshall Law Library, Special Collections, The University of Maryland School of Law)

approaching matters political and his failure to value the social connections of American politics may be seen in his letter to John Quincy Adams in 1819 discussing the qualifications of Thomas Bland for the position of District Judge.[79] While other letter writers, such as William Wirt and Supreme Court Justice Gabriel Duvall addressed only the abilities of the alternative candidate, Elias Glenn, Hoffman directly attacked Bland, and those, like the influential Marylander William Pinkney, who supported Bland:

> Mr. Pinkney has, I am informed, expressed a favorable opinion of Wm. Bland. This appears to me not only irregular, but unaccountable, as Mr. Pinckney's views on all matters connected with learning and learned men are so uniformerly sound. He must, I should suppose, have perceived that an increase of Wm. Bland's knowledge has generally tended to confusion rather than illumination...Mr. P. cannot be unacquainted with his [Bland's] other deficiencies. Learning in a judge is no doubt, essential, but a little learning guided by good sense, has always been found more efficient and useful, than undigested knowledge under the direction of an imbecile mind.[80]

In 1841 Daniel Webster, who was then serving as Secretary of State, offered Hoffman the opportunity to serve as a Commissioner to Mexico. Had Hoffman accepted this lesser position and built upon it he might have achieved the political influence he sought. Instead he turned the offer down.[81]

By the time Hoffman next sought a political appointment in the Foreign Service he had been too long *out of the loop* and possessed little political capital to offer an old Washington hand like Daniel Webster. Hoffman himself may have recognized this as his request for a foreign mission post is more pleading than persuasive.[82] Of the two posts that Hoffman sought, Spain and Austria, the first was held by Washington Irving (1842-1846) while the second was not filled during Webster's tenure.[83]

Hoffman probably did not help himself in his application to Webster for the Austrian mission by citing only personal and family reasons for desiring the position while all the while maintaining that the President had "assured him" of an appointment once a position came open.[84] Hoffman's approach to Webster again illustrates how his self-absorbed personality often hindered his own efforts. Convinced that he had been promised the position outright Hoffman assumed that his social position, legal training and past Whig politics qualified him for the appointment. All the while Hoffman was either oblivious to, or perhaps he thought he was above, the "tit for tat" nature of political appointments. His inability to secure the appointment comes as no real surprise considering how poorly qualified Hoffman was, in terms of temperament, for a position that would have required a great degree of discretion. The politically astute Webster, who had worked with Hoffman in the past, probably had a greater understanding of Hoffman's abilities and shortcomings than Hoffman himself did.

Author and Social Critic

Not content with his already threefold career Hoffman also embarked on a literary career penning a collection of amusing and pointed commentaries on life in America under the pen name of "Anthony Grumbler of Grumbler Hall."[85] He also proposed to write a multi-volume history of the world under the title of *Cartaphilus, the Wandering Jew*.[86] David Hoffman's literary efforts offer a view of his career that has often been overlooked. Historian Robert Ferguson suggests that Hoffman represents the type of lawyer who viewed literary efforts as important but that they should not distract from the primary purpose of legal training - creating a nation of laws.[87] While this is essentially true, such a limited perspective fails to take into account the seriousness with which Hoffman approached his few literary efforts. Like Washington Irving,[88] or Hoffman's fellow Baltimorean John Pendleton Kennedy,[89] Hoffman hoped that by using his training and skills to respond satirically to the changes that he saw developing in American society he could re-direct attitudes and opinions. His curmudgeonly persona of Anthony Grumbler of Grumbler Hall served as more then just an amusing (and telling) pseudonym; he was the voice for educated elites who feared that the potential greatness of the Nation was being undercut by the common ways and broad democratic participation of the 1830s. One way this change manifested itself in Grumbler/Hoffman's view was in the loss of prestige that Hoffman thought had normally been reserved for educated lawyers:

> Miscellaneous Thoughts on Men, Manners and Things
> (Thurgood Marshall Law Library, Special Collections, The University of Maryland School of Law)

What does the term esquire now import? If nothing, it ought to be disused- if something, it then must confer a title of some precedence. Counsellors at law, justices of the peace and aged gentleman were formally entitled to it, more by reputation than in strict right. But now, no one can venture to address a youth who has passed twenty-one, -a merchant, or even a haberdasher, without esquiring him! Where is this title of precedence so strangely abused as in Eromitlab [Baltimore]?-And though it can break no bones, nor pick any pockets, it is still hugely out of keeping, and strongly indicative of the "ultraism" of our democracy. Would it not be far better wholly to abolish every title of precedence, than to use them without the least discrimination?[90]

It is not a stretch to conclude that the resurgent outcry against trained lawyers, and in fact against all professions, increasingly common in the 1830s, deeply offended Hoffman's aristocratic sensibilities and drove his literary ambitions.[91]

In 1839 Hoffman continued this theme in his work *Viator: or a Peep into My Note Book* wherein he compared the "sterling character of the British nation" with the "ultraism" and constant desire for change in America:

> Innovation...prompts men to think that change must be improvement-but which the cautious venerators of literature, the law, and the manners of the olden times, have so often to deplore...[men] in their eagerness for change, will root up the sturdy oaks, with the noxious tares.[92]

Hoffman's concerns over the democratization of American society would remain virtually unchanged during his life. Although Hoffman tempered his elitist views while recruiting emigrants in the 1840s for John Fremont's California land sales, in his final non-legal work (*Cartaphilus*) Hoffman returned to his earlier theme urging tolerance but only within acceptable boundaries:

> Only a few words more unto thee, oh Albion! - Thou mayest be either the Savior, or the Destroyer of Man's best hope on Earth, and in Heaven, - for there are in thee two signal virtues flowing from the Source of all Good - "TOLERATION" and "LIBERTY" - the just use of either of which is heavenly- the abuse of which is diabolic! .... Doubt it not, oh Albion, that the "Toleration," without conservative limitations, and thy "Liberty," without its essential restrictions, are fascinating thee into the abyss thou wouldst avoid.[93]

Hoffman's literary efforts, while certainly sincere, serve most effectively as a means to highlight his own political views and growing dissatisfaction with life in America.

Social & Personal Life

One of the few contemporary acknowledgements of Hoffman's literary efforts was an invitation to join Baltimore's "Monday Club" - a local literary and drinking society founded by John Pendelton Kennedy.[94] "The Monday Club" was envisioned by its members as a successor of sorts to the "Tuesday Club" of Annapolis and claimed as members such Maryland luminaries as George Calvert, Benjamin Howard, and John Latrobe.[95]

Hoffman does not appear to have been invited to join an earlier literary society – the Delphian Club- to which both Latrobe and Kennedy had belonged.[96]

"The Monday Club" was only one of Hoffman's stops on the Baltimore social circuit. He was a regular guest of Robert Gilmore, Dr. Ashton Alexander (Secretary of the Medical and Chirurgical Faculty of Maryland), and fellow Law Faculty member William Frick.[97] Hoffman also served on many boards and associations in Baltimore, including the Maryland Academy of Science and Literature, where he served with Baltimore lawyer William Donaldson.[98] Donaldson was, coincidentally, also one of the "investigators" employed by the State of Maryland to examine the actions of the militia following the 1812 riots.[99] Hoffman was a leading supporter of the Whig Party in Baltimore and was in regular contact with many local and national Whig leaders.[100] This is in addition to the many political and professional contacts in Philadelphia that he gained through his marriage to Mary McKean, the granddaughter of former Pennsylvania Governor Thomas McKean.[101]

While his marriage to Mary McKean appears to have been stable, Hoffman's family life was filled with loss. Of the children born to the Hoffman's only one daughter survived and Hoffman and his wife almost lost her as well.[102] In 1833, during his struggles with the University of Maryland Trustees, his only son died and

Hoffman expressed his grief and sense of loss to Joseph Story writing that "this has been a miserable day to me. A week ago I received the first confidential intelligence concerning my beloved, my only son. I was compelled to keep it to myself - I could not venture to communicate it to my wife. A day or two ago I made a partial communication of the sad news, I need not tell you how miserable we have been."[103] While the chances of losing a child through illness or accident were high in the 1830s, the loss of two, almost three, would make any parent feel both beleaguered and anxious for the future. These feelings are certainly present in Hoffman's letter to Story and may account for the pleading tone of his request for a foreign mission post to Daniel Webster.[104]

By this time Hoffman was greatly dissatisfied with his life in the United States. Frustration over the changing nature of life in America, coupled with a dwindling interest in his legal work and fear for the health of his family led Hoffman to depart for England, intending to remain permanently. In an 1847 letter to Henry Wheaton Hoffman urged Wheaton to assist him in disposing of his unsold publications so at to not be burdened with them after his departure. Offering to sell the unbound sheets at $1.50 a piece Hoffman refused to take less than $1.25 for the remaining stock, threatening to destroy the remaining sheets himself rather than be embarrassed by such a poor showing for his work. Hoffman was determined, he told Wheaton, to "bid adieu to the American shores."[105]

England and Land Speculation

England was the scene of Hoffman's final career effort. After his failure to secure a foreign mission post he undertook for himself the role of a promoter for emigration to unsettled lands in the United States. He began, in typical grandiose Hoffman fashion, with a published announcement listing not only the attributes of the region he sought to promote (portions of Southern Ohio and Northern Kentucky) but also six lengthy points on why such an endeavor should be considered.[106] His plan was to create a "British-American Land and Emigration Company" that would purchase land for re-sale to immigrants, draw up maps and charts and create a journal which would focus on emigration to the U.S. and finally, to sell stock in the company.[107] The scheme was, even for Hoffman, unusually audacious, and depended in part not only on investors accepting his proposals but also on the State of Ohio somehow gaining control of a substantial portion of land in northern Kentucky.[108]

Hoffman's pamphlet also affords an insight into his changing views: on the issue of slavery. Hoffman seemed to have adopted the belief, common among many Americans, that left to its natural course free labor would put an end to slavery.[109] With respect to the "leveling of society" Hoffman, who had encouraged only the participation of "gentlemen" in his scheme, also urged those who considered moving to the western lands to leave their sense of class or position behind:

> It is especially observed that no one should think of settling in the United States who is attached to English social distinctions and who is disinclined toward democratic institutions and their natural consequences. Everyone before making up his mind to join this company should take the trouble to become acquainted with the character of the climate, the condition of the country and the state of the society. [110]

Whether this truly represents a genuine change in Hoffman's views or was merely an effort to attract as many investors as possible to his plan is not clear. Whatever the motivation, it is a public departure from the view he advocated years before in *Men, Manners and Things*.[111]

Hoffman's finances and schemes took yet another downward turn in 1851 when he became the sole British agent involved in an effort to sell land in California that had been purchased and mapped by John C. Fremont.[112]

As demand for this California land increased Hoffman became involved in a public newspaper battle with a competitor that was so embarrassing to Fremont, and so disruptive to efforts to sell the land, that Hoffman was relieved of his position as Fremont's agent.[113] An open letter in the *London Times* from Hoffman to John Duncan, the attorney for Thomas Sargent who claimed to control some of the land Hoffman was trying to sell, again exemplifies Hoffman's personal and aggressive style in his dealings with the many claimants to Fremont's land in California:

Letter to John Duncan, Esq.*
10 Conduit Street, 1st March, 1852

Sir - In reply to your note of the 28th, received this morning I have to state as follows:-
1st. I cannot at all admit that I was in the least benefited by the perusal of the copies you permitted me to see, only by the unavoidable compulsion of your case; but I acknowledge freely your courteous manner whilst I was examining them.
2nd. I regard then, and much more now, your situation as most eminently perilous.
3rd. Sargent, I repeat, is not the purchaser of an inch of the Mariposas.
4th. He never will be.
5th. He has been the architect of his own certain ruin, and of the sure disgrace of many.
6th. Your suits against me for Sargent, and also for the ridiculous Mr. Green, are nuts for me to crack hereafter. Proceed with them at your and their peril.
7th. My powers and numerous letters are not to be inspected by you. Hundreds have seen them and fully. That is for me quite sufficient.
8th. The horrible contrivance will come out in due time. I know it all—all.
9th. You cannot, I fear, duly appreciate your own dreadful condition, and my own strict adherence to justice, and my total indifference to all motives, save those of rigid truth.
10th. I have no vengeance in my nature; but Sir, do not, for your own sake, press me further.
11th. You are a man of talents (so say all), but talents alone will serve no man.
12th. Write me no more notes; I have neither inclination nor time to even read them—certainly not to reply to them.
13th. My previous information between the 24th of February and this 1st of March was complete.

14th. My letters received this 1st of March, 1852, are more than ample for me and for the public, here and in the United States, and as to which you and they will hear in due season.
I am, Sir, your most obedient servant,
David Hoffman

Unfortunately for Hoffman, John Fremont was not completely truthful in his dealings with his London agent. Throughout this period Fremont continued to sell, and even give away, land to his father-in-law, Thomas Benton. Benton, in turn, was selling the land to others oftentimes in conflict with Hoffman's own efforts on behalf of Fremont. This would eventually leave Hoffman, not discounting his own aggressive approach, in a professional and financial bind. Dismissed by Fremont and unable to secure financial support for his own Ohio plans, Hoffman reluctantly returned to the United States where, upon arriving in New York, he died quite suddenly.[114]

Final Thoughts

David Hoffman, committed to his profession and the idea of America as a nation of laws, devoted his life to reforming the legal community through education, codification and his own personal example. In fact, Hoffman lived the type of life and career that, according to Robert Ferguson, many of his contemporaries sought after.[115] Yet throughout his life Hoffman proved to be self-centered, short-sighted and, in many ways, *his own worst enemy*. Oftentimes Hoffman failed to realize that what he felt was his due, because of social position and training, his contemporaries saw only as inflated vanity. While Hoffman did contribute to the creation of a "Republican Culture," as suggested by Professor Maxwell Bloomfield, the resulting society was hardly one that Hoffman would have embraced as his own.[116]

Hoffman's death in 1854 warranted only one brief paragraph in the *Baltimore Sun*.[117] He had, in the years since his move to England, become increasingly isolated from the American legal community. Although his 1817 outline continued to serve as a guide for scholarly lawyers,[118] the law itself had undergone fundamental changes by mid-century.[119] Despite Hoffman's vision of creating an elite class of academically trained lawyers and politicians the practice of law was moving in another direction. It was becoming primarily a craft performed by competent but increasingly narrowly trained practitioners.[120] That Hoffman was either unaware of this shift or unwilling to endorse it is reflected in the extension of his *Course of Legal Study* in 1836 and the publication of his 1846 *Legal Hints*. In both instances Hoffman's belief that the needs of practicing attorneys would best be answered by philosophical works that could assist them in their future education and scholarship was at odds with the growing demand for "practical" publications that by mid-century represented the bulk of legal publishing and the direction of legal education in America.[121]

While Hoffman's personal ideals did not keep pace with changes in the law his theories on how to teach the law were not a complete failure. There are echoes of Hoffman's methodology in the early curriculum design at New York University[122] and in Joseph Story's early efforts at Harvard University.[123] Hoffman's method for training lawyers even served, in an age before bar exams, as a model for evaluating the quality of would-be attorneys in states as far away as Louisiana and Alabama.[124] That Hoffman's influence continues to be felt can be seen in the more recent claims for him as the "father of American legal ethics."[125] Today the legal community can look to this dynamic Maryland scholar as the founder of a multi-disciplinary academic model that remains central to the mission of many contemporary law school programs.[126]

Endnotes

1. Thomas L. Shaffer, "David Hoffman's Law School Lectures, 1822 - 1833," *Journal of Legal Education*, 32 (1982): 127.; Judith L. Maute, "Changing Conceptions of Lawyer's Pro Bono Responsibilities: From Chance Noblesse Oblige to Stated Expectations," *Tulane Law Review*, 77 (2002-2003): 103.
2. Maxwell Bloomfield, "David Hoffman and the Shaping of a Republican Legal Culture," *Maryland Law Review*, 38 (1979): 678-679.
3. Anthony Grumbler, *Miscellaneous Thoughts on Men, Manners, and Things* (Baltimore: Published by Coale & co., 1837). Thurgood Marshall Law Library, Special Collections, The University of Maryland School of Law.
4. Wilbur S. Shepperson, "Thomas Rawlings and David Hoffman: Promoters of Western Virginia Immigration," *West Virginia History*, 15 (1954): 311.
5. David Hoffman, *A Course of Legal Study; Respectfully Addressed to the Students of Law in the United States* (Baltimore: Published by Coale and Maxwell, 1817). Thurgood Marshall Law Library, Special Collections, The University of Maryland School of Law.
6. David Hoffman, *Chronicles Selected From the Originals of Cartaphilus, The Wandering Jew Embracing a Period of Nearly XIX Centuries* (London: T. Bosworth, 1853). Maryland State Law Library.
7. Two articles that look at Hoffman's legal career and provide biographical information are: Bloomfield, "David Hoffman and the Shaping of a Republican Legal Culture," note 2 and Shaffer, "David Hoffman's Law School Lectures," note 1.
8. Whitman H. Ridgway, *Community Leadership in Maryland, 1790 - 1840* (Chapel Hill: The University of North Carolina Press, 1979). Mary A. Seitz, *The History of the Hoffman Paper Mills in Maryland* (Towson: The Holliday Press, 1946), 24-26.
9. William H. Ridgway, *Community Leadership in Maryland, 1790-1840*. Also, Maxwell Bloomfield, "David Hoffman," 675.

Descendants of William Hoffman. Unpublished typescript. Library of the Baltimore County Historical Society.
10. Bloomfield, "David Hoffman," 674.
11. Alfred S. Konefsky and Andrew J. King, *The Papers of Daniel Webster: Legal Papers, Volume 1 – the New Hampshire Practice* (Hanover, N.H.: University Press of New England, 1982). *See* chapter 1 generally for Webster's and others dissatisfaction with the content and nature of legal education as an apprentice.
12. The nature of legal education in Maryland, like legal education across the United States, was extremely varied in the opportunities that were available to students. A very good discussion of the type of training afforded most attorneys can be found in John E. Semmes, *John H.B. Latrobe and His Times* (Baltimore: The Norman, Remington Co., 1917), 100.
13. Bloomfield, "David Hoffman," 675.
14. Dumas Malone, Editor, "David Hoffman," *Dictionary of American Biography*, (New York: Charles Scribner's Son, 1932), 5:111. (hereafter *DAB*).
15. See note 5 above.
16. *DAB* 5:111. See also, Shaffer, "David Hoffman's Law School Lectures," 127.
17. Hoffman, *Course of Study*, xi - xii.
18. Paul D. Carrington, "The Revolutionary Idea of University Legal Education," *William & Mary Law Review*, 31 (1990): 527.
19. Hoffman, A Lecture being the second of a series of lectures introductory to a course of lectures now delivering in the University of Maryland. (Baltimore: John Toy, 1825), 2.
20. Charles M. Cook, *The American Codification Movement: A Study of Antebellum Legal Reform* (Westport: Greenwood Press, 1981), 61.
21. Hoffman, *Course of Study*, xv.
22. Ibid.
23. Ibid., xvii.
24. Ibid., xxx.
25. Ibid., 273.
26. *DAB*, 5:111.

27. *An Act to Authorise the Raising a Sum of Money by a Lottery or Lotteries to Build an Arsenal for the City of Baltimore, and for Other Purposes*, Chapter 125. *The Laws of Maryland, From the End of the Year of 1799* (Annapolis: Printed by J. Green, Printer of the State, 1813).
28. Bernard C. Steiner, "History of Education in Maryland," *Contributions to American Educational History* (Washington: Government Printing Office, 1895), 136. Also identified as *United States Bureau of Education, Circular of Information, No. 2, 1894*.
29. Among researchers there is some difference of opinion as to when Hoffman actually began his Institute at the University. The *DAB* gives a date of 1823, while Shaffer and Bloomfield both cite 1822 as the first year that Hoffman began to lecture using his method. Bernard Steiner in an 1894 report to the U.S. Bureau of Education writes that Hoffman announced his program in the *American & Commercial Daily Advertiser* in 1822 but did not begin actual instruction until 1823. Hoffman's own records – in his letter to the Trustees of the University claims to have begun in 1822 and it is this date, from his own writing, that I have accepted as the "official" date for his Institute to have begun.
30. *See* David Hoffman, *The Trustees of the University of Maryland in relation to the law chair*. (Baltimore: J.D. Toy, 1826). Maryland Historical Society.
31. "Minutes of the Faculty of the University of Maryland," September 28, 1821. The University of Maryland Health Sciences and Human Services Library, Special Collections, The University of Maryland, Baltimore.
32. Ibid.
33. George H. Callcott, *A History of the University of Maryland* (Baltimore: Maryland Historical Society, 1966), 55.
34. Ibid., 72-75.
35. David Hoffman, *A Circular to Students at Law in the United States*. Philadelphia: Barrett and Jones, Printers, 1844. The Making of Modern Law. Thomson-Gale, 2004. (viewed 11/24/2010). http://www.galegroup.com/ModernLaw/
36. Calcott, *History of the University of Maryland*, 69.

37. "A Letter to the Trustees," 1826. Minutes of the Faculty, 1839. The University of Maryland Health Sciences and Human Services Library, Special Collections, The University of Maryland, Baltimore.
38. Hoffman did prepare a series of open letters to the Trustees expressing his concerns over finances, competition with the medical faculty, and the overall structure of the law institute, concerns which apparently were never addressed to his satisfaction. *David Hoffman, To the Trustees of the University of Maryland in relation to the law chair* (Baltimore: J. D. Toy, 1826). Maryland Historical Society.
39. Ibid.
40. Calcott, 37.
41. An Act Regulating the Admission of Attorneys to Practice Law in the Several Courts of this State, Chapter 286. *Laws Made and Passed by the General Assembly of the State of Maryland* (Annapolis: Printed by J. Green, Printer of the State,1832). One part of this law allowed attorneys to practice with only two years of education, considerably less than what Hoffman believed was necessary if a student was to be an able lawyer.
42. An Act limiting the time for the collection of the Fees of Attorneys, Solicitors, Clerks, Registers, Sheriffs and other officers of the State, Chapter 258. *Laws Made and Passed by the General Assembly of the State of Maryland* (Annapolis: Printed by J. Green, Printer of the State, 1834). The Act limited to three years the amount of time in which an attorney could try to collect any fees. Also, "Letter to the Trustees" at 38 above.
43. Calcott, 68.
44. Ibid.
45. An Additional Supplement to the Act, Entitled An Act for the Benefit of the University of Maryland, Chapter 270. *Laws Made and Passed by the General Assembly of the State of Maryland*, (Annapolis: Printed by J. Green, Printer of the State, 1832). This law allowed a group of medical faculty, including Nathaniel Potter, to bring an action against the Trustees for the reimbursement of personal funds expended on behalf of the University.
46. David Hoffman, *A Course of Legal Study, Addressed to Students and the Profession Generally* (Baltimore: Published by

Joseph Neal, 1836). Thurgood Marshall Law Library, Special Collections, The University of Maryland School of Law.
47. Faculty list. Records of the University of Maryland. Health Sciences and Human Services Library, Special Collections. The University of Maryland, Baltimore.
48. *Eugene Cordell, University of Maryland, 1807-1907* (New York: The Lewis Publishing Co., 1907) Volume 2, p.7.
49. Dumas Malone, Editor, "Brantz Mayer," *Dictionary of American Biography*, (New York: Charles Scribner's Son, 1932), 6: 449.
50. John Neal, *Wandering Recollections of a Somewhat Busy Life: an autobiography* (Boston: Robert Brothers, 1869), 167.
51. David Hoffman, *Hints on Professional Deportment of Lawyers, With Some Counsel to Law Students* (Philadelphia: Thomas, Cowperthwait, 1846). *See also* Thomas L. Shaffer, "David Hoffman's Law School Lectures, 1822 - 1833," *Journal of Legal Education*, 32 (1982): 127.; Judith L.Maute, "Changing Conceptions of Lawyer's Pro Bono Responsibilities: From Chance Noblesse Oblige to Stated Expectations," *Tulane Law Review*, 77 (2002-2003): 103.
52. Eugene Cordell, *University of Maryland, 1807-1907* (New York: The Lewis Publishing Co., 1907), 347.
53. Bloomfield, "David Hoffman," 683.
54. *See* Chace against Vasquez, 24 U.S. 429 (1826), The Arrogante Barcelones, 20 U.S. 496 (1822) and *Chirac* v. *Reinecker*, 27 U.S. 612 (1829); also, Peter Gustier, *Memorial and argument in the case of the ship Blaireau, praying a return of tonnage and duties, erroneously paid in1803: addressed to the Senate of the United States* (Baltimore: J.D. Toy, 1826).
55. *Trials of the mail robbers, Hare, Alexander and Hare. With the testimony, the proceedings of the court, and the arguments of counsel at length. William Wirt, esq., attorney general of the United States; Elias Glenn, esq., district attorney; Thomas Kell and Reverdy Johnson, esqs., for the prosecution. General Winder, David Hoffman, Charles Mitchell and Ebenezer L. Finley, esqs. for the prisoners. Reported by Edward J. Coale. To which is added, the trial and proceedings before the Circuit*

of the United States, in Philadelphia, in the case of William Wood, an accessary [sic.] before the fact. Reported for the Franklin gazette, by Richard Bache, esq. (Baltimore: Edward J. Coale, 1818). Maryland Department, Enoch Pratt Free Library.
56. *James Sheppard* v. *Lemuel Taylor*, 30 U.S. 675 (1831). *Robert Oliver* v. *James Alexander and seventy-seven others*, Seamen of the Warren, 31 U.S. 143 (1832).
57. *Sheppard* v. *Taylor*, 30 U.S. 675.
58. Ibid.
59. *Oliver* v. *Alexander*, 31 U.S. 143.
60. Here Hoffman refers to the Union Bank in Baltimore; one of Andrew Jackson's "pet banks," whose President at the time was Thomas Ellicott. *See* Richard Walsh and William Lloyd Fox, Ed. *Maryland: A History, 1632-1974* (Baltimore: Maryland Historical Society, 1974), 271.
61. David Hoffman, "Letter to Joseph Story," 1832. Joseph Story Papers, The Massachusetts Historical Society.
62. This effort recognizes that there may be many more cases that did not reach court that Hoffman might be associated with. Many of these are in the records of Baltimore County and are available at the Maryland State Archives.
63. *Barron* v. *Baltimore*, 32 U.S. (7 Pet.) 243 (1833). The case, familiar to most constitutional law scholars, was one of the last decided by the Marshall Court and dealt with the application of the 5th Amendment to individual states.
64. Descendants of William Hoffman. Unpublished typescript. Library of the Baltimore County Historical Society.
65. Records of cases decided in the Supreme Court of the United States at January term, 1833. National Archives and Records Administration. Microfilm edition.
66. "Letter to William Sullivan, Feb. 13, 1833." The Pierpont Morgan Library, New York. 1833-0214.
67. Armed Forces Occupation Acts. 5 Stat. 502. Chap. 122 (August 4, 1842).
68. Treaty of Amity, Settlement and Limits between the United States of America and His Catholic Majesty. 8 Stat. 252 (Feb. 22, 1819).

69. [David Hoffman]. The Second Protest of Richard S. Hackley's Heirs, respecting the lands in East Florida, Addressed to His Excellency James K. Polk, President of the United States. June 27, 1845 (S.l: s.n., 1845). George Peabody Library, Johns Hopkins University.
70. *Memorial and argument in the case of the Ship Blaireau, praying a return of tonnage and duties erroneously paid in 1803: Addressed to the Senate of the United States* (Baltimore: Printed by J.D. Toy, 1826).
71. [David Hoffman], "Construction of a Power of Attorney, and of a Deed," American. *Jurist & Law Magazine*, 3 (1830): 52.
72. Cook, *Codification Movement*, 72.
73 Journal of the Proceedings of the Maryland House of Delegates, March 17, 1837, pp.675-677, 722. Journal of the Proceedings of the Senate of Maryland, 1836. p. 44 (Index).
74. "Letter to Joseph Story from David Hoffman." 1832. Massachusetts Historical Society Library. "Letter to Henry Wheaton," 1847. The Pierpont Morgan Library. Ma995.
75. John E. Semmes, John H.B. Latrobe And His Times, 1803-1891, 366-367. Hoffman was a committed member of the Whig party while Latrobe is quoted as being a supporter of Jackson.
76. Robert J. Brugger, *Maryland: A Middle Temperament, 1634-1980* (Baltimore: Published by The Johns Hopkins University Press, in Association with the Maryland Historical Society, 1986), 178.
77. Alexander Contee Hanson. *To the Voters of the Congressional District composed of Montgomery and Part of Frederick* [Frederick, Md.,1812?]. Maryland Department, Enoch Pratt Free Library.
78. For example, in 1840 Hoffman served as a Presidential Elector for William Henry Harrison. Cordell, *University of Maryland*, 347. Calcott, *History of the University of Maryland*, 35.
79. Peter Graham Fish. *Federal Justice in the Mid-Atlantic South: United States Courts from Maryland to the Carolinas, 1789-1835* (Washington, DC: Administrative Office of the United States Courts, 2002), 225-229.
80. David Hoffman, Letters of Application and Recommendation During the Administration of James Monroe, 1817-1825. Record

group M439, roll 7, at 568-571. National Archives of the United States.
81. Harold D. Moser, Editor, *The Papers of Daniel Webster, Correspondence, 1840-1843* (Hanover: Dartmouth College, University Press of New England, 1982), 5: 412. The letter is mentioned in the calendar of 1841.
82. David Hoffman, "Letter to Daniel Webster," Feb. 1, 1843. Microfilm version of the Papers of Daniel Webster. The Library of Congress, Special Collections.
83. For a discussion of Daniel Webster's various appointments see volume one, series three of The Papers of Daniel Webster, Diplomatic Papers (1841-1843).
84. Ibid.
85. Anthony Grumbler, Miscellaneous Thoughts on Men, Manners, and Things. Thurgood Marshall Law Library, Special Collections, The University of Maryland School of Law.
86. David Hoffman, *Chronicles Selected From the Originals of Cartaphilus*. See also *Syllabus of a course of lectures upon ecclesiastical and civil history during the first ten centuries, upon a plan ... based upon the first three volumes in manuscript, of a work entitled "Chronicles of Cartaphilus."* Baltimore: John D. Toy, 1841. Maryland Historical Society.
87. Robert A Ferguson, *Law and Letters in American Culture* (Cambridge: Harvard University Press, 1984), 91-92.
88. Washington Irving, *A History of New York* (1809), Ed. Michael L. Black and Nancy B. Black (Boston: Twayne Publishers, 1984).
89. John Pendleton Kennedy, *Swallow Barn; or, A Sojourn in the Old Dominion* (1832), with an Introduction by Lucinda H. MacKethan (Baton Rouge: Louisiana State University, 1986).
90. Grumbler, *Miscellaneous Thoughts*, 35.
91. The outcry against learned professions and lawyers in particular was not new. The dislike for attorneys began almost as soon as colonist arrived and never really ceased although its intensity may have ebbed and flowed. *See* Maxwell Bloomfield, *American Lawyers in a Changing Society, 1776-1876* (Cambridge: Harvard University Press, 1976). How accurate Hoffman's interpretation of anti-lawyer sentiment was is difficult to gauge but

there can be no doubt that Hoffman, writing as Grumbler, believed it to be very real.

92. David Hoffman, *VIATOR: or, A Peep into My Note Book* (Baltimore: Plaskitt & Cugle, 1839), vi.

93. David Hoffman, *Chronicles Selected From the Originals of Cartaphilus*.

94. Hoffman was not invited to be a founding member of the Club. It is likely that it was more for his prestige in Baltimore, which was still considerable, rather than his skills as an author that eventually engendered the invitation. John Pendleton Kennedy, in commenting on Hoffman's *Cartaphilus* said, "I would not be surprised if it be all ready for the press in huge and painful volumes...with immense resource of reading and authority scattered through voluminous notes." Bloomfield, "David Hoffman," 686.

95. William D. Hoyt, Jr. "The Monday Club," *Maryland Historical Society Magazine*, 49 (1954): 301.

96. John Earle Uhler, "The Delphian Club," *Maryland Historical Society Magazine*, 20 (1925): 305.

97. "The Diary of Robert Gilmore," *Maryland Historical Society Magazine*, 17 (1922): 241.

98. Laws of Maryland, Chapeter 123. 1826.

99. The personal library of the Donaldson family, which contains a gift book from Hoffman, became – through the gift of Maryland Judge Frederick Brune - the core of the Thurgood Marshall Law Library's rare book collection.

100. Along with those already mentioned Hoffman was known to have been in communication with William Henry Harrison and Henry Clay. The latter was prevailed upon to put in a word or two on Hoffman's behalf when he sought the foreign mission position from Webster. *See* Robert Seager II, Editor, Melba Porter Hay, Assoc. Ed. *The Papers of Henry Clay, The Whig Leader, January 1, 1837 - December 31, 1843* (Lexington: The University Press of Kentucky, 1988), 9: 458.

101. *DAB*.

102. Ibid.

103. David Hoffman, "Letter To Joseph Story," July 18, 1833. Joseph Story Papers, The Massachusetts Historical Society.

104. David Hoffman, "Letter to Daniel Webster," Feb. 1, 1843. Microfilm Version of the Papers of Daniel Webster. The Library of Congress, Special Collections.
105. David Hoffman, "Letter to Henry Wheaton," 1847. The Wheaton Papers. The Pierpont Morgan Library.
106. David Hoffman, Letter By An American Citizen, Permanently Resident in England, Addressed to British Capitalists (London: John Miller, 1849). The George Peabody Library, Johns Hopkins University.
107. Wilbur S. Shepperson, "Thomas Rawlings and David Hoffman," 316.
108. Hoffman, Letter By An American Citizen, 8.
109. Ibid. 5. For a discussion of the inconsistencies in this position *see* Samuel Olken, Chief Justice John Marshall and the Course of American Constitutional History. *John Marshall Law Review*, v. 33, no. (summer, 2000) at note 175.
110. Ibid. 16.
111. Anthony Grumbler, *Miscellaneous Thoughts on Men, Manners, and Things* (Baltimore: Published by Coale & co., 1837).
112. Shepperson, "Thomas Rawlings and David Hoffman," 319.
113. Ibid.
114. *DAB*.
115. Robert A. Ferguson, "The Emulation of Sir William Jones in the Early Republic," *The New England Quarterly*, v. 52, no. 1 (March, 1979).
116. Bloomfield, "David Hoffman."
117. Baltimore Sun, Vol. 35, No. 154 (Nov. 13, 1854), page 2, column 1.
118. Ferguson, *Law and Letters in American Culture*, 29.
119. Ferguson, Part III. *See* generally, Morton Horowitz. *The Transformation of American Law, 1780 - 1860* (Cambridge: Harvard University Press, 1977).
120. Ferguson, 201.
121. Examples of publications representing the antithesis of Hoffman's ideals include John Collyer's *A Practical Treatise on the Law of Partnership* (1848); Isaac Redfield's *A Practical Treatise Upon the Law of Railways* (1858); David Graham's *A*

Treatise on the Law of New Trials in Cases Civil and Criminal (1855); and Isaac Edwards' *A Treatise on Bills of Exchange and Promissory Notes* (1857).

122. Ronald L. Brown, Editor, *The Law School Papers of Benjamin F. Butler, New York University School of Law in the 1830's* (New York: Greenwood Press, 1987). Brown provides a detailed discussion of both similarities and departures from Hoffman's ideals.

123. Bloomfield, "David Hoffman," 686.

124. Warren M. Billings, "A Course of Studies: Books That Shaped Louisiana Law" (unpublished manuscript - made available through the courtesy of Professor Billings); Carol Rice Andrews, et. al, "Gilded Age Legal Ethics: Essays on Thomas Goode Jones' 1887 Code and the Regulation of the Profession." (Tuscaloosa, Alabama: Occasional Publications of the Bounds Law Library, 2003).

125. Shaffer, "David Hoffman's Law School Lectures," at 127.

126. University of Maryland School of Law, Maryland Law, Embracing the Real World, 1997 Admissions Information 5. In describing the goals of the program the Law School takes a very Hoffman-like stance on legal education - "Courses exploring the relationship between law and other disciplines reflect the faculty's view of the importance of a good lawyer's perspective on the law. Among these disciplines are the humanities, social science, health care policy, environmental policy, economic development and others."

DAVID HOFFMAN
TIME LINE

1784 December 24 - David Hoffman born.
1802 - Hoffman attends Saint John's College in Annapolis, Maryland.
1802-1804? - Legal training.
1812 - The University of Maryland Chartered.
1812 - Hoffman and others involved in riot and street battles over President Madison's declaration of war.
1813 - *An Act to Authorize the Raising a Sum of Money by a Lottery or Lotteries to Build an Arsenal for the City of Baltimore, and for other purposes.*
1814 - Receives appointment as Professor of Law at the University of Maryland.
1816 January - Marries Mary McKean of Philadelphia, PA.
1816 November - Son Frederick is born.
1817 - *A Course of Legal Study* is published.
1818 November - Daughter Anne McKean is born.
1818 May - Argues (as co-counsel representing the defendants) *United States v. Hare* in the Circuit Court of Maryland.
1819 March - Daughter Anne dies.
1822 - Appears before the U.S. Supreme Court in *The Arrogante Bacelones.*
1822 - Appears before the U.S. Supreme Court in *The Santa Maria.*
1822 - Hoffman announces in the American Commercial & Daily Advertiser the start of his program, which he calls a "Law Institute," at the University of Maryland.
1823 - Hoffman begins publishing his University lectures in pamphlet form.
1824 - Publishes *An Address to Students of Law*.
1826 - Appears before the U.S. Supreme Court in *Chace against Vasquez.*

1828 - Publishes *Memorial and argument in the case of the ship Blaireau, praying a return of tonnage and duties, erroneously paid in 1803: addressed to the Senate of the United States.* (Guistier petition)

1828 - Appears before the U.S. Supreme Court in *Benjamin Buck & Thomas Hendrick v. The Chesapeake Insurance Company.*

1829 - Petition on behalf of Peter Guistier rejected by the United States Congress.

1830 - Argues *Kalkman vs. Causten* in the Maryland Court of Appeals.

1830 - *The Construction of a Power of Attorney, and of a Deed* by Hoffman published in the *American Jurist & Law Magazine.*

1830 - Appears before the U.S. Supreme Court in *James Sheppard v. Lemuel Taylor* ("Warren I").

1832 - Hoffman announces his intention to close the "Law Institute" at The University of Maryland.

1832 - Appears before the U.S. Supreme Court in *Robert Oliver v. James Alexander and Seventy-seven others, Seamen of the Warren* ("Warren II").

1833 - Hoffman's son Frederick dies.

1833? - Hoffman travels to England.

1836 - Revises *A Course of Legal Study,* published in both Baltimore and London.

1837 - Writing as "Anthony Grumbler" Hoffman publishes *Miscellaneous Thoughts on Men, Manners and Things.*

1839 - *VIATOR; Or, A Peep Inside My Notebook* published.

1839 - Helps university faculty to prepare a statement to the Trustees on the possible take over of the University by the State of Maryland.

1840 - Serves as Presidential Elector for Harrison.

1841 - Publishes second edition of *Miscellaneous Thoughts.*

1843 - University trustees formally accept Hoffman's resignation from the University of Maryland.

1843 - Hoffman seeks foreign mission post from Secretary of State Daniel Webster, expresses an interest in either Austria or Spain.

1844-1847 - Conducts a private law school in Philadelphia, PA.

1845 - Publishes *The Second Protest of Richard S. Hackley's Heirs, Respecting their Lands in East Florida:Addressed to his Excellency James K. Polk, President of the United States: June 27, 1845.*
1846 - *Hints on Professional Deportment of Lawyers, With Some Counsel to Law Students* published.
1847 - Moves to England.
1847 - Writes series of articles on life in America for *The London Times.*
1848 - *Views on the Formation of a British and American Land and Emigration Company* published.
1849 - *Letter by an American Citizen, Permanently Resident in England Addressed to British Capitalists* published.
1850 - 1851- Employed by John C. Fremont to help sell land in California.
1853 - Publishes volume one of *Chronicles Selected from the Originals of Cartaphilus, the Wandering Jew Embracing a Period of XIX Centuries.*
1854 - Returns to the United States, dies in New York City.

Part Two

INTRODUCTORY LECTURES,

AND

SYLLABUS

OF A

COURSE OF LECTURES,

DELIVERED IN THE UNIVERSITY OF MARYLAND,

BY DAVID HOFFMAN.

NOW RE-PUBLISHED IN REFERENCE TO THE RECENT RESIGNATION OF THE MEDICAL AND LAW PROFESSORSHIPS IN THAT INSTITUTION.

BALTIMORE:
JOHN D. TOY, PRINTER.
1837.

Composite volume title page
(Law Library of Congress, Washington, DC)

Syllabus

of a Course of Lectures on Law Proposed to be Delivered in the University of Maryland, 1821

SYLLABUS

OF

A COURSE OF LECTURES

ON

LAW;

PROPOSED TO BE DELIVERED IN

THE UNIVERSITY OF MARYLAND,

ADDRESSED

TO THE

Students of Law in the United States.

BY DAVID HOFFMAN.

BALTIMORE:
PUBLISHED BY EDWARD J. COALE.
1821.
JOHN D. TOY, PRINTER.

PREFACE.

The following Syllabus, though it may have faults of enumeration and arrangement inevitable in an analysis, (in a great degree prospective) of so large a variety of topicks, contains the substance of a Course of Lectures long proposed to be delivered in this institution. The actual execution of this plan will undoubtedly suggest to the author the amendment of errours, which the more learned may detect at once; few of which, however, will, he hopes, be found very material.

Instruction by *Lectures* gives some obvious facilities to students of Law, although it is not indispensable in this as in some physical sciences, where reasoning requires the aid of experiment. A lecturer gives greater latitude to his illustrations, and presents his subject in a greater variety of aspects, than is consistent with the compass, or with the condensed language of iv

books; and besides these advantages, which will be most valued by such as have pursued their law studies unaided and solitary, he can combine in one view the points and principles which in this science, perhaps beyond all others, are to be sought in many books, and are mingled with much matter that is either useless in itself, or darkly and barbarously set forth.

Whoever looks on the numerous volumes of Institutes, Abridgments, Digests and Reports, will see the benefit of possessing some summary of principles, of distinctions, and of topicks, which, however imperfect in itself, may show him the points which are to be sought over this wide surface, the train of investigation which is to lead him to each, and the order in which they are to be pursued. The author attempted this selection and arrangement in his Course of Legal Study." In the following course of lectures, which he supposes will occupy an hour every day for ten months in the year,—he expects to treat, in order, all the important topicks of the law, with a minuteness which will give students a knowledge of them that will leave few difficulties in their private studies.

This mode of instruction is particularly convenient, nay necessary, to American students. The laws of England, with unimportant excep-

V

tions, are to be studied as much in detail by them as by English students; to which must be added the laws of the United States, those of the state in which they practise, and such of the laws of the individual states as relate to topicks of universal concern. If they would keep pace too with the growth of the science, as it is measured by the numerous volumes which emanate from English and American presses, they must have some acquaintance with a mass of books truly appalling. Scarcely a week passes in England, without ushering to light a new treatise of law. The Reports, too, are becoming alarmingly numerous.

Since the beginning of the reign of the second Edward, there have been published in England not less than six hundred volumes of reports, one third of which are large folios, and perhaps two thirds of them are the product of the last hundred years. The number of English law treatises since the time of Glanville and Bracton, cannot easily be ascertained; but there have been several thousand. Notwithstanding this prodigious accumulation, the ground does not seem to be looked on as occupied: the last ten years have been prolifick of law works beyond former example, and much beyond that of the Roman law writers at any period. America has not been sparing in her contributions neither.

vi

From the publication of Mr. Kirby's Connecticut Reports in 1789, till the year 1804, the American books of Reports did not exceed eight volumes, whereas they amount, at this time, to about *one hundred and seventy!* It is therefore manifest enough to the student, that if the science is to be studied in these reports and treatises, his means, his time, and his industry are seldom likely to last him; nor is it necessary to enlarge on the utility of a Course of Lectures, the author of which has anticipated many of their difficulties, and digested, as far as his ability went, the knowledge of some part of these voluminous works.

Though Law is a moral science, and is unsusceptible, as was before observed, of the experimental demonstrations of physicks, it may be advantageously taught by means of lectures, and ought to constitute a part of University instruction. European nations have all introduced the subject of their municipal Law into the course of University studies: nay, as far back as history gives us any knowledge of this science, we find it taught as an important branch of learning, in publick Seminaries, Colleges and Universities. In Egypt, Rome, Constantinople, Berytus, Bagdad, Bologna, and, more recently, in most of the European countries, Law has been taught by lectures, and degrees have been conferred in

vii

this as in other departments of knowledge.
Irnerius, Bartolus, Cujacius, Baldus, Voetius,
Accursius, Heineccius, Gentilis, Gothofrede,
Lampredi, Buddæus, Gravina, Pothier, Imola,
Zouch, Blackstone, Wooddeson, and Sullivan,—
all members of universities,—are great and imposing names as lecturers in this science: and the
reasons which have made it to be considered
worthy of a place in the university education of
other countries, are of yet greater weight in a
nation whose fundamental principles of government invite all, without distinction of rank, to
the participation of political power, and to the
administration of its laws.

The present undertaking, we are aware, is one
of great extent. Hitherto this wide subject has
either been partitioned out to several professors, or the *institutes* only have been taught;
the object of the present course is to treat each
of its branches, and to investigate every important one in detail. This enterprise, however laborious and responsible, will be prosecuted with
all the industry and zeal which the author can
command, provided it should meet with encouragement sufficient to compensate him for the
sacrifices inevitable to so great an undertaking.
As he is prompted to it by no pecuniary necessity, and by no want of extensive practice, his
chief motive is to be found in a fondness for

viii

these subjects, and his reward must be the consciousness of being useful. He looks to this to sustain and enliven him in the many hours of exhaustion incident to his enterprise. He begs leave to say, however, that his regular business at the bar *will not be interfered with in any degree,* nor the interest of his clients neglected. The nature of the studies connected with the present undertaking, is such as to advance him beyond any other plan in the knowledge necessary and proper to forensick business; and he has always looked to it as abundant compensation, should any accident defeat his proposed scheme of lecturing, that every hour expended in preparation for it, has disciplined him more strictly in the learning of his profession.

The University of Maryland is, we apprehend, the only institution in this country which professes to teach through the medium of lectures exclusively. There are at present fourteen professorships and two lectureships in the University, eight of which are in operation, under circumstances of rare and gratifying promise, and several others, it is contemplated, will commence in October next. The subjects designed to be lectured on, as arranged by the Faculties and according to the Charter, are the *Institutes of Medicine, Anatomy,* the *Principles and Practice of Surgery,* the *Theory and Practice of* ix

Physick, Chemistry, Materia Medica, and *Obstetricks; Theology; Law,* national municipal and civil; *Mathematicks, Humanity, Rhetorick and Belles Lettres, Moral Philosophy,—Natural Philosophy, Geology* and *Mineralogy—Botany,* and *History.* As a Medical school, there is no institution in the country which offers such numerous facilities for the acquisition of its peculiar learning. No pains nor expense has been withheld in the erection of the buildings, and in providing those accommodations particularly necessary in the prosecution of these studies. The chemical apparatus is more modern and extensive than any in this country, and is annually augmented by importations from Paris, under the direction of the able gentleman who fills the chemical chair. An extensive museum contains the preparations of Professor Pattison. These specimens, illustrative of morbid anatomy, are among the most valuable of the kind in the world, having been collected with great care and expense, in part, by the celebrated Allan Burns of Glasgow, and partly by his friend and successor, the present Professor of Anatomy in this institution. The Mineralogical department is respectable and growing. From the extent and perfection of the philosophical apparatus also, and the learning and zeal of the Professor, we calculate on much in this department. Botany languishes, at present, for want of a botanical

X

garden, &c.; but as the pecuniary resources of the University are augmenting, and it is within the view of the Regents both to fill all the chairs, and to furnish them with the requisite means of instruction, it is hoped that this auxiliary to the department of Materia Medica will meet with due attention.

These remarks on the situation and prospects of the University of Maryland, will not seem out of place to the student who remembers the intimate relation between all divisions of human knowledge. It was quaintly but truly observed by Finch, that "the sparks of all the sciences in the world, are raked up in the ashes of the Law;" and Sir Matthew Hale, perceiving this *commune vinculum*, used to say that "no man could be the master of any profession, without having some skill in all the sciences." In this institution, then, the law student may have the advantage of acquiring this knowledge in the most easy and pleasant way. At present, it is a part of the learning of a gentleman, to know the outlines of anatomy and physiology; something of the various and agreeable learning of natural philosophy, and of the astonishing, and no less valuable discoveries of chemistry,—a topick which constantly obtrudes its lessons or its interrogatories in society or solitude, at home or in the field. We know no mode of acquiring this kind of knowledge, which is so ready or so easy xi

as attending an able course of lectures, in which precept is constantly enforced by entertaining experiment and palpable demonstration; and we know of no manner in which those many hours can be better filled up, in which the mind is hardly adequate to very vigorous exertion, but which are too valuable to be thrown entirely away.

For the advantageousness of instruction by lectures, we have the authority of Doctor Watts, who, in his "Improvement of the Mind," enumerates the reasons of this preeminence, which are nearly those which we have already ascribed to them. These are in the first place, the greater liveliness with which ideas are impressed on the mind by oral instruction, than by the silent and retired labours of the closet; the compendious views which lecturers can give, after researches which were either difficult or unprofitable to students; the familiarity of example and illustration in which they may indulge; and the opportunity which is afforded of solving by private study the doubts which may arise during the lectures,—a circumstance, we will add, which impresses a truth with double force on the mind; and he comments, a little farther on, on the narrow views, and limited range of inquiry, to which the most assiduous private student is subject.

We had hoped to have it in our power to say

xii

with certainty that the Lectures would commence in October next; but the accomplishment of this desire has been prevented, in part by the extensiveness of the scheme of instruction, of which the following Syllabus is the outline, and in part by the imperfect state and deficient funds of the University. The exertions of the institution having been liberally aided by the patronage of the state, the accommodations for students having already been greatly increased and improved, and the extensive original plan being likely to be completed during the ensuing summer; the medical professorships being filled by men of well known talent and knowledge; and the prospects of the University, from these advantages, its situation, and the increase of students during the last session, being on the whole extremely flattering,—we have every encouragement in this point of view. At the same time, as it is essential that we previously ascertain the probable attendance of a respectable class,—students of this country who mean to attend, or who have a reasonable expectation of doing so, will please address letters to me, at any time between this and the first day of next October. Proper means will be afterwards taken to inform them when the lectures commence, and of any other matters which it may be interesting to them to know.

UNIVERSITY OF MARYLAND. } *April* 1, 1821.

SYLLABUS.

TITLE I.

LECTURE I.

OF THE ORIGIN AND NATURE OF MAN, HIS PHYSICAL AND MORAL CONSTITUTION.

(1) OF the propriety of treating of Man's nature previously to the consideration of the science which unfolds his rights and duties. (2) Idea of some antient philosophers as to a triple nature of the soul. (3) Man not merely a *gregarious*, but a *social* animal. (4) Man endued with reason, and progressive in knowledge. (5) Man a religious animal. (6) Man's free agency. (7) His actions imputable or not. (8) Society, Government, Religion, and Knowledge congenial to man, and essential to his happiness. (9) What is meant by the natural equality of Man.

10

LECTURE II.
OF MAN IN A STATE OF NATURE.

(1) Why the state of nature is treated of. (2) Its various meanings. (3) Merely theoretical and metaphysical. (4) Its real and only useful meaning. (5) Whether this supposed state of nature be one of war or peace; and herein of the opinions of Hobbes, Puffendorf, Grotius, Montesquieu, &c. &c. (6) Of the inconveniencies and miseries of this state of nature.

LECTURE III.
OF THE RIGHTS OF NATURE.

(1) Various meanings of the word *right*. (2) Rights perfect, imperfect, natural, adventitious, alienable, unalienable. (3) In what the rights of nature consist; as,—to life and the integrity of our body; to the fruits of mental and bodily labour; to reputation; to liberty, and herein of *natural* liberty, as distinguished from *savage* liberty, &c. (4) Liberty subject by natural law to three species of restriction.

LECTURE IV.
OF THE ORIGIN OF PRIMARY SOCIETY, AND OF CIVIL GOVERNMENT.

(1) Of primary society as distinguished from political or civil society. (2) Of the motives which induced men to establish civil society and government, and herein, *First*, of the theory which ascribes the origin of government to Divine command. *Secondly, of the theory* which supposes man originally a soli-

11

tary animal, and that society and government sprung from various causes, such as
    1. The social principle.
    2. Sense of impotency.
    3. Natural hostility.
    4. Wants.
    5. Sexual passion.
    6. Desire for knowledge.

(3) Political science more indebted to authentick history, and a knowledge of man's physical and moral nature, than to systems.

LECTURE V.
OF THE RIGHT OF CIVIL GOVERNMENT.

(1) Division of this right into original and subsequent. (2) Of the original right arising, *First*, from Divine command. *Secondly*, from the consent of the governed. (3) Of the subsequent right of civil government, and herein *First*, of the opinion that all government, original and subsequent, rests on *consent*. *Secondly*, of the opinions that the subsequent right of government rests either on
    1. Possession.
    2. Inheritance.
    3. Prescription.
    4. Antient consent of governed.
    5. Virtues of political rulers.
    6. Expediency.

LECTURE VI.

OF THE EFFECTS OF SOCIETY OR JURISDICTION ON THE NATURAL RIGHTS OF MAN.

(1) Jurisdiction and law the necessary result of the change from a state of nature to that of civil union. (2) Men not reduced to a *state of nature* by a dissolution of the government. (3) Effects of civil union on the right of personal security. (4) Effects of civil union on the right to the fruits of mental and bodily exertion. (5) Effects on the right to reputation. (6) Effects of the union as to personal liberty, and herein

    1. Of social, as distinguished from natural liberty.
    2. Of civil, as distinguished from political liberty.
    3. Of that liberty which consists in simple freedom from confinement.
    4. Of relative liberty.
    5. Extent to which liberty is alienable.

LECTURE VII.

Of Law in the *abstract*, or the signification of the term "Law"—or "The Law." Of Law in the *concrete*, its fourfold division into Divine, Natural, National, and Civil or Municipal Law. The present Course to embrace the three last divisions, the first belonging exclusively to the chair of Theology.

(1) Of the various definitions of Law as a *genus*, and herein of the errour of most authors in defining the *species* when the *genus* was intended.

13

(2) Professor's definitions of Law, as a *genus* and *species*.

(3) Of the general properties of Law, as applied to the regulation of human conduct, and herein
1. How Law is distinguished from contract; how from counsel or advice.
2. Whether permissions, in any respect, can be regarded as laws.
3. That Laws should speak a general language, and not attempt to comprehend all possible cases.
4. That Laws should not only be general in their phraseology, but universal in their operation.
5. That Laws should be of a legal nature, and their language simple and perspicuous.
6. That Laws should have a possible, reasonable, and useful object.
7. That Laws should not be needlessly multiplied, but be as few in number as the genius of the government, and the state of society will admit.
8. That Laws should contain a sanction.
9. Obligation essential to laws, and herein
    1. Meaning of the word obligation.
    2. Various definitions of obligation.
    3. Division into *perfect, imperfect, external, internal.*
    4. Cause, or origin of obligation, and
        1. Of the obligation of moral Law.
        2. Of the obligation of civil Law.

14

5. How obligation differs from sanction.

10. Laws should operate *in futuro*. [This property of law will be hereafter fully considered, when we come to examine the Constitution of the United States, Art. 1. Sec. 9—10. relative to *ex post facto laws*.]

LECTURE VIII.

OF THE LAWS OF NATURE, APPLIED TO MAN INDIVIDUALLY, WHETHER IN A STATE OF NATURE, OR OF SOCIETY AND GOVERNMENT.

(1) This subject partly treated in the previous Lectures. Foreign to the design of this course to dwell on these topicks; but shall endeavour to combine all that is *really* valuable on this extensive learning, in a small compass.

(2) Definitions of the Law of nature. Best definition.

(3) Opinion of those who consider the Laws of nature common to man and brute; and how far the Law is common to God and man.

(4) Difference between the Laws of nature, and divine positive Law.

(5) Of the opinion that this Law is derived from the consent of mankind, and herein of the doctrine of Aristotle.

(6) Of the idea of those who maintain that we are to look for this Law in the manners and customs of nations, and of those, on the other hand, who contend that the Law relates exclusively to actions in-

15

trinsically good or evil, independent of all positive Law.

(7) Whether Hobbes' doctrine, that nature did not institute *society*, but *discord* among men, justifies the conclusion of his criticks, that society is against the design of nature.

(8) Laws of nature the dictates of right reason, and herein of the opinion of Hobbes, that these dictates should not be regarded as *laws*, only so far as they have been enacted by God, in his scriptures.

(9) Of the matters referred to the Laws of nature *reductively*, and of the distinction between those things which are commanded or prohibited, and those which are merely permitted by, or are consentaneous to, the laws of nature.

(10) Division of the laws of nature into laws relative

    1. *To man's duty to himself*, which consists principally, *first*, in the cultivation of his moral and religious character; *Secondly*, in the improvement of the intellectual faculties by the acquisition of all useful knowledge; *thirdly*, in the preservation of his health of body and mind; *fourthly*, in the acquisition of property; *fifthly*, in the pursuit of salutary pleasure.

    2. *To man's duty to his fellow-creatures*, which may be considered, *first*, ABSOLUTE, or such as oblige all men, in all countries, and independently of all human institutions.

16

Secondly, Hypothetical, or such as arise after the establishment of society, and which are nevertheless founded on the condition of mankind, considered in general, and herein of the difference between this hypothetical natural law, and positive or civil law.

LECTURE IX.

OF POLITICAL, AS DISTINGUISHED FROM CIVIL LAW, AND OF THE VARIOUS FORMS OF CIVIL GOVERNMENT.

(1) Of Political Law, what it is, and how distinguished from Civil Law. Political state, how different from Civil state.

(2) Of the exercise of governmental power, relative, or not, to the constitutional and fundamental laws of a state, and herein

First, Definition of a *Constitution.*

Secondly, That the constitution and laws should have reference to the natural and constitutional character of the governed, as no one form of government would answer for every nation; and herein of the errour of Montesquieu in carrying this doctrine too far.

Thirdly, That the constitution and laws should vary according to the *great and radical* changes in the genius and disposition of a people, effected by the gradual de-

17

velopement and expansion of the energies of the nation; due veneration, however, being had at all times for existing laws, and a wholesome jealousy of innovations.

(3) **Of** the various forms of Government.
>
> *First.* Form of Government defined, and how different from Constitution.
>
> *Secondly.* Of the influence of Government on individual and national character.
>
> *Thirdly.* Various divisions of the forms of government, and herein of the division
>> 1. Of Plato.
>> 2. Of Socrates.
>> 3. Of Aristotle.
>> 4. Of Machiavel.

(4) Division of Civil Governments into
> 1. Pure and simple, as
>> 1. Simple Monarchy.
>> 2. Simple Aristocracy.
>> 3. Simple Democracy.
>
> 2. Pure and mixed, as,
>> 1. Monarchy combined with Aristocracy.
>> 2. Monarchy combined with Democracy.
>> 3. Aristocracy combined with Democracy.
>> 4. Monarchy, Aristocracy, and Democracy combined.

        5. Single Republic.
        6. Confederate Republic.
    3. Corrupt and Simple, as,
        1. Despotism, or Tyranny.
        2. Oligarchy.
        3. Ochlocracy.

(5) **Of Patriarchal Government.** The Theocracy of the Jews, and herein of the former, as referred to simple monarchy, and the latter, as referred by Sidney to Aristocracy, and by Filmer, to Monarchy.

(6) The above forms of government illustrated and exemplified.

LECTURE X.

OF THE ELEMENTARY AND CONSTITUTIONAL PRINCIPLES OF THE MUNICIPAL LAW, AND HEREIN

    I. Of the Feudal Law.

LECTURE XI.

    II. Of the Institutes of the Municipal Law generally.

TITLE II.

OF THE LAW OF REAL RIGHTS AND REAL REMEDIES.

I. OF REAL RIGHTS.

LECTURE XII.

Introductory observations. (1) On the study of the Real Law. (2) On the propriety of treating first of the *jura rerum*, Justice Blackstone's method, when unfolding the Institutes merely, being proper, but Mr. Sullivan's and lord Hale's opinion preferable, when the science is to be studied in detail. (3) Real Remedies, why nearly obsolete. (4) Whether the change from real to personal and mixed remedies, be advantageous. (5) Of the Real Law in this country; why much studied in the United States; why formerly more than at present, particularly in the Atlantic states. (6) Ejectment law on *location*, nearly peculiar to this country, and why. (7) Little of this law to be found in our Books of Reports; traditionary; important that it should be reduced to system, and no longer remain *Lex non scripta*. (8) Some account of distinguished writers on the doctrines of the

26

Realty; and of some eminent real lawyers of this country.

(9) Things Real we shall consider in order and in detail, in *five* points of view, viz.
> I. As regards the *Objects,* or several kinds of real property.
> II. The *Estate,* or interest which may be had in real property.
> III. The *Time of Enjoyment* of estates in real property.
> IV. The *Number* and *Relation* of owners of real property.
> V. The *Modes* of *Acquiring* title to real property.

(10) In a minute exposition of the various learning of the Realty, the present division of our subject preferable to that of Sir William Blackstone, and why.

(11) The *Tenures* by which Estates may be holden, need not be further treated than has been done in our observations on the Feudal Law. (Vide Lecture X.)

LECTURE XIII.

I. OF THE OBJECTS OF REAL PROPERTY, VIZ. LANDS, TENEMENTS, HEREDITAMENTS, CORPOREAL AND INCORPOREAL.

LECTURE XIV.

Of Incorporeal Hereditaments—Ten in number. Six only worthy of particular notice, viz.
> 1. Rents.
> 2. Annuities.

24

 3. Offices.
 4. Franchises.
 5. Ways.
 6. Common.

LECTURE XV.

II. OF THE ESTATE OR INTEREST WHICH MAY BE HAD IN REAL PROPERTY.

(1) **Why** preferable to treat of *all* the objects of real property, corporeal and incorporeal, prior to the consideration of the estate or interest which may be had in them, and reasons for departing from the method adopted by Mr. Cruise.

(2) Under the subject of estates we shall treat in order,

 1. Estate in fee simple.
 2. Estate tail.
 3. Estate tail after possibility, &c.
 4. Estate for life.
 5. Estate for life, and occupancy.
 6. Estate for years.
 7. Estate from year to year.
 8. Estate at will.
 9. Estate at sufferance.
 10. Estate by courtesy.
 11. Estate in dower and jointure.
 12. Estates upon condition.
 13. Mortgage.

(3) **Of an Estate in Fee simple.**

LECTURE XVI.

OF AN ESTATE TAIL, ITS ORIGIN AND VARIOUS KINDS.

LECTURE XVII.

History of the Tenant in Tail's power over the Estate, and the various devices for defeating the Donor's intention. Some account of the Estate Tail in this country, statutory modifications in different states, and important decisions in American Courts.

LECTURE XVIII.

OF THE ESTATE TAIL AFTER POSSIBILITY OF ISSUE EXTINCT.

LECTURE XIX.

OF ESTATES FOR LIFE, POUR AUTER VIE, OCCUPANCY.

LECTURE XX.

OF AN ESTATE FOR TERM OF YEARS.

LECTURE XXI.

SAME SUBJECT CONTINUED.

LECTURE XXII.

OF ESTATES AT WILL, FROM YEAR TO YEAR, AND AT SUFFERANCE.

LECTURE XXIII.

OF AN ESTATE BY COURTESY.

LECTURE XXIV.
OF AN ESTATE IN DOWER.

LECTURE XXV.
SAME SUBJECT CONTINUED.

LECTURE XXVI.
SAME SUBJECT CONTINUED.

LECTURE XXVII.
OF JOINTURES.

LECTURE XXVIII.
OF ESTATES UPON CONDITION, AND OF THE ORIGIN AND VARIOUS KINDS OF MORTGAGE.

LECTURE XXIX.
OF THE ESTATE OF MORTGAGOR AND MORTGAGEE AT DIFFERENT TIMES.

LECTURE XXX.
OF THE EQUITY OF REDEMPTION, AND THE MANNER IN WHICH THE MORTGAGE IS TO BE SATISFIED.

LECTURE XXXI.
OF THE ORDER IN WHICH MORTGAGES SHALL BE PAID, AND OF THE DOCTRINE OF TACKING.

24

LECTURE XXXII.

HOW MORTGAGES ARE ENFORCED IN LAW, AND IN EQUITY.

LECTURE XXXIII.

III. OF THE TIME OF ENJOYMENT OF ESTATES IN REAL PROPERTY.

Introductory observations. (1) On Estates in *possession*, and *expectancy*. (2) On the origin of remainders. (3) Of the distinction between vested and contingent remainders. (4) Certain rules relating to remainders.

LECTURE XXXIV.

OF VESTED REMAINDERS.

(1) General division of estates into *vested* and *contingent;* further division necessary, viz. into *executed* and *executory*, as there are some executory estates, which are neither vested nor contingent, and herein of the defect of Mr. Fearne's division, and of Mr. Preston's view of the subject. (2) Various instances of Vested Remainders.

LECTURE XXXV.

OF CONTINGENT REMAINDERS.

(1) General observations. (2) Mr. Fearne's division of Contingent Remainders into *four* kinds, each stated *generally*. (3) Exceptions to the *third* kind. Exceptions to the *fourth* kind—these touched on, as

25

they will be hereafter particularly considered. (4) Of Conditional Limitations, as distinguished from the *first* class of contingent Remainders.

LECTURE XXXVI.

OF THE EXCEPTIONS TO THE THIRD CLASS OF CONTINGENT REMAINDERS.

LECTURE XXXVII, XXXVIII, XXXIX.

OF THE *FIRST* EXCEPTION TO THE *FOURTH* CLASS OF CONTINGENT REMAINDERS, OCCASIONED BY THE CELEBRATED RULE IN *SHELLY'S* CASE, AND HEREIN

(1) Statement of the rule. (2) Origin of the rule. (3) Policy of the rule. (4) Cases within the rule, where conveyance is by deed. (5) Cases out of the rule, where conveyance is by deed. (6) Cases within the rule, where conveyance is by devise, &c. (7) Cases out of the rule, in devises, &c. (8) Mr. Butler's view of this celebrated rule. (9) Mr. Blackstone's view of it. (10) Mr. Hargrave's admirable exposition of the rule. (11) American cases on this doctrine.

LECTURE XL.

OF THE *SECOND* EXCEPTION TO THE *FOURTH* CLASS OF CONTINGENT REMAINDERS.

26

LECURE XLI.

OF THE *THIRD* EXCEPTION TO THE *FOURTH* CLASS OF CONTINGENT REMAINDERS.

1. This not generally treated of as a distinct exception to the fourth class of contingent Remainders, and why.
2. As much so as either of the others, and why.

LECTURE XLII.

OF THE SPECIES OF UNCERTAINTY WHICH CHARACTERIZES A CONTINGENT REMAINDER.

LECTURE XLIII.

OF THOSE CONDITIONS ANNEXED TO A PRECEDING ESTATE WHICH *ARE*, OR ARE *NOT*, CONDITIONS PRECEDENT TO GIVE EFFECT TO ULTERIOR LIMITATIONS.

LECTURE XLIV.

OF THE NATURE OF THE CONTINGENCY ON WHICH REMAINDERS MAY BE LIMITED; AND OF THE ESTATE REQUIRED TO SUSTAIN CONTINGENT REMAINDERS.

LECTURE XLV.

WHEN CONTINGENT REMAINDERS MUST VEST; AND HOW THEY MAY BE DESTROYED.

27

LECTURE XLVI.

OF TRUSTEES TO PRESERVE CONTINGENT REMAINDERS; AND OF OTHER MATTERS RELATING TO THEM.

LECTURE XLVII.

OF CROSS REMAINDERS.

(1) Express or implied. (2) Raised *first* by deeds at common law. *Secondly* by limitations of an use. *Thirdly*, by limitations by will. (3) Of cross remainders between two, three, or four persons.

LECTURE XLVIII.

OF EXECUTORY DEVISES.

(1) Origin and history of executory devises. (2) This subject more properly considered under the third head, which treats of *"The time of enjoyment of estates in real property"* than under the fifth, which speaks of the *"modes of acquiring title to real property."* Mr. Cruise's method therefore departed from. (3) Executory devise defined. (4) Executory devises either vested in interest, contingent in interest, or neither vested nor contingent in interest. (5) Errour of Mr. Fearne in classing such executory devises with *contingent estates*, as are dependent on an uncertain event, they being executory, but neither vested nor contingent estates. (6) Division of executory devises into *three* classes. (7) Mr. Fearne's phraseology in defining the *second* Class of executory devises, departed trom.

28

LECTURE XLIX.
OF THE *FIRST* CLASS OF EXECUTORY DEVISES.

LECTURE L.
OF THE *SECOND* CLASS OF EXECUTORY DEVISES

LECTURE LI.
OF THE *THIRD* CLASS OF EXECUTORY DEVISES.

LECTURE LII.
OF THE DISTINCTIONS BETWEEN AN EXECUTORY DEVISE, AND A CONTINGENT REMAINDER; OF THE GENERAL QUALITIES OF, AND OTHER MATTERS RELATING TO, EXECUTORY DEVISES.

LECTURE LIII.
OF ESTATES IN REVERSION.

LECTURE LIV.
IV. OF THE NUMBER AND RELATION OF OWNERS OF REAL PROPERTY.

(1) **Of** an estate in joint-tenancy.

LECTURE LV.
OF THE SEVERANCE AND DESTRUCTION OF A JOINT TENANCY.

29

LECTURE LVI.

(2) Of an estate in coparcenary.

LECTURE LVII.

(3) Of tenancy in common.

LECTURE LVIII.

V. OF THE MODES OF ACQUIRING TITLE TO REAL PROPERTY.

Introductory observations. (1) On the nature of *title* to things real in general. (2) Of the four degrees of title. (3) Of the different kinds of title, viz. by *descent* and *purchase*.

LECTURE LIX.

OF DESCENT.

(1) Natural law of descent. (2) Descent among the Jews, Greeks, Romans, Lombards, &c. &c. generally considered. (3) Common law of descent.

LECTURE LX.

OF THE CANONS OF DESCENT.

LECTURE LXI.

OF THE DESCENT OF REMAINDERS, REVERSIONS, AND ESTATES TAIL.

LECTURE LXII.

OF THE DESCENT OF REAL PROPERTY BY THE LAWS OF MARYLAND.

LECTURE LXIII.

OF PURCHASE.

Introductory observations. (1) On the distinction between descent and purchase. (2) Of the *five* modes of acquiring title to real property by purchase, viz. *escheat; occupancy; prescription; forfeiture; alienation,* of four kinds, viz. by deed, record, custom, devise.

LECTURE LXIV.

OF TITLES BY ESCHEAT, PRESCRIPTION, OCCUPANCY AND FORFEITURE.

LECTURE LXV.

OF TITLE BY ALIENATION.

(1) History of the Potestas alienandi. (2) Of the different modes of alienation.

LECTURE LXVI.

OF TITLE BY DEED, AND HEREIN

(1) Of the essentials to a deed.

LECTURE LXVII.

(2) Of the Orderly Parts of a Deed.

34

LECTURE LXVIII.

(3) **Of** the Covenants in a deed, and herein particularly of the covenant of Warranty.

LECTURE LXIX.

(4) **Of** the different kinds of deed, and herein of Foeffment, Gift, Grant.

LECTURE LXX.

OF EXCHANGE, RELEASE, CONFIRMATION.

LECTURE LXXI.

OF PARTITION, SURRENDER, ASSIGNMENT, DEFEASANCE.

LECTURE LXXII.

(5) **Of** deeds deriving their efficacy wholly or in part from the statute of uses, and herein

    I. OF THE ORIGIN OF USES.

LECTURE LXXIII.

II. OF THE NATURE OF USES PRIOR TO THE STATUTE 27th HENRY 8th Ch. 10.

LECTURE LXXIV.

III. OF THE NATURE OF USES BY THE STATUTE 27th HENRY 8th Ch. 10.

32

LECTURE LXXV.

IV. OF THE VARIOUS MODIFICATIONS OF USES, ARISING FROM THE CONSTRUCTION OF THE STATUTE OF USES.

LECTURE LXXVI.

OF THE ORIGIN OF TRUSTS, AND OF THE RULES WHICH GOVERN TRUST ESTATES OF *FREEHOLD*.

LECTURE LXXVII.

OF THE RULES WHICH GOVERN TRUST *TERMS*.

LECTURE LXXVIII.

OF THE ESTATE AND DUTY OF TRUSTEES.

[Having fully investigated the nature of *Uses* and *Trusts*, we may now proceed to the consideration of such Deeds as derive their operation wholly, or in part, from the statute of uses.]

LECTURE LXXIX.

(6) Of the deed of bargain and sale.

LECTURE LXXX.

(7) Of the deed of covenant to stand seized to uses.

LECTURE LXXXI.

(8) Of a lease and release.

33

LECTURE LXXXII.

(9) Of deeds to lead and declare uses.

LECTURE LXXXIII.

(10) Of powers of revocation and appointment; and of the execution of powers.

LECTURE LXXXIV.

(11) Of powers to jointure and lease, and of the extinguishment of powers.

[☞ Where the defective execution of a power will be aided in equity, will be hereafter considered under Title IV.]

LECTURE LXXXV.

(12) Of registering and inrolling deeds, and of the laws of Maryland on this subject.

LECTURE LXXXVI.

(13) Of avoiding deeds, and of the interpretation, or the construction of deeds.

[☞ We now proceed to the *second* species of alienation, viz. by matters of record, of which there are four kinds, by *Act of Parliament, King's Grant, Fine, Recovery,* and shall close our inquiry into the "modes of acquiring title to real property" by an

34

examination of the title by Devise, entirely omitting, as useless, the subject of alienations by *special custom*, and which will also close the extensive learning of acquisitions by *purchase*.]

LECTURE LXXXVII.
OF TITLE TO REAL PROPERTY BY PRIVATE ACT OF PARLIAMENT, AND BY KING'S GRANT.

LECTURE LXXXVIII.
OF TITLE TO REAL PROPERTY BY FINE.

LECTURE LXXXIX.
OF TITLE TO REAL PROPERTY BY RECOVERY.

LECTURE XC.
OF TITLE BY DEVISE.

(1) Of the origin and nature of devises. (2) Who may devise, and to whom real property may be devised.

LECTURE XCI.
WHAT THINGS AND INTERESTS MAY BE DEVISED.

LECTURE XCII.
OF THE SOLEMNITIES REQUIRED IN A DEVISE.

35

LECTURE XCIII.

OF THE REVOCATION AND REPUBLICATION OF DEVISES; AND OF VOID DEVISES.

LECTURE XCIV.

OF THE MODES OF CONSTRUING DEVISES.

LECTURE XCV.

OF THE WORDS REQUISITE TO CREATE A DEVISE; TO DESCRIBE THOSE WHO ARE TO TAKE; AND THE INTEREST AND THINGS TO BE TAKEN.

II. OF REAL REMEDIES.

LECTURES XCVI, XCVII.

(1) Of real actions in former times, and at present. (2) Division of real actions. (3) Of droitural actions, writs of right, properly so called, and writs, in the nature of writs of right. (4) Of writs of entry upon disseisin, intrusion, alienation. (5) Of the various kinds of auncestral possessory actions. (6) Of real actions in the United States.

[Having finished the abstruse and extensive doctrine of the Realty, in which the student, though he may find some obsolete law, will discover most of the important principles and analogies of the entire system of municipal jurisprudence, we shall now proceed to an equally minute investigation into the learning of what has been denominated the Personalty.]

TITLE III.

OF THE LAW OF PERSONAL RIGHTS, AND PERSONAL REMEDIES.

LECTURE XCVIII.

Introductory. (1) Of the rights of persons. (2) Of persons in freedom, or in slavery. (3) Commentaries on some of the chapters of Magna Charta. (4) Commentaries on some of the sections of the Maryland Declaration of Rights.

LECTURE XCIX.

OF MARRIAGE AND DIVORCE, AND OF BASTARDY.

LECTURE C.

OF BARON AND FEME.

LECTURE CI.

OF GUARDIAN AND WARD, AND OF INFANCY AND AGE.

LECTURE CII.

OF IDIOTS AND LUNATICKS.

37

LECTURE CIII.
OF ALIENS, OF AMBASSADORS, OF PREROGATIVE.

LECTURE CIV.
OF CORPORATIONS.

LECTURE CV.
OF BY-LAWS; AND OF STATUTES.

LECTURE CVI.
OF WILLS AND TESTAMENTS.

LECTURE CVII.
OF EXECUTORS AND ADMINISTRATORS.

LECTURE CVIII.
SAME SUBJECT CONTINUED.

LECTURE CIX.
OF LEGACIES.

LECTURE CX.
SAME SUBJECT CONTINUED.

LECTURE CXI, CXII, CXIII.
OF CONTRACTS OR AGREEMENTS.

38

LECTURE CXIV.
OF OBLIGATIONS, ASSIGNMENT, AUTHORITY.

LECTURE CXV.
OF FRAUD, OF DURESS.

[The law of personal rights being thus far unfolded, we shall, before we inquire into the various remedies and actions to enforce these rights, examine into the organization of the tribunals, or courts of judicature, which have been constituted to ascertain, define, and execute such rights, and also into the peculiar *powers* of these courts.]

LECTURE CXVI.
OF COURTS AND THEIR JURISDICTION IN GENERAL; AND OF THE COURT OF PARLIAMENT.

LECTURE CXVII.
OF THE COURTS OF KING'S BENCH AND COMMON PLEAS.

LECTURE CXVIII.
OF THE COURT OF EXCHEQUER; THE COURT OF THE JUSTICES OF ASSISE AND NISI PRIUS, AND OF ECCLESIASTICAL COURTS.

LECTURE CXIX, CXX.
OF THE OFFICERS OF COURTS.

(1) Attorney. (2) Sheriff. (3) Coroner. (4) Constable.

39

LECTURE CXXI, CXXII.

OF THE POWERS OF COURTS OF JUDICATURE.

(1) Attachment. (2) Fine. (3) Amercement. (4) Habeas Corpus. (5) Prohibition. (6) Certiorari. (7) Mandamus.

OF THE LAW OF PERSONAL REMEDIES.

LECTURE CXXIII.

OF ACTIONS IN GENERAL, AND OF THE ACTION OF ACCOUNT.

LECTURE CXXIV.

OF THE ACTIONS OF DEBT AND COVENANT.

LECTURE CXXV.

OF THE ACTIONS OF DETINUE AND TROVER.

LECTURE CXXVI.

OF THE ACTION ON REPLEVIN.

LECTURE CXXVII.

OF THE ACTION ON THE CASE.

LECTURE CXXVIII.

OF THE ACTION OF ASSUMPSIT.

40

LECTURE CXXIX.
SAME SUBJECT CONTINUED.

LECTURE CXXX.
SAME SUBJECT CONTINUED.

LECTURE CXXXI.
OF THE ACTION OF TRESPASS.

LECTURE CXXXII.
OF THE ACTION OF EJECTMENT.

LECTURE CXXXIII.
OF THE ACTIONS FOR SLANDER AND LIBEL.

LECTURE CXXXIV.
OF THE ACTION OF ASSAULT AND BATTERY.

LECTURE CXXXV.
OF ARBITRAMENT AND AWARD.

LECTURE CXXXVI.
OF ACCORD AND SATISFACTION.

LECTURE CXXXVII.
OF ACTIONS LOCAL AND TRANSITORY, OF VENUE, OF ABATEMENT, OF MISNOMER AND ADDITION.

LECTURES CXXXVIII, CXXXIX, CXL, CXLI.

OF PLEADING.

LECTURE CXLII.

OF AMENDMENT AND JEOFAIL, OF NONSUIT, OF SUMMONS AND SEVERANCE.

LECTURE CXLIII.

OF ESCAPE IN CIVIL CASES, OF RESCUE, OF BAIL IN CIVIL CASES, OF JURIES.

LECTURES CXLIV, CXLV, CXLVI.

OF EVIDENCE.

LECTURE CXLVII.

OF TRIAL, VERDICT, DAMAGES, COSTS.

LECTURE CXLVIII.

OF BILLS OF EXCEPTION, OF ERROUR, OF SUPERSEDEAS.

LECTURE CXLIX.

OF SCIRE FACIAS, OF AUDITA QUERELA, OF INJUNCTION.

LECTURE CL.

OF EXECUTION.

42

[The student having attended us through the important and interesting topicks of *personal rights* and the *ordinary remedies* for their enforcement, We shall close the subjects embraced by our *Third Title*, by an inquiry into that *extraordinary* remedy founded on the customs of London, Exeter, &c. and established in most of the states of our union by statute, under the denominations of foreign and domestic attachment.]

LECTURES CLI, CLII.
OF FOREIGN AND DOMESTICK ATTACHMENTS.

TITLE IV.

OF THE LAW OF EQUITY.

LECTURE CLIII.

HISTORY OF CHANCERY JURISDICTION; EQUITY DEFINED; FOUR GREAT DIVISIONS OF CHANCERY JURISDICTION.

1. Common law jurisdiction.
2. Equity jurisdiction.
3. Statutory jurisdiction.
4. Delegated jurisdiction.

LECTURE CLIV.

OF THE COMMON LAW JURISDICTION OF THE CHANCELLOR; AND THE GENERAL OBJECTS OF EQUITY JURISDICTION; VIZ.

(1) Accident. (2) Mistake. (3) Account. (4) Fraud. (5) Infants. (6) Specifick performance of agreements. (7) Trusts *express*, *first*, Marriage Settlements. *Second*. Conveyances to purchasers. *Third*, Mortgages, &c. for payment of debts. *Fourth*, Choses in action. *Fifth*, Trusts created by

44

will. (8) Trusts *implied, first,* from the office of executor or administrator, and herein of the administration of assets, and payment of legacies. *Second,* from purchases in the name of another. *Third,* Purchases with notice of trust.

LECTURE CLV.

OF THE STATUTORY JURISDICTION OF THE CHANCELLOR.

(1) Admiralty jurisdiction. (2) Bankrupts. (3) Charitable uses. (4) Habeas corpus. (5) Arbitration. (6) Infant trustee.

LECTURE CLVI.

OF THE DELEGATED JURISDICTION.

(1) Idiots and Lunaticks. (2) Petition of right.

[The four cardinal divisions of chancery powers having been summarily treated, we shall proceed to a more minute examination of the subjects embraced in the second head, viz. "*Equity jurisdiction,*" this being, by far, the most extensive and important branch of our subject.

Previously to this, however, we shall speak of the organization of the court in which chancery law is administered.]

LECTURE CLVII.

OF THE COURT OF CHANCERY IN ENGLAND, AND IN THE STATE OF MARYLAND.

45

EQUITY JURISDICTION OF THE CHANCELLOR.

LECTURE CLVIII.

OF ACCIDENT AND MISTAKE.

Of *accidents* in case. (1) Of deeds and bonds lost. (2) Unsettled boundaries. (3) Penalties and Forfeitures.

Of *mistakes*. (1) In the execution of deeds. (2) Execution of Powers. (3) In Settlements. (4) In Bonds. (5) In Policies of insurance. (6) In Judgements. (7) In Pleadings. (8) In Arbitrators. (9) In settled accounts. (10) In Wills. (11) As to Law.

LECTURE CLIX.

ACCOUNT.

(1) Origin of this jurisdiction. (2) Between tradesman and customer. (3) Landlord and tenant. (4) Felling timber, &c. (5) Factor. (6) Partnership dealings. (7) Opening stated accounts.

LECTURE CLX.

FRAUD.

(1) Prolifick source of jurisdiction. (2) Definition of fraud. (3) *Suppressio veri,* and *Suggestio falsi.* (4) Of purchases made by persons in fiduciary relations—Trustee and *Cestui que Trust*—dealings between Attorney and Client—Guardian and Ward—Sales by expectant heirs.

46

LECTURE CLXI.

OF AVOIDING DEEDS, FINES, LETTERS PATENT, &c. WHEN OBTAINED BY FRAUD.

LECTURE CLXII.

OF AVOIDING CONTRACTS FOR FRAUD, DEDUCED FROM THE *INTRINSICK* NATURE OF THE AGREEMENT.

LECTURE CLXIII.

OF AVOIDING CONTRACTS FOR FRAUD, APPARENT FROM THE *CIRCUMSTANCES* OF THE CONTRACTING PARTIES.

LECTURE CLXIV.

OF AVOIDING CONTRACTS MADE IN FRAUD OF CREDITORS; AND OF COMPOSITION DEEDS.

LECTURE CLXV.

OF AVOIDING CONTRACTS MADE IN FRAUD OF PURCHASERS.

LECTURE CLXVI.

OF AVOIDING CONTRACTS MADE IN FRAUD OF MARITAL RIGHTS; AND OF MARRIAGE AGREEMENTS.

LECTURE CLXVII.

OF AVOIDING CONTRACTS WHOSE NULLITY ARISES RATHER FROM *PUBLICK POLICY*, THAN FROM FRAUD, AND HEREIN

47

(1) Of marriage and office brocage contracts. (2) Of contracts founded on the consideration of unlawful sexual intercourse. (3) Contracts for money won at play, &c.

LECTURE CLXVIII.

OF OTHER MATTERS OF FRAUD COGNIZABLE IN EQUITY.

LECTURE CLXIX.

OF THE AUTHORITY OF THE CHANCELLOR OVER INFANTS, AND OF THE LIGHT IN WHICH EQUITY VIEWS THEIR CONTRACTS.

LECTURE CLXX.

OF THE POWER OF CHANCERY TO DECREE THE SPECIFICK EXECUTION OF CONTRACTS.

(1) Origin of this power. (2) What kind of contracts will be thus executed. (3) Of the specifick performance of contracts out of the statute of frauds and perjuries. (4) Specifick performance of other contracts.

LECTURE CLXXI.

WHEN EQUITY WILL REFUSE TO DECREE SPECIFICK PERFORMANCE, AND OF OTHER MATTERS RELATIVE TO THE EXERCISE OF THIS POWER.

LECTURE CLXXII.

OF CHANCERY JURISDICTION IN CASES OF EXPRESS TRUST.

(1) General observations. (2) Of marriage settlements. (3) Of trust terms, or conveyances to purchasers in bar of dower. (4) Conveyances or trusts for payment of debts. (5) Of the assignment of choses in action.

LECTURE CLXXIII.

OF EXPRESS TRUSTS CREATED BY WILL, AND HEREIN OF THE DISTINCTION BETWEEN *EXECUTED* AND *EXECUTORY* TRUSTS.

LECTURE CLXXIV.

OF IMPLIED TRUSTS, AND HEREIN OF THE ADMINISTRATION OF ASSETS, &c.

LECTURE CLXXV.

OF IMPLIED TRUSTS, AND HEREIN

(1) Of the origin of chancery jurisdiction in case of *Legacies*. (2) Various kinds of legacies. (3) Other matters relative to legacies.

LECTURE CLXXVI.

OF IMPLIED TRUSTS RESULTING

(1) From a conveyance made to A. of an estate purchased with the money of B. (2) From purchases of property bound by a *trust* known to the purchaser.

49

[☞The powers of chancery being fully considered, we shall finish the subjects of our *Fourth Title*, with a few Lectures on the practical proceedings in chancery courts.]

LECTURE CLXXVII.
OF CHANCERY PRACTICE.

(1) General observations. (2) Institution of a suit. (3) Analysis of a bill in equity. Mode of compelling appearance. (5) Analysis of answer to a bill in equity. (6) Necessary parties to a bill. (7) Amendment of bills. (8) Mode of procuring evidence. (9) Defence to a suit.

LECTURE CLXXVIII.

(1) Of publication. (2) Of bringing the cause to hearing. (3) Of the decree. (4) Of rehearsing and review. (5) Of enforcing the decree.

LETURE CLXXIX.
OF THE VARIOUS KINDS OF BILLS IN EQUITY.

LECTURE CLXXX.

OF VARIOUS PETITIONS, MOTIONS, ORDERS, &c. AND OF THE STATUTORY PROVISIONS RELATIVE TO CHANCERY PROCEEDINGS IN THE STATE OF MARYLAND.

TITLE V.

OF THE LAW OF CRIMES AND PUNISHMENTS.

LECTURE CLXXXI.

Introductory observations. (1) Of the words *Crime, Misdemeanour, Offence, Transgression, Sin, Guilt.* (2) Origin and right of punishment. (3) Ends of punishment. (4) Measure of punishment. (5) Right, and necessity of capital punishment. (6) Of the criminal jurisprudence of various nations.

LECTURE CLXXXII.

ANALYSIS OF THE WORK OF MR. BENTHAM, ENTITLED,

"*Théorie des Peines, et des Récompensès.*"

LECTURE CLXXXIII.

I. OF CRIMES AGAINST RELIGION AND PUBLICK MORALS, AND PARTICULARLY OF THE STATUTES OF MARYLAND ON THIS HEAD.

LECTURE CLXXXIV.

II. OF CRIMES AGAINST SOVEREIGNTY; AND HEREIN CHIEFLY OF *TREASON* AGAINST THE UNITED STATES, AND THE STATE OF MARYLAND.

51

LECTURE CLXXXV.

III. OF CRIMES AGAINST THE PERSON.

(1) Of Homicide in general, and *first* of *Murder*, and herein of the *degrees* of Murder, by the law of Maryland. *Secondly*, of *Manslaughter* and *Suicide*.

LECTURE CLXXXVI.

OF JUSTIFIABLE AND EXCUSABLE HOMICIDE.

LECTURE CLXXXVII.

OF MAYHEM, ASSAULT, BATTERY, RAPE.

LECTURE CLXXXVIII.

OF FALSE IMPRISONMENT, KIDNAPPING, &c. &c.

LECTURE CLXXXIX.

IV. OF CRIMES AGAINST PROPERTY.

(1) Of Arson. (2) Of Burglary.

LECTURE CXC.

OF LARCENY AND ROBBERY.

[☞ The law of Piracy, will be fully considered under Title X.—"Laws of the United States."]

52

LECTURE CXCI.

OF CHEATS.

(1) At common law. (2) Under the statutes.

OF FORGERY.

(1) By the laws of England. (2) In Maryland. (3) A general view of the Penal Code of Maryland.

LECTURE CXCII.

V. OF PRACTICAL PROCEEDINGS IN CRIMINAL CASES.

(1) Arrest. (2) Bail. (3) Presentment and Indictment. (4) Arraignment and standing mute. (5) Pleas. (6) Evidence. (7) Judgment. (8) Reversal of Judgment. (9) Reprieve and Pardon. (10) Execution.

TITLE VI.

OF THE LEX MERCATORIA.

LECTURE CXCIII.

Introductory observations. (1) Every branch of this extensive subject will *not* be treated by us with our usual minuteness, *first*, because not equally interesting to the students of every state; *Secondly*, as the doctrines are simple, and sufficiently attractive to induce the student to bestow an ample portion of his time on them; *Thirdly*, as this law is so much practised in some of the states, as necessarily to insure a minute acquaintance with it, and the design of these Lectures being to dwell on, and to enforce such portions of the law as are apt to be in some degree neglected, either from their *abstruseness*, or the infrequency of occasion to investigate them. (2) The present course, however, will exhibit a full analysis of the principles, enforced by all of the important decisions of the Lex Mercatoria. (3) Definition of Lex Mercatoria. (4) History of the progress of this law in England, France, and the United States. (5) Grand divisions of the Lex Mercatoria—viz. into law.

54

1. Of Principals, Agents, Factors, and Brokers.
2. Of Bills of Exchange.
3. Of Promissory Notes.
4. Of Partners and Joint Traders.
5. Of Marine Insurance.
6. Of Owners and Masters of ships.
7. Of Mariners, and their Wages.
8. Of Bills of Lading, and Stoppage in Transitu.
9. Of Freight, Charter Party and Demurrage.
10. Of Average and Salvage.
11. Of Bankruptcy.

(6) The above eleven divisions will embrace every topick of this varied and useful system of law.

LECTURE CXCIV.
OF THE LAW OF PRINCIPAL, AGENT, &c.

LECTURE CXCV.
SAME SUBJECT CONTINUED.

LECTURE CXCVI, to CCII.
OF THE LAW OF BILLS OF EXCHANGE AND PROMISSORY NOTES.

LECTURE CCIII.
OF THE LAW OF PARTNERSHIP.

LECTURE CCIV.
SAME SUBJECT CONTINUED.

55

LECTURES CCV, CCVI, CCVII, CCVIII.
OF THE LAW OF INSURANCE.

LECTURES CCIX, CCX, CCXI, CCXII.
OF OWNERS AND MASTERS OF SHIPS.

(1) **Of Vessels of the United States.** (2) **Of foreign vessels.** (3) General duties of the master. (4) His powers of Hypothecating, &c. (5) Owners' interest in vessel. (6) Duty of Owner or Owners. (7) Responsibilities of Owner. (8) **Of Clearance, Manifest, Report, Entry, &c.**

LECTURE CCXIII.
OF MARINERS.

(1) How employed. (2) American and foreign. (3) Their duties. (4) Common law remedy for wages. (5) Other matters relative to Seamen. [☞ The subject of Mariners' wages will be fully considered under Title VIII. of "Admiralty and Maritime Law."]

LECTURE CCXIV.
OF BILLS OF LADING, AND STOPPAGE IN TRANSITU.

LECTURE CCXV.
OF FREIGHT, CHARTER PARTY, AND DEMURRAGE.

56

LECTURE CCXVI.
SAME SUBJECT CONTINUED.

LECTURE CCXVII.
OF AVERAGE AND SALVAGE.

[☞ The latter subject will be more particularly considered under Title VIII.]

LECTURE CCXVIII.
OF BANKRUPTCY AND THE INSOLVENT LAWS OF THE STATE OF MARYLAND.

TITLE VII.

OF THE LAWS OF NATIONS.

LECTURE CCXIX.

(1) History of the Law of Nations as a science. (2) Various definitions of the Law of Nations. (3) Professor's Definition. (4) Division of the Law of Nations into
    1. Universal, Necessary, or Natural Law of Nations.
    2. Voluntary, or Presumed Law of Nations.
    3. Customary, or Tacit Law of Nations
    4. Conventional, or Express Law of Nations.
(5) Of the different views of Grotius and Puffendorf as to a *Positive* Law of Nations.

LECTURE CCXX.

(1) Of the Laws of Nations as they respect the threefold relations of states with each other, viz.
    1. Of Peace.
    2. Of War.
    3. Of Neutrality.

58

(2) OF PEACE, and herein, *first* definition of Peace. *Secondly* of certain rights and duties appertaining to nations in a state of peace, and herein

    1. Of the right of sovereignty, and absolute equality and independence in all matters of self government.
    2. The extent of national jurisdiction.
    3. Of commercial and other intercourse between nations.
    4. Of the reciprocal right of Embassy.

LECTURE CCXXI.

OF *WAR*, AND HEREIN

(1) Definition of War. (2) To whom the right of making war appertains. (3) War perfect, imperfect, offensive, defensive. (4) Of the justifying causes of war. (5) Of the time and modes of commencing war, and herein

    1. Declaration of War.
    2. Manifestoes.
    3. Warlike Embargoes.
    4. General Reprisals.
    5. Commencement of Hostilities.
    6. Belligerant's treatment of enemies found in the country when war commences, or is declared by or against the country.

LECTURE CCXXII.

OF THE MEANS TO BE USED IN CONDUCTING THE WAR.

    1. Of killing, or enslaving an enemy.
    2. Of quarter.

59

3. Of confiscation by belligerant of enemy's property taken within his dominions.
4. Of conquest.
5. Of capture of moveables.
6. Of recapture and the *jus postliminii*.
7. Of the use of Privateers.
8. Of Persons exempted.
9. Of Things exempted.

LECTURE CCXXIII.

(1) Of the illegality of commerce between alien enemies, &c. (2) Exceptions and qualifications of this rule. (3) Of those who are deemed alien enemies, as to certain purposes, by acquiring a *hostile character*, and of the various modes in which this character may be impressed.

LECTURE CCXXIV.

OF TERMINATING THE WAR.

(1) In case of conquest, and herein,
    1. Of exterminating the inhabitants.
    2. Of enslaving them.
    3. Of subjecting them to the laws of the conqueror.
    4. Of simply annexing them to the conqueror's dominion.
(2) Without conquest, and herein,
    1. Of Mediation.
    2. Of Negotiation.

60

3. Of Amnesty.
4. Of Arbitration.
5. Of Conferences, Congresses, &c.

LECTURE CCXXV.

OF *NEUTRALITY.*

(1) Definition of neutrality. (2) Of the right of remaining neutral. (3) General duties of neutrality. (4) Different kinds of neutrality. (5) The consideration of neutrality leads us to inquire.

    1. As to the conduct of neutrals towards either of the belligerants.

    2. As to the conduct of belligerants towards neutrals.

(6) Enumeration of the rights and duties of neutrals.

(7) Enumeration of the rights and duties of belligerants.

LECTURE CCXXVI.

OF THE CONDUCT OF NEUTRALS TOWARDS BELLIGERANTS.

(1) Of the strict impartiality required by neutrals. (2) Of the right of neutrals to carry on their accustomed trade, with the exceptions *to blockaded places;* in *contraband* articles, and of liability to *visitation* and *search.* (3) Of the commerce of neutrals with belligerants in contraband articles. (4) Of the universal and positive law of nations with respect to contraband, and of the three classes of contraband articles.

61

LECTURE CCXXVII.

OF TRADE BY NEUTRALS WITH A PLACE BLOCKADED OR BESIEGED.

LECTURE CCXXVIII.

OF THE TRADE OF NEUTRALS, ALLOWED BY EITHER BELLIGERANT IN TIME OF *WAR*, BUT WHICH IS FORBIDDEN IN TIME OF *PEACE*. OF THE RULE OF THE WAR OF 1756, AND THE RELAXATIONS THEREOF.

LECTURE CCXXIX.

OF THE CONDUCT OF BELLIGERANTS TOWARDS NEUTRALS.

(1) Of the conduct of a belligerant in passing through a neutral country. (2) Of the respect due from belligerants to neutral limits. (3) Of the exception, contended for by some jurists, as to the right to consummate a capture within neutral limits, which had its inception beyond them. (4) Of the exemption of *neutral* property from seizure when found in enemy's vessel. (5) Of the seizure of *enemy's* property on board a neutral vessel, and of the doctrine that "Free ships make free goods."

LECTURE CCXXX.

SAME SUBJECT CONTINUED.

(1) History of the right of visitation and search. (2) Of this right *first*, where neutral vessel has *contraband* property; *secondly*, where vessel is proceed-

62

ing to a *blockaded* or *besieged* place, *thirdly*, for *enemy's goods*. (3) Of the right of belligerants to carry their prizes into neutral ports for sale.

[☞ Various doctrines of international law will necessarily be considered under Title **VIII**. viz. of "Maritime and Admiralty Law."]

TITLE VIII.

OF THE MARITIME AND ADMIRALTY LAW.

LECTURE CCXXXI.

ORIGIN OF THE ADMIRALTY, AND ITS COURTS; AND OF THE GENERAL PRINCIPLES OF ADMIRALTY AND MARITIME LAW.

LECTURE CCXXXII.

OF THE CIVIL AND PRIZE DROITS, OR PERQUISITES OF THE ADMIRALTY.

LECTURE CCXXXIII.

OF THE CRIMINAL JURISDICTION OF THE ADMIRALTY.

(1) Murder. (2) Treason. (3) Piracy. (4) Felonies. (5) Violations of Truce and Safe Conduct.

LECTURE CCXXXIV.

OF CONTRACTS COGNIZABLE IN THE INSTANCE COURT OF THE ADMIRALTY.

64

LECTURE CCXXXV.

OF TORTS COGNIZABLE IN THE INSTANCE COURT.

LECTURE CCXXXVI.

OF THE JURISDICTION OF THE PRIZE COURTS.

LECTURE CCXXXVII.

OF THE JURISDICTION AND LAW OF THE DISTRICT COURT OF THE UNITED STATES IN CIVIL CAUSES, OF AN ADMIRALTY AND MARITIME NATURE, AS,

 1. Of Maritime capture.
 2. Of Maritime torts or injuries to the person or property of citizens, or foreigners.
 3. Of Ransoms.
 4. Of Salvage.
 5. Of Derelict.
 6. Of Seaman's Wages.

(1) Of Maritime capture. (2) Of Maritime Torts, &c.

LECTURE CCXXXVIII.

OF RANSOM, OF SALVAGE, AND OF DERELICT.

LECTURE CCXXXIX.

OF SEAMAN'S WAGES.

65

LECTURE CCXL.

OF THE PRACTICE OF THE PRIZE AND INSTANCE COURTS OF ENGLAND, AND OF THE DISTRICT COURTS OF THE UNITED STATES, AND HEREIN OF *PROCEEDINGS IN REM.*

(1) Libel. (2) Attachment. (3) Monition. (4) Appearance, *absolute* or *under protest*. (5) Cautions. (6) Claim, by *Counsel, Agent, Owner*. (7) Answer. (8) Receiving the property on stipulation. (9) Of the power of the court to order stipulators to give further security when they become incompetent, or *lapsi facultatibus*. (10) Default. (11) Sales under perishable monition. (12) Appraisement and sale for other reasons. (13) Publication. (14) Disposition of proceeds. (15) Libel for wages. (16) Libel on Hypothecation and Bottomry Bonds. (17) Other Libels *in rem*.

LECTURE CCXLI.

OF PROCEEDINGS *IN PERSONAM*.

(1) Of Injuries to the *person*. Libel for Assault and Battery; Answer to such Libel. (2) Injuries to *property*, as, *first*, Libel for collision, *secondly*, Libel for recovery of damages for injuries, or illegal seizures of property at sea; *thirdly*, Libels by Ambassadors or Consuls, for recovery of damages where seizure was *jure belli*, but by persons violating the neutrality or laws of that nation in whose court jurisdiction is claimed. (3) Answer and Defence to these Libels. (4) Decree. (5) Mode of enforcing decree. (6) Of Appeals and Writs of Errour, and

9

66

herein of the distinction between these modes of removing causes. (7) Of the extent of the further security to be given on appeals, after the property claimed has been given to the claimant on stipulation.

[☞ The above is necessarily a very imperfect enumeration of the interesting and various topicks of Maritime and Admiralty Law. The subject is so extensive and diversified, that the bare mention of all the items of consideration, with the subjects yet to be stated, would swell this Syllabus much beyond its contemplated size.]

TITLE IX.

OF THE CIVIL OR ROMAN LAW.

LECTURE CCXLII.

Introductory observations. (1) On the excellence of the Civil Law. (2) Its intimate connexion with many of the most important branches of the Common, National, Admiralty and Maritime Law. (3) Of the *Corpus Juris Civilis,* as reduced by the order of the Emperor Justinian. (4) Of the *Basilica.* (5) Of the "*Pandectæ Justinianæ in novum ordinem digestæ,*" of M. Pothier. (6) Of the modes of citing the *Institutes, Digest, Code,* and *Novels.* (7) Of the most distinguished works on the Civil Law. (8) Of the study of the Civil Law in Europe and America, and of the chief schools in which it has been taught in Europe; and of the vast importance and extent of the subject, and the necessity of distinct Professorships in this country.

LECTURE CCXLIII.

I. OF THE STATE OF PERSONS.

[*De Statu hominum.*]

(1) In what the state of persons consists. (2) Division into natural and civil state. (3) The *status*

68

naturalis as it regards persons, either *to be born* (*nascituri*,) or *born* (*nati*.) (4) Natural state founded on *sex, age, birth*. (5) The *status civilis*, or civil state, had relation to the person's *Liberty, Country*, or *Family*. (6) The *first* as it regarded persons in freedom or in slavery. (7) The *second*, as Roman citizens, or strangers. (8) And the *third*, as fathers of a family, and children subject to their authority. (9) The first and third only considered, which give rise to the great relations in civil life, of *Husband and Wife, Parent and Child, Master and Slave or Servant*.

LECTURE CCXLIV.
OF HUSBAND AND WIFE.

(1) General observations. (2) Of Marriage, and herein of *Matrimonium, Nuptiæ, Connubium, Conugium, Consortium, Contubernium*, each explained. (3) Definition of *matrimonium*, and how distinguished from *nuptiæ;* sometimes used indiscriminately. (4) Regarded only as a civil contract. (5) The subject but little noted in the Institutes.

LECTURE CCXLV.
OF CONTRACTING MARRIAGE.

(1) Of matters essential to the contract, and herein of the *will* and *ability* to contract. (2) Of temporal disabilities, and herein of *infancy, want of consent of parents or guardians, alienage*. (3) Of the disability arising from *turpitude*, which may be *inces-*

69

tuous, indecorous, noxious, [included in the last.]
(4) Of consanguinity and affinity, and of *natural* and *civil* incest. (5) Of the degrees of proximity. (6) Mode of computing degrees by the *Civil, Canon, English* and *American* Laws. (7) Of the disability flowing from what was considered *indecorum*. (8) Of noxious disabilities, and herein of marriage between Christian and Jew; Guardian and Ward; of Clergy or others after vow; of Polygamy.

LECTURE CCXLVI.
SAME SUBJECT CONTINUED.

(1) Of the *actual consent,* in concurrence with *will* and *ability,* requisite in marriage; and herein of Precontract, *per verba de prasenti, and per verba de futuro,* and of the doctrines of the *canonists* in regard to these contracts. (2) Of consent founded in Errour, and herein of errours *de substantia,* and *de qualitate.* (3) Of the *forms,* &c. sometimes required to be added to *willingness, ability,* and *consent,* and herein of marriages either solemn (*solennes.*) unsolemn, or less solemn (*minus solennes,*) the former contracted by Confarreation (*confarreatione,*) Coemption (*coemptione,*) or by use (*usu.*) (4) Of unsolemn marriage, and herein of the marriage *ex usu,* why classed with solemn marriages. (5) Of certain ceremonies which attended Roman marriages. (6) Of inducements to marry, and of restraints on marriage.

70

LECTURE CCXLVII.

OF THE EFFECTS RESULTING FROM MARRIAGE.

(1) Husband and Wife *not* considered as one person, having one will, but as distinct individuals who might enjoy separate property, rights, &c. and be subjected to correspondent duties. (2) Of suits by Husband against Wife, and *e converso*. (3) Of suits by or against them individually. (4) Not responsible for each other's debts, injuries, or illegal acts. (5) Of Husband and Wife inheriting each other's property. (6) Of the *Dos adventitia*, and *Dos profectitia*. (7) Of their disability to testify for or against each other, though distinct persons. (8) Of the Husband's power over his Wife.

LECTURE CCXLVIII.

OF DIVORCE AND REPUDIATION.

(1) History of the right of Divorce among the Romans. (2) Of the distinction between *Divortium* and *Repudium*, though sometimes confounded. (3) Causes of divorce of Husband from Wife, and of Wife from Husband. (4) Of the ceremonies attendant on Divorces. (5) Distinction between Divorces *a vinculo matrimonii*, and *a mensa et thoro*, unknown to the Civil Law, and herein of the causes of the present distinction.

LECTURE CCXLIX.

OF PARENT AND CHILD.

(1) History of parental power among the Romans; how acquired, and its extent, *first* over the person of

71

the child, *secondly* over his property. (2) Of the son's *peculium*. (3) Of the obligations of parent and child to each other. (4) Of the termination of parental authority, and herein of the *death, relegation, deportation, punishment,* and *captivity* of the father. (5) Of Emancipation.

LECTURES CCL, CCLI.

OF MASTER AND SLAVE.

(1) Division of Persons into *freemen* and *slaves*. (2) Of freemen who are *sui juris*, and such as are not, and of those who are *ingenui* or *libertini*. (3) Definitions of slavery and of freedom, and of classing slaves under the head of *Homo*, but not of *Persona*. (4) Of slavery arising from captivity. (5) Of slavery arising from birth, and herein of the maxim *Partus sequitur ventrem*. (6) Of slavery arising from consent. (7) Of slavery, the consequence of crimes and offences. (8) Of the master's power over the *person* of his slave. (9) Of the master's power over the property of his slave. (10) Of the slave's *peculium*. (11) Of the slave's general condition. (12) Of the manumission of slaves, either *solemn* or *less solemn;* the former, as by enrolment, (*census,*) the Lictor's Wand, (*vindicta,*) by *Will,* (*Testamentum,*) in the face of the Church, (*in ecclesiis.*) The less solemn, as by Letter, (*per epistolam,*) before Friends, (*inter amicos,*) by being constituted Heir or Tutor, by Nomination, by Admission to his master's table, (*per convivium,*) &c. (13) Emancipation not to be made in fraud of creditors. (14) Of

72

other matters relating to manumission. (15) Of the Laws made to ameliorate the slave's condition.

LECTURE CCLII.

OF TUTELAGE AND CURATION.

(1) Tutelage defined. (2) Distinguished from curation. (3) Who were subject to tutelage, as Infants, Idiots, Lunaticks, Women, Prodigals. (4) Of the modes of appointing tutors, by Law or by the Magistrate. (5) Of Testamentary tutors. (6) Of Legal tutors. (7) Of tutors appointed by Magistrates or Bishops. (8) Of the duties and powers of the tutor. (9) Of the obligations of the minor to his tutor. (10) When and how tutelage terminates.

LECTURE CCLIII.

OF CURATION.

(1) Of the office of curators. (2) Mode of their appointment. (3) Who are subject to curation (4) Of the duty and power of curators. (5) Of the duties of those under curation. (6) Of the causes excusing those nominated curators or tutors from serving. (7) Of suspected curators and tutors.

[Having treated of individuals or *natural* persons, we shall finish this branch of our subject with an examination of the Law relative to those *artificial* bodies composed of several individuals, denominated Universities, Communities, or Corporations, considered as Persons.]

73

LECTURE CCLIV.

OF COMMUNITIES, CORPORATIONS, OR UNIVERSITIES.

(1) Origin of artificial persons. (2) Several kinds of corporations. (3) All corporations are aggregate. (4) How corporations were constituted. (5) Of the capacities and incapacities of corporations. (6) Of their power of self government by by-laws. (7) Of their contracting and being contracted with. (8) Of their power to receive donations. (9) Of their power to elect members to fill vacancies. (10) Of their suing or being sued. (11) Of their acting by syndics. (12) By what kind of majority corporations were obligated. (13) Of the dissolution of corporations. (14) University a word of generical import, comprehending every species of corporation or community, and herein of Universities for the advancement of the Sciences and Liberal Arts.

[The material doctrines under the head *"De statu hominum,"* or as we might express it, *The Rights of Persons*, having been considered; we now proceed to investigate the Law of *Things*, a learning more extensive and important, and in *some respects* bearing a nearer similitude to the *jura rerum* of the Common Law, though on the doctrines of the *realty* often very dissimilar.]

74

II. OF THINGS.

LECTURE CCLV.

(1) Civil Law doctrine as to the origin of property. (2) Of things *in patrimonio,* or *extra patrimonium.* (3) Of things extra patrimonium, *in common, publick, universitatis,* [or belonging to some community,] lastly *nullius,* the property of no one, comprehending things either *sacred, religious,* or *holy.* (4) The division of things by *Caius,* followed by Taylor and other civilians, preferable.

LECTURE CLCVI.

OF THINGS IN PATRIMONIO.

(1) Of things considered as corporeal moveable, corporeal immoveable, and incorporeal. (2) Of things incorporeal *lato sensu.* (3) Of usus fruct. (4) Of use and *res fringibiles.* (5) Of habitation. (6) Of Prœdial services, *rural* and *city.*

LECTURE CCLVII.

OF THE ESTATE OR QUANTITY OF INTEREST IN THINGS.

(1) The numerous and refined distinctions of the Common Law, between *real* and *personal* estates, unknown to the Civil Code. (2) Of the *dominium eminens,* and the *dominium vulgare.* (3) Of the *dominium directum, dominium utile, dominium plenum, dominium minus plenum.* (4) Of substitutions Vulgar,

75

Papillary, Quasi Papillary, and Fiduciary. (5) Of the Fidei Commissary Substitution, and herein of their resemblance to the Common Law estates in *Tail, Remainder,* and *Trust.* (6) Courtesy and dower unknown to the Civil Law—Estates for life very unusual. (7) Of *Emphyteusis,* perpetual or long *leases;* how Emphyteusis may be created, and the obligations of the Emphyteuta.

LECTURE CCLVIII.

OF THE ACQUISITION OF THINGS JURE NATURÆ.

(1) Of Occupancy. (2) Of Accession. (3) Of Delivery.

[These are subjects of considerable extent and nicety, and will be minutely examined and compared, in all material respects, with the doctrines and decisions of the Common Law. The subject of *Delivery,* however, will be more particularly examined in the 6th section of the ensuing Lecture.]

LECTURE CCLIX.

OF THE ACQUISITION OF THINGS JURE CIVILI.

(1) Of Prescription. (2) Of *Caduca,* or devolutions of property to the Exchequer. (3) Of the *Cessio Bonorum.* (4) Who might alien, what could not be aliened. (5) Of the modes of alienating. (6) Of Proper Gifts, or *donatio inter vivos.*

76

LECTURE CCLX.

(1) Of Improper Gifts, first *propter nuptias*, secondly *causa mortis*. (2) Of Inheritance, first by Testament; secondly by Law, or Right of Descent; thirdly the *Bonorum Possessio* of the Prætor; these three now briefly considered.

LECTURE CCLXI.

OF INHERITANCE OR SUCCESSION BY TESTAMENT.

(1) Whether the right of disposing of property by will be the creature of positive law. (2) Definition of Testament, and of the four kinds of Testament. (3) Of solemn testaments, common to all. (4) Of unsolemn, particular, or privileged testaments. (5) Of Codicils.

LECTURE CCLXII.

(1) By whom testaments could be made. (2) Of things devisable or not. (3) Of testamentary heirship, who might become heirs, and of the rights and duties of such heirs. (4) Of executors, as distinguished from testamentary or instituted heirs. (5) Of Legacies.

LECTURE CCLXIII.

(1) Of annulling testaments, first *by law*, as by implication, cancellation, express revocation, subsequent testament; secondly *by the judge*, for inofficiousness, for fraud in their acquisition, arrogation, &c. (2) Of the constructions of wills. (3) Of the proof of wills.

77

LECTURE CCLXIV.

OF LEGAL INHERITANCE, OR SUCCESSION AB INTESTATO.

(1) Definition of heirship. (2) Difference between the legal heir and the *hœres factus*. (3) Of the ideal unity of ancestor and heir, and consequences flowing from this doctrine. (4) Division of heirs into *necessarii, sui et necessarii,* and *extranei*. (5) Succession to moveable and immoveable property the same; the common law distinction between real and personal estate being unknown.

LECTURE CCLXV.

(1) Of the rules of descent of property, and of the order of heirship. (2) Of the computation of degrees. (3) Of succession *per capita* and *per stirpes*. (4) Of succession in the descending line. (5) Of succession in the ascending line. (6) Of succession in the collateral line. (7) Comparison of the canons of descent with those of the common law, and the rules of descent in Maryland. (8) Of the Bonorum Possessio. (9) Of the Collatio Bonorum.

LECTURE CCLXVI.

OF HYPOTHECA (MORTGAGE) AND OF PIGNUS (PAWN.)

(1) Hypotheca and Pignus defined and distinguished. (2) Three species of mortgage. (3) Of conventional hypothecation, as a security only for debt, interest and costs, and herein of the several respects in which the Roman Hypotheca differs from

78

the common law mortgage. (4) Of the modes in which the creditor satisfied himself out of the hypothecated property. (5) Of matters common to hypotheca and pignus. (6) Of the various kinds of pledges. (7) Of Subrogation, the various kinds, and consequences resulting from such assignments.

LECTURE CCLXVII.

OF JOINT ESTATES.

(1) General observations. (2) Of the *jus accrescendi*. (3) Of *communio Bonorum*, and the actions *communi dividudno et familiæ erciscundæ*. (4) Of services charged, in case of unequal division, similar to the common law rent charge, for *owelty* of partition.

LECTURE CCLXVIII.

OF OBLIGATIONS, CONTRACTS, AND PACTS.

(1) Of obligations, natural, civil, and mixed. (2) Obligation distinguished from contract or covenant. (3) Definition of covenant, either *nude* or a *contract*. (4) Definition of contract—contracts either *nominate* or *innominate*. (5) Nominate contracts enumerated. (6) Innominate contracts explained, and divided into classes. (7) Of obligations arising *ex contractu, quasi ex contractu, ex delicto,* and *quasi ex delicto,* generally explained.

LECTURE CCLXIX.

OF OBLIGATIONS ARISING EX CONTRACTU.

(1) Of Nominate or true contracts, proceeding *ex re,* from a thing done; *ex verbis,* from words; *ex literis,* from writing; *ex consensu,* from consent. (2) Of nominate contracts, *ex re,* viz. Mutuum, Commodatum, Depositum, and Pignus, fully treated of, except the *last,* which has been considered in Lecture CCLXII. (3) Of nominate contracts *ex verbis,* viz. *stipulation* and *surety.* (4) Of nominate contracts *ex literis.*

LECTURE CCLXX.

OF NOMINATE CONTRACTS EX CONSENSU.

(1) General observations. (2) Of the distinction between consensual and real contracts. (3) Division of consensual contracts, and *first* of the contract of sale, *emptio-venditio, secondly* of the contract of hiring, *locatio-conductio,* which has been in part considered in Lecture CCLIII. *thirdly* of the contract of partnership, *societas; fourthly* of the contract of commission or authority, *mandatum.*

LECTURE CCLXXI.

OF INNOMINATE CONTRACTS, AND OF OBLIGATIONS ARISING QUASI EX CONTRACTU.

(1) General observations. (2) Of the *actio in factum,* and the *locus pœnitentiæ.* (3) Of improper or

80

quasi contracts. (4) Of the *negotiorum gestio,* and how different from *mandatum.* (5) Of the *Tutelæ Administratio, Judicium, finium regundorum, Aditio hœreditatis, Solutio indebiti.* (6) Of obligations proceeding from accidents and frauds.

LECTURE CCLXXII.

(1) Of contracts *bonæ fidei,* and *stricti juris.* (2) Of the interpretation of contracts. (3) Of the termination of contracts, and herein of Payment, Consignation, Acceptilation, Confusion, Novation, Compensation, Mutual Consent, and Oblation.

LECTURE CCLXXIII.

OF OBLIGATIONS ARISING EX DELICTO.

(1) Of the nature of the obligation occasioned by the commission of publick and private offences, and of the difference, in this respect, between the civil and common law. (2) Of private crimes, or rather offences, *delicta et quasi delicta,* as distinguished from publick crimes, *crimina.* (3) Of delicta or proper offences, viz. Theft, *furtum,* Robbery, *rapina,* Damage, *damnum,* Injury, *injuria.*

LECTURE CCLXXIV.

OF OBLIGATIONS ARISING QUASI EX DELICTO.

(1) Of private, improper offences, or *quasi delicta.* (2) Of the seven species of *quasi torts,* and herein *first,* of an erroneous Judgment of a Judge, through

81

ignorance; *secondly,* of carelessly throwing any thing out of a house, &c. whereby another suffers harm; *thirdly,* of loss of property committed to innkeepers or masters of a vessel; *fourthly,* of placing or suspending any thing on high, near a house, so that persons *may* be injured; *fifthly,* of harm contemplated from a work about to be erected; *sixthly,* of harm expected to arise from a work already built, and herein of the *nuntiatio, cautions,* and proceedings of the Prætor in the two last cases; *seventhly,* of harm from beasts.

LECTURE CCLXXV.

OF OBLIGATIONS ARISING FROM CRIMES, PROPERLY SO CALLED.

(1) Preliminary observations on the Penal Laws of the civil code. (2) Of Blasphemy. (3) Of Treason, *læsa majestas.* (4) Of Adultery and Stuprum. (5) Of Bigamy. (6) Of Incest. (7) Of Sodomy. (8) Of Homicide. (9) Of Parricide. (10) Of Witchcraft. (11) Of Banishment. (12) Of House-burning. (13) Of Theft, after it became criminal. (14) Of the Crimen Falsi. (15) Of Robbery, after it became criminal, and herein of *effractores, latrones, pirates,* and *expilatores.* (16) Of the Crimen Peculatus. (17) Of the Crimen Residui. (18) Of Bribery, *crimen repetundarum.* (19) Of the Crimen Ambitus. (20) Of Plagium, or man-stealing, Saccularii, Abigei, Balnearii. (21) Of Forestaling and Monopolizing, Crimen Fraudatæ Annonæ.

82

LECTURE CCLXXVI.

(1) Of the division of crimes into ordinary and extraordinary. (2) The ordinary crimes having been fully considered, we now proceed to the latter, viz. Procuring Abortion. (3) Threatening death or bodily harm, *scopelisinus*. (4) Violating tombs. (5) Prostration of the dams of publick rivers. (6) Coucussion, or extortion of money &c. by various illegal devices. (7) Prevarication, or collusion between Informer and Defendant. (8) Abigeatus, or stealing a specifick number of cattle. (9) Harbouring criminals. (10) Enticing and harbouring bondmen, &c. (11) Exposure of Infants. (12) Stellionate, or undefined cheats and frauds. (13) Removing landmarks. (14) Unauthorised Universities or communities. (15) Perjury. (16) Breaking prison. (17) Desertion by soldiers. (18) Taking unlawful pledges or distresses. (19) Purchasing silks and purple. (20) Attempts on chastity. (21) Polluting publick waters.

LECTURE CCLXXVII.

OF THE ORGANIZATION OF THE ROMAN COURTS OF JUDICATURE, AND FORMS OF PRACTICE.

(1) Of the office and power of a Judge. (2) Of contentious and voluntary jurisdiction. (3) Of exceptions to the jurisdiction, and of challenging the Judges. (4) Of the Assessor to the Judge. (5) Of the distinct duties of the Judge and Magistrate, and of the modes of appointing them. (6) Of the parties to an action, Actor, *plaintiff*, Reus, *defendant*, and

88

herein, who may sue or be sued. (7) Of the oath of calumny. (8) Of taking the complaint *pro confesso*. (9) Of the duties of the Advocate and Proctor. (10) Of Apparitors and Notaries.

LECTURE CCLXXVIII.

OF ACTIONS.

(1) Definition of action. (2) Division of actions into Civil, Criminal, Real, Personal, Mixed, Petitory, Possessory, Prejudicial, Persecutory, Noxal, Bonæ fidei, Stricti juris, &c. each explained. (3) Of Real actions or Vindications. (4) Of Personal actions, or Condictions. (5) Of Mixed actions. (6) Of the Cession of actions. (7) Of the Cumulation of actions. (8) Of Interdicts.

LECTURE CCLXXIX.

OF ACTIONS (CONTINUED.)

(1) Of Citation. (2) Of the Libel. (3) Of the Litis Contestatio. (4) Of the Answer. (5) Of Exceptions, dilatory and peremptory. (6) Of the Replication. (7) Of the *fidejussory, pignoratitious, juratory,* and *promissory* Cautions. (8) Of Intervention, Laudation, Nomination, Transaction, and Arbitration. (9) Of Trials *pro tribunali* and *de plano*.

LECTURE CCLXXX.

OF ACTIONS (CONTINUED.)

(1) Of the Evidence or Proof; and herein of General, Particular, Plena, and Semi-plena proof, and the

84

topicks of argumentation. (2) **Of Particular** proof arising from Confession, Presumptions, either *juris*, or *juris et de jure*. (3) **Of Witnesses**, and herein of their number, qualification, and mode of giving their testimony. (4) **Of Instruments**, and herein of Publick and Private instruments, *cautio, apocha, antipocha, syngraphia, chirographia, litera,* Merchants and Tradesmen's *books,* and herein of the Suppletory Oath. (5) **Of Oaths**, how, and to whom administered, when and how far proof. (6) **Different kinds of Oaths**, as *decisive, ad litem, suppletory, juramentum calumniæ,* of *expenses,* of *truth* &c.

LECTURE CCLXXXI.

OF ACTIONS, (CONTINUED.)

(1) **Of** the submission, or argument of the cause. (2) **Of the Decree**, interlocutory or final. (3) **Of Appeal** and stay of Execution. (4) **Of Supplication**. (5) **Of** *Restitutio in integrum*. (6) **Of Remedium Syndicatus**, and Appeals from a *nullity*. (7) **Of Rehearsing**. (8) **Of Executions**.

TITLE X.

OF THE CONSTITUTION AND LAWS OF THE UNITED STATES OF AMERICA.

LECTURE CCLXXXII.

OF A CONFEDERATION, A CONSTITUTION, AND OF THE DIVISION OF GOVERNMENTAL POWERS.

(1) Of the objects of confederation, deduced from an historical view of national associations. (2) Of a Constitution, its true meaning, and advantages. (3) Of the rule requiring the Legislative, Judicial, and Executive functions to be distinct and separate.

LECTURE CCLXXXIII.

OF THE CONSTITUTION OF THE UNITED STATES, AND FIRST OF THE NATIONAL LEGISLATURE.

(1) All Legislative power vested in Congress, consisting of a Senate, and House of Representatives.

(2) *House of Representatives*, how composed, its Duration, Qualifications of Electors and of Representatives, Apportionment of Representation, Vacancies how filled up, Powers of the House in the choice of Officers, in Impeachments, in originating Revenue Bills, &c.

86

(3) *Senate*, of whom composed, how chosen, its Duration, Division into three classes, and Mode of voting, Vacancies how replenished, Qualifications of Senators, Powers of the Senate in the choice of its Officers; as a Court for the trial of Impeachments; in relation to Revenue Bills; in making Treaties, Appointment of Ambassadors, &c.

(4) Of Powers, Duties, and Privileges common to both houses, or the members thereof, and herein of holding elections for senators and representatives, and of the power of Congress herein. Of the assembling of Congress. Of the Power of either house to decide on the election of its own members. Of the quorum required in certain cases. Of the Power of each house to regulate its internal government, and of the power of adjournment, &c. Of the compensation of members. Of exemption from arrest, and of certain incapacities of members. Of enacting Laws, after the dissent of the Executive.

LECTURE CCLXXXIV.

OF THE POWERS EXPRESSLY DELEGATED TO CONGRESS BY THE CONSTITUTION.

LECTURE CCLXXXV.

OF THE POWERS EXPRESSLY DENIED TO CONGRESS BY THE CONSTITUTION AND AMENDMENTS THERETO.

87

LECTURE CCXXXLVI.

OF MATTERS OBLIGATORY ON THE SEVERAL STATES OF THE UNION.

(1) Of the articles for the preservation of the rights of the several States and of the People. (2) Of the amendments to the Constitution proposed by Congress, but not ratified by the States.

LECTURE CCLXXXVII.

OF THE EXECUTIVE POWER.

(1) President and Vice-President, how chosen. (2) Duration of office. (3) Qualifications of President; his compensation; oath of office; when his powers devolve on the Vice-President. (4) Commander in chief of the Army, Navy, and Militia in actual service of the United States. (5) Powers of the President in making Treaties, appointment of Ambassadors, filling up vacancies in the Senate which occur during the recess; to pardon or reprieve. (6) When he may convene or adjourn Congress.—Of his duty to inform Congress of the state of the Union —to propose measures for their consideration—to receive Ambassadors and Publick Ministers—to see that the Laws are executed—to Commission all the officers of the United States. (7) Of the removal from office of the President, Vice-President and other civil officers.

88

LECTURE CCLXXXVIII.

OF THE JUDICIAL POWER.

(1) Judicial Powers how distributed. (2) Tenure of office. (3) Compensation of the Judges. (4) Extent of the Judicial powers.

LECTURE CCLXXXIX.

OF OTHER PROVISIONS IN THE CONSTITUTION.

(1) Of Trial by Jury. (2) Of the Guarantee from the United States of a Republican form of go ern-ment to every State, and their protection against invasion or domestick violence. (3) Of the debts and engagements prior to the adoption of the Constitution. (4) The Constitution, Laws, and Treaties the Supreme Law of the Land. (5) Of excessive Bail, Fine, and Cruel and unusual Punishments.

OF THE LAWS OF THE UNITED STATES.

[In our Commentaries on the *Constitution* of the United States, much has necessarily been said of those Laws, enacted in virtue of the powers delegated by the Constitution to Congress. This, however, is not sufficient. We shall, therefore, proceed to treat of the most important of those Laws, and in our observations thereon, shall introduce all of the *leading* decisions which have occurred in our courts of Judicature in exposition of the Laws. In treating of the *Laws* of the United States, we shall generally adopt a very simple method, viz. the *Alphabetical,*

89

as we presume that the student, who has proceeded thus far with us in our inquiries, which have been as regardful of *method* as practicable, stands no longer in need of a more philosophical arrangement.]

LECTURE CCXC.

OF ALIENS, AND HEREIN

Of the Laws enacted under Art. 1. Sec. viii. 4. of the Constitution, by which "Congress shall have power to establish an uniform rule of Naturalization."

LECTURE CCXCI.

OF THE BANK OF THE UNITED STATES.

(Art. 1. Sec. viii. 2. 17.)

(1) Of the constitutionality of the Acts, 5th of February, 1791, ch. 84, and 10th of April, 1816, ch. 44. (2) Of the establishment of Branches, or Offices of Discount and Deposite within any state. (3) Of the State's right to tax such Branch or Office. (4) In what courts the Bank of the United States, or its Branches, may sue or be sued.

LECTURE CCXCII.

OF COPY RIGHT AND PATENT.

(Art. 1. Sec. viii. 8.)

[In the foregoing Lectures we have purposely omitted to treat of the rights of Authors and Inventors, and shall, therefore, at this time fully consider the English and American Law on these subjects.]

90

LECTURE CCXCIII.

OF CRIMES AND PUNISHMENTS.

(Art. 3. Sec. 2. ch. 3. Sec. 3. ch. 1. 2. Art. 4. Sec. 2. ch. 2.)

LECTURE CCXCIV.

OF DUTIES ON IMPORTS AND TONNAGE, AND OF DRAWBACKS.

[On this numerous class of Laws, nothing more will be attempted than to present the important decisions which have been made on any of them, and to bring to the student's notice such of the laws on this subject as may be deemed material.]

LECTURE CCXCV.

OF THE JUDICIAL SYSTEM OF THE UNITED STATES.

(Art. 3. Sec. 1. ch. 1. Sec. 2. ch. 1. 2. 3. Art. 4. Sec. 1. ch. 1. Art. 11. Amendments.)

(1) Division of the United States into Districts. (2) Division of the United States into Circuits. (3) Division of the Judicial Power and herein

>   1. Of the *Supreme Court;* its Organization, Powers and Jurisdiction, *first* Original and exclusive; *secondly* Original but not exclusive; *thirdly* Appellate.
>   2. Of the *Circuit Courts,* their Organization, Powers, and Jurisdiction, *first* Original exclusive, *secondly,* Original concurrent, *thirdly,* Appellate.

91

3. Of the *District Courts*, their Organization, Powers, and Jurisdiction, *first*, exclusive Original; *secondly*, concurrent.

———

[In treating of the Organization, Powers and Jurisdiction of the courts of the United States, we shall embrace the entire Judiciary system, and present to the student the material decisions thereon.]

LECTURE CCXCVI.

OF THE LAWS RELATIVE TO NAVIGATION, POST OFFICES, AND POST ROADS.

LECTURE CCXCVII.

OF THE LAWS RELATIVE TO SEAMEN.

———

[Under the Titles of *"Lex Mercatoria,"* and *"Admiralty and Maritime Law,"* we have spoken fully of Seamen's Wages, and incidentally of several other matters, growing out of the various acts of Congress relating to Seamen. Many Laws, however, have not been mentioned, which, together with some important Judicial decisions yet remain for the present Lecture.]

LECTURE CCXCVIII.

OF SHIPS OR VESSELS, AND OF THE SLAVE TRADE.

LECTURE CCXCIX.

OF THE STATE, TREASURY, NAVY, AND WAR DEPARTMENTS.

TITLE XI.

LECTURE CCC.
OF LEGAL BIOGRAPHY AND BIBLIOGRAPHY.

LECTURE CCCI.
OF PROFESSIONAL DEPORTMENT.

[The Author has in a state of considerable forwardness an entire new abridgment of Lord Coke's Reports, with such notes and references to English and American authorities, as exhibit the law in its present state. This work will be comprised in three volumes octavo.]

ERRATA.

For counsel read consul	page 65.
conugium read conjugium	68.
Frangibiles read Fungibiles	74.
Dele (,) between judicium and finium	80.

A Lecture

Introductory to a Course of Lectures Now Delivering in the University of Maryland, 1823

A

LECTURE,

INTRODUCTORY TO A

Course of Lectures,

NOW DELIVERING IN THE

UNIVERSITY OF MARYLAND.

BY DAVID HOFFMAN.

PUBLISHED AT THE REQUEST OF THE FACULTY OF LAW.

Baltimore:
PRINTED BY JOHN D. TOY,
Corner of Market street and St. Paul's lane.
October, 1823.

INTRODUCTORY LECTURE, &c.

THE science of jurisprudence, as it concerns the topicks most interesting to human understanding, and human happiness, is also that of the widest extent, and most numerous particulars. As it relates to the conduct of man, it is a moral science of great sublimity; as its object is individual and national prosperity, it must be, of all others, the most important; as it regards the actions, both of communities and individuals, it is infinitely various; and as it concerns all the rights and obligations derived from, or due to God, our country, and ourselves, it is a science endlessly diffusive, whose "seat is," indeed, "the bosom of God, and whose voice is the harmony of the world."

6

Lawgivers have, in all ages, been esteemed the largest and most transcendant benefactors of the race; not only because their institutions have obviously promoted the tranquillity and elegance of societies, but because it was equally obvious how large a share of observation, how clear a discernment of causes and effects, and how judicious an adjustment of various principles, were requisite to the success of any form of policy. Scarcely less accurate or admirable, too, is that perspicacious talent by which the expositor of laws is led to the recognition of these general principles,— to use them in the interpretation of old, and in the framing of new enactments; or that steady, and liberal understanding by which general consequences are regarded, instead of particular, and general justice is distributed, without reference to private or partial inconvenience.—These are, or ought to be the characteristicks of the three great classes of lawyers.—Legislators, who make, Jurisconsults, who expound, and Judges, who both interpret and distribute, the laws of policed societies.

We are not then to expect, and far be it from me to inculcate the opinion, that such a science requires no extraordinary powers of genius, of application, or of both. That which has been

7

aptly described by Burke, as the *"pride of the human intellect, and the collected wisdom of ages, combining the principles of original justice with the boundless variety of human concerns,"* cannot be acquired, but by the steady, and methodical application of a well regulated mind.

You will doubtless find, in the very largeness of the career on which you are entering—in the difficulties by which it is environed—in the strong thought, and assiduity which it enforces, additional motives of admiration, and (to bold and generous minds) additional causes of ambition, and of emulation. Were your profession of vulgar and easy attainment, there would be no just reason for the high veneration with which we regard the great masters, and luminaries of the science; nor should I have any motive for proffering the aids, which, among others, I have proposed for the progress of the student; or for stimulating your industry and emulation. I am earnestly of opinion that few, perhaps none, have ever attained *"unto the depths of learning,"* in any science, without industry and talent, regulated by method, and accompanied by a love of study, bordering on enthusiasm. To use the strong language of Gesner, in relation to knowledge in general, and which is emphatically appli-

8

cable to law, "He who would be learned, must cry after knowledge, and lift up his voice for understanding: he must seek her as silver, and search for her as for hidden treasures."—Yet when I use this language, which may, perhaps, seem discouraging, I must be understood to speak of students who desire to study and practise law, as one of the most *honourable, profitable,* and *laudable* professions, and not of such as desire to rank the knowledge of its general principles, among the number of their elegant accomplishments; between whom, and professional men, there is as wide a difference, as between the polite man of science, who in his closet, studies the philosophy of mechanicks, and the learned mechanician, who applies them to the erection of complex machinery, or the edification of perfect models of architecture. To the professional student, then, we must be understood to address ourselves, when we discourse of the largeness of the science enveloped in his profession, and of the zeal, the method, and enduring perseverance with which it is essential to pursue it.

Students of law, in common with others, partake of those obstacles which science (in this age) herself erects to the followers of science. Not only are the boundaries of legal, as well as other

9

learning, greatly enlarged, and its topicks equally multiplied, but the literature of the age, even that which solicits your regard, as kindred to your legitimate studies, are vastly extended, and diversified. To these allurements of polite, and general learning, it is necessary to oppose the greatness, and importance of your own particular science, and to urge you to the remembrance of the maxim, now more just than ever, *"non omnia possumus omnes."* On this point I presume, I shall not be misunderstood—as in a work, some time since, addressed by me to American students of law, I insisted on the necessity of preparing their mind for its legal studies, by imbuing it with general and liberal learning, thus previously acquiring information on subjects, which the study of their profession will seldom permit to be extensively, and minutely inquired into afterwards; and at the same time of framing their minds to habits of research and diligence. This is not, however, designed to exclude altogether the study of other sciences, or of polite literature, *cotemporaneously* with that of law: the most indefatigable student has either from external circumstances, or from mental exhaustion, many intervals of time, in which he revolts from his immediate pursuit through he would gladly fill them with less labo-

10

rious avocations. The mind is unwilling to be forever contending with difficulty, or excited to the full measure of its strength: the most diligent require some relaxation of employment, some change to diversify the rugged track of investigation. The sage Ascham, the erudite Erasmus, the deeply thinking Montesquieu, and the sublime Newton, were accustomed to unbend the mind, in the moments stolen from their intellectual toils, by the perusal of the fancies of Dante, or of Tasso, or of some of the voluminous tales and romances of the times.

The student who desires to economise time, should therefore indulge these variations of the mental appetite, and tempt this intellectual satiety with every modification with which genius has adorned literature, or disguised the harshness of science. Such an occupation of the fragments of time, often idly and unprofitably thrown away, under the plea of mental exhaustion, would enable the law student to accomplish himself in the principles of universal science, without, in any degree breaking in upon those hours which should be sacred to the study of his profession. It is fortunate that the instruction which the mind rejects in one shape, it will often receive in another.

11

Like a chemical *menstruum*, it may be saturated with one species of matter, and imbibe a different, even with avidity. In this nice art of supplying it with various food, and at suitable times, of courting, or commanding it, consists the principal difficulty of study. But whilst a law student should endeavour previously to treasure up a fund of general and diversified knowledge, and aim during his professional studies, to fill its occasional intervals by the pursuits of analogous or elegant science, he should beware of an overweening attachment to the *literæ humaniores*, and more especially avoid the jejune, though fashionable trifles which modern literature pours perpetually from the press, no less than the noisy verbiage and the speculative and passionate vituperation of the day. These considerations are the more important at this time, when not only the *deliciæ* of letters are served up in innumerable attractive shapes, but, as I have intimated, the fashion of the age, in knowledge and reading, is excursiveness and generality, rather than system and correctness;—a method of reading no less destructive of taste than of time, and which has the additional disadvantage of loosing, in the crowd, the pure and ancient standards of literary excellence. Leave then to the Reviewers, the too often un-

12

profitable labour of skimming the wide surface of ephemeral literature, and reserve for the acknowledged models of thought and the true fountain of science, the brief and precious hours of occasional leisure. It is the peculiarity, however, of a long habit of research into a science, however vast and various, that the mind acquires, in no small degree, powers of methodising, of selecting, and investigating, which every day renders its labours less fatiguing, and its search less perplexing. Thoughts and topicks arrange themselves insensibly; the scientifick, and technical divisions suggest themselves with little effort; what is known, becomes so, not more from memory, than from system; and what is unknown is speedily found, because we have learned towards what point to direct our search. In this respect the adept in a science resembles the captain of a host; where the vast number is weilded without disorder, because it is symmetrically classified; and every thing takes, or is found in its proper place, because it is arranged there by an invariable system.

There have been times in which learning was chiefly measured by the mere knowledge, or rather multiplicity of facts, treasured up by the *memory*. Before the invention of printing, it was

13

extremely difficult, and scarcely possible, to become learned in the science and literature of the age, without a retentive memory. This was considered a faculty admirable in itself, and, in consequence of its utility, was then allowed to hold a more dignified position among the intellectual powers, than modern metaphysicians are willing to grant it. In those days of primitive knowledge, we hear of the most surprising instances of the cultivation of this faculty. We read of *Portius Latro*, who remembered every word of every oration he ever spoke. We are told that *Seneca* could repeat two thousand words after once hearing them, and strictly preserve their order, though they had no dependence whatever on each other. Demagogues, also, who were desirous to please the people, often knew the names of all their fellow citizens, as *Cyrus* knew that of every soldier in his numerous army. We likewise read of an ambassador from *Pyrrhus* to the Romans, who in one day learnt the names of his spectators, and on the following, saluted the Roman senate, and all the assembled populace, each by his name! An incredible story, certainly, unless the crowd were less moved than in our own day, by vulgar curiosity. In more modern times, but prior to the revival of letters in Europe, a man who had read

14

a few manuscripts, and committed them to memory, was deemed learned, and regarded as a national treasure. He could travel from place to place, and by repeating from Aristotle, Plato, Homer, Eusebius, or St. Jerome, not only live, but thrive by his learning.

Knowledge, however, which is deposited in the memory, is not necessarily valuable. Natural, and even acquired memory, are not frequently accompanied by the higher mental endowments; by the power of philosophical arrangement, of analysis, and synthesis; and we find that the most able and learned philosophers have not relied on this species of knowledge, or on the arduous cultivation of this faculty, as is forcibly illustrated in the history of Bacon, of Voltaire, Franklin, Montaigne, and others, and remarkably, in the case of Sir Isaac Newton, who, of all philosophers, perhaps, thought most deeply, and in an eminent degree possessed the power of arranging his extensive knowledge to useful purposes; yet, he, according to Doctor Pemberton, was often at a loss, even when conversation turned on his own discoveries, and excellent writings.

A consciousness of his own inventive powers, of his perfect ability again to analyze and arrange, prevented his taking much pains in treasuring in

15

his memory the details of his knowledge. On this subject Dugald Stewart has a pertinent remark. "A man of original genius," says he, "who is fond of exercising his reasoning powers anew, on most points as they occur to him, and who cannot submit to rehearse the ideas of others, or to repeat by rote the conclusions which he has deduced from previous reflection, often appears to superficial observers to fall below the level of ordinary understandings; while another, destitute both of quickness, and invention, is admired for that promptitude in his decisions, which arises from the inferiority of his intellectual abilities." Who now regards with veneration the astonishing memory of the *Abbé de Longuerue*, whose erudition was said to be so vast as to have been called terrible—who spoke all languages, knew all facts of history—had recorded in his memory all the places and times of geography and chronology, and who actually wrote a history of France, purely from memory, and without consulting a single volume! Or, who delights to remember the learning of the Florentine Librarian, *Magliabechi*, who is said to have read six large rooms full of books! Both of these prodigies of the erudition of the memory, were however remarkably deficient in the powers of induction, of philosophi-

16

cal analysis, and arrangement, and of all those qualities, which, at the present day, are considered as really valuable, and indicative of mental ability. The Abbé admired an antiquarian commentator on Homer, more than Homer himself, and the learned librarian left, for the benefit of posterity, but one line of his own composition, and that was round a medal of his own likeness, and contained neither sentiment, knowledge nor wit. Fortunately for the jurisprudent, his attainments do not depend exclusively on a faculty which ranks so low among the intellectual powers; and I cannot but express, on this occasion my disapprobation of the mode recently recommended by an able lawyer of a neighbouring state, who insists, (strange as it may appear) on students actually getting by rote the whole of Blackstone's Commentaries, and some other elementary works. I would urge you, on the contrary, to study the general and pervading principles of the science. Treasure up its maxims, their meaning, and application. Cultivate it in all its bearings and analogies. Search into its philosophy with care, and be sure that you understand what you read. Study much but all with *method*. Let your inquiries be censorial, as well as expository; and trust to your knowledge of the reasons and

17

grounds of law, added to your recollection of the sources of information, rather than to the vain hope of treasuring up its *particulars*. Should these rules be regarded, the entire science may be open to your view, though nearly all of its facts be but imperfectly remembered by you. If your mind be deeply imbued with its philosophy, your acquaintance with the paths and sources of knowledge will soon enable you to obtain, with certainty, the special information you desire.

To your profession you must devote yourself as the industrious merchant to his gains, and with a zeal and steadiness the greater, as your pursuit is more laborious, more noble and more profitable in all that enriches and adorns life. Nor can I but confess, as I have just remarked, that your task is a great one, if you design to complete it as you should; and it requires certainly the steadfast application of all the high powers, which attract dignity and respect to the human understanding. And while I thus speak my candid sentiments on this point, I trust you will only be incited by them to a higher, and more earnest emulation; to a respect for the profession itself, and an admiration for those illustrious sages, who have bent almost the whole splendour, and

18

force of their genius, to the most profound, as well as the most excellent of human sciences.

It is fortunate, indeed, that the study of the law has a nearer alliance than any other with the business of the world, and all the high concerns of human life. Its collateral topicks, also, fit him better for the business and conversation of men, amidst which his vocation lies than those which engage the divine and the physician.

The lawyer, then, it particularly behoves to be uninfected with those prejudices and peculiarities of mind, those excentricities of manner and expression, which often arise from men's avocations, which colour and too frequently circumscribe the operations of their talents, and which the illustrious Bacon has quaintly, but forcibly placed under the general head of *idola specus*.— He should studiously guard against the little remaining pedantry of his science, and endeavour to soften the strong impressions made on his mind by his chief and favourite pursuit, by mingling them with such as are derived from his intercourse with other men, and other books. This consideration is still more important in America, where the lawyer and the politician pass into each other by so easy a transition; more easy at least, than is found by the votaries of other pursuits.

19

And as it is from those who have been *students* of this profession, if not from its *practitioners*, that the nation draws the largest portion of its legislators and statesmen, there is an obvious reason for somewhat enlarging the circuit of the law student's acquirements, arising from this probable combination of the counsellor with the politician. The studies of these two, their habits of extemporaneous discipline, their converse with society resembles each other; and as there is, with us, no privileged class, the maker is often found in the expositor or distributor of laws. This circumstance exerts a happy influence on our profession, first, as it offers its members the chance of advancement in two roads of life; and secondly, as it cannot fail to unfetter them from the technical narrowness, too often the result of an exclusive devotion to a single science: and hence a lawyer without materially diverting his mind from the topicks of his profession, has a field, abundantly large, and various for the active and pleasing employment of his intellectual powers.

The sedentary and studious have, indeed, to contend with obstacles peculiar to themselves. Secluded of necessity, for the larger portion of their time, from the business and bustle of men, their ideas insensibly assume a monotonous aspect,

20

and receiving little ventilation from the constant current of novelties, which refresh those who are engaged in active and crowded scenes, are apt to stagnate into languor and melancholy.—It is little wonderful that intellectual exertion should become irksome, when thus accompanied by despondency; and that the student should find the lapse to indolence and relaxation so easy, and the return to his solitary avocations so painful—a painfulness most generally augmented by a consciousness of neglect of duty, which he is happy to drown in the pleasures or bustle of society, rather than brood over in the stillness of his study.—Instead of attempting to remedy this tendency by total seclusion, it is better, gentlemen, to indulge it with moderation; and to mingle business and pleasure in those proportions, which will equally prevent the fatigue of too much exertion, and the satiety of too much enjoyment. Hermits, whether in religion or in science, have generally found their scheme of exclusive and solitary devotion to a single pursuit, to issue in lassitude and indolence. But with occasional relaxation from society; with exact and uniform attention, and strict economy in the occupation of your time, together with a rigid adherence to method in your studies, and the devotion of your leisure time to the pursuit of

21

miscellaneous literature, or general science, you will find your chief study, that of law, to be not only easy, but pleasing. There is no difficulty in cultivating even a passion for this study; and though a lawyer should be, in some degree, acquainted with the whole circle of human science, so that he may be as occasion may require, a philosopher to detect, a logician to reason, a poet to describe, and an orator to persuade, yet, believe me, that excellence in a single scientifick profession, is all that our reasonable expectations should embrace.

"One science only can one genius hit,
"So vast is art, so narrow human wit."

A student, who is animated by a just zeal to attain the summits of professional learning and renown, is not to be surprised, or discouraged by the prospect of a thousand nights devoted to research, and a thousand days employed in the practical application of its results.—No eminence, that is worth having, is attainable *per saltum;* nature has included in steady application the seeds both of mental sanity and pleasure; and while, to the pursuit of amusement, she has destined a sickly appetite, inevitably and speedily cloyed, business and study, on the contrary, not only reap a reward in themselves, but quicken the relish of unaccustomed relaxation. Science, if not like the

22

well, which my lord Coke quaintly describes, is perhaps, like the grotto, or the mine,—to which the access is uninviting and fatiguing, but which often rewards him who is content to groupe awhile with pains and patience, with the view of unexpected beauties, wealth and wonders. It is true, indeed, that to taste the pleasures which spring from legal research, we must have entered into the principles, discovered the harmonies, and arranged with method and curiosity the innumerable topicks of the science; as in the caverns of the earth the accomplished and inquisitive mineralogist and geologist reap a satisfaction, and an interest unknown to the uninformed spectators.

With these views of the science, to which you are pledged to devote yourselves, the number and variety of its subjects, instead of alarming your patience, should animate your enterprise.

A profession so liberal and extended, so sublime and important, should be cultivated by those only who are actuated by principles of the purest, and most refined honour. Regarding law as a science equally venerable from its objects, and noble from the ingenuity and mental expansion employed and excited in its acquisition and practice, it should be the ardent desire of its votaries to see its shrine unprofaned by knavery and igno-

23

rance, and its retainers not more eminent, from the importance of their functions, than from the honesty and skill with which they discharge them. It is true, we cannot reasonably expect that this can ever be fully accomplished: it is incident to the best things to be the most perverted; and while we may admire and emulate the portraiture which the sincere lovers of this science have been fond to appropriate to its professors, we must be content to see its dignity sometimes debased by the ignorant, and its liberality by the mercenary. We believe that, in most cases, enlarged knowledge, and noble studies exercise, in themselves, a happy influence on those who have pursued them. The very acquisition of liberal knowledge, supposes the acquisition of liberal ideas; so that, in most cases, the possession of intellectual power begets correctness in its application to the purposes of life; and the complexion of its pursuits seems to be, almost necessarily, accompanied by more sound, more enlarged, and more honourable views, than we find in those whose knowledge has been circumscribed. But, if the intrinsick excellence of the profession, and its natural tendency to beget elevated and honest dispositions, be not sufficient to check the wayward proclivity of some men's minds towards vice and dishonour, it is for-

24

tunate that our profession has a powerful control over its members, in the authority possessed by courts of justice (whose officers lawyers are, and under whose commission alone, are they competent to act) to suspend them, or wholly to deprive them of the privilege of practice; and, if this be once done, by any court of judicature, all others, by courtesy, would, at once, adjudge them unworthy members, and close every hope of amending their condition, by a change of residence.

You have then, every motive for exerting the utmost assiduity in your studies, and the most sacred honour in the practice of your profession. Respect and influence in society, professional reputation, the highest stations of honour and profit, in a great and enlightened republick, and all the goods of intellectual and worldly wealth are proffered to you. The character of a lawyer who does justice to his profession, and to the important station he holds in life, is, indeed, truly excellent and dignified. He is one, whom early education has imbued with the principles of probity, and habituated to labour and research, in that which enlarges, and refines the mind. He desires to impart lustre to the utility of his learning, by fostering every honourable and amiable affection. The fountains of liberal science and polite letters

25

he has tasted of, before he enters on the pursuit of his more technical studies, and has thus protected himself from pedantry and narrow views. Versed in the sciences most necessary to the purposes of society, he naturally obtains over it a large and legitimate control, which he exercises only that he may become in it a more useful member. He is the asserter of right, the accuser of wrong, the protector of innocence, and the terror of crime. He labours not for those alone who can afford the *honorarium*, but the widow, the fatherless, and the oppressed are ever in his mind. No prospect of gain will ever induce him to advise the pursuit of law against right, or sober judgment; nor will any man's greatness be a shield against the justice due to his client. If he assist in the enaction of laws, which he may afterwards be called on to vindicate, it is done with an eye solely to his country's good, and whilst he respects its legislature and judiciary, he learns to reverence the constitution more than either.—History is his field, as he learns in it the rudiments and revolutions of his science. Rhetorick and logic are the weapons by which he imparts to his oratory warmth and grace, force and clearness. From his knowledge of man he learns truth, and he cultivates rectitude for the more useful exercise

26

of his powers. Destitute of these, he is either unprofitable, or mischievous to society, and endued with them, he is one of its *chiefest ornaments* and *firmest safeguards.*

Most of you, gentlemen, are no doubt apprised of my intention to deliver a course of Lectures in this University, on every branch of jurisprudence, in any degree applicable to this country, or which may be useful to the American student of law.—The actual execution of this laborious enterprise has been delayed, in part, by the extensiveness of the scheme of instruction, of which the Syllabus, which I sometime since addressed to you, and the course of Legal Study, previous to that, contain the outline; and in part, by the imperfect state and deficient funds of the University, which have prevented those accommodations which are essential. This wide subject has hitherto, either been partitioned out to several professors, or the *institutes* only have been taught; but the object of the course, now to be delivered in this University, is to treat all of its branches, and to investigate every important one in detail: and though this be perhaps the first attempt of the kind in England or in this country, the enterprise, however laborious and responsible, will certainly be prosecuted with all the industry and zeal which I

27

can command; relying on such encouragement from students of law throughout the Union, as may compensate me for the sacrifice inevitable to my undertaking.

Though law has been publickly taught in Great Britain, it is a little remarkable that no attempt has been made to go beyond the institutes of the science. *Sir William Blackstone's* immortal work presents only a bird's eye view of this various, extensive, and complicated science: and though it be admitted, by so competent a judge as Sir William Jones, to be "the most correct and beautiful outline that was ever exhibited of any human science,"—yet this accomplished scholar unites with Hargrave, Redesdale, Brown, Story, Tucker, and others, in the decided opinion that it presents nothing beyond the mere rudiments of English law; and, to use the well known language of Sir William Jones, "these beautiful commentaries will no more form a lawyer, than a general map of the world, how accurately and elegantly soever it may be delineated, will make a geographer."

The lectures of the second Vinerian Professor, *Dr. Wooddeson,* have prosecuted some of the topicks more at large; but still the whole work is strictly rudimental.

28

Doctor Sullivan's Lectures, which are comprised in one volume, are solely on feudal learning, and the first principles of the English constitution, and some of its laws; and those of *Doctor Brown*, delivered in the University of Dublin, do not aspire to any thing beyond the presentation of a well arranged contour of the Roman Civil Law, and the law of the Admiralty; and it cannot, with justice, be said, that even this design has been accomplished, as there are several, even important branches, in no way alluded to, and others, which are merely named.

There have been several elementary courses delivered in this country, with what success, and how far meritorious, I regret I have not the means of judging, as they have never been published, with the exception of Lectures by the late Doctor Wilson, of Philadelphia, which, even as a course of elementary *legal* instruction, are extremely imperfect, and better suited, (from their general and indefinite legal information, embellished by the ornaments of literature) for polite scholars, or students, in the course of their collegiate inquiries, than for the regular student of law. We entertain great respect for the character and learning of this gentleman, and had his scheme been more extensive, his lectures, no doubt, would

29

have proved highly valuable to American law students.

The lectures which for many years past have been delivered at Litchfield, in the state of Connecticut, by the venerable Judge Reeves, and his able associate, Judge Gould, we are persuaded, are well entitled to the high reputation they have ever maintained. The eminence of many lawyers who now adorn our country, and who were students in that institution, are the best proofs of the excellence of the scheme of instruction which is there pursued. Massachusetts and Virginia also, have not been inactive in the laudable endeavour to promote our favourite science through the medium of lectures: and the state of New-York possesses, in the genius, learning, and highly embellished mind of its late Chancellor, an inestimable resource, could that able lawyer and civillian be induced to devote a portion of his time in this way.* As far, however, as my acquaintance with these various enterprises extends, I believe that no attempt has yet been made to embrace even the rudiments of the *entire science*.

The enterprise, then, in which I am now engaged, has been hitherto unessayed: the expe-

* We are happy to learn that our wishes in this respect are about to be realized, Chancellor Kent having removed to the city of New-York with the view of delivering a course of lectures in the University of that state.

30

rience of others, if it afford me no cause of very flattering expectation, at least gives me no anticipation of disappointed efforts. Inclination, and judgment, bid me proceed; and I am unwilling to believe, what diffidence sometimes whispers to me, that my design may not meet an adequate encouragement. As long as this is the case, I shall endeavour to enliven and sustain myself, in the many hours of exhaustion incident to this enterprise, with the confident hope and belief of receiving sufficient to gratify my ambition, as well as all other reasonable expectation. Should all this fail, I am not vain, in hoping that the failure may be softened by the remark, "*Magnis tamen, excedit ausis.*"

But let us now proceed to other topicks:—

The tendency of science, as she enlarges her acquisitions, is to methodize and arrange them. As want is the obstacle to the first steps of her progress, so abundance is that of her later stages. If in the gradual accessions to human learning, the base could be accurately separated from the precious—the certain from the obscure and the impenetrable, the task of the modern scholar were comparatively easy; and if his *memory* were burdened, his *judgment* would be relieved and anticipated. Such, however, are the revolutions

31

of human opinion, such the motive for reverting often to systems and doctrines deemed to be exploded—that scarcely any thing which has been written can be thrown entirely aside, as having been tested to be false, or unfit for the purposes of instruction. Scarcely any, so to speak, of the *old furniture of the mind,* is to be thrown entirely out of doors.

If such is the case in regard to the sciences more metaphysical and theoritick, it is manifestly more so in such as are positive and arbitrary. In them, as in municipal law, for example, it is not sufficient to establish only general principles, whose application is left for the individual, in each particular case as it occurs. As these principles are continually compared with the emergencies of life, as their seeming collision, in particular cases, is explained and reconciled, and as it is important to know distinctly their operation on our interests and conduct, cases decided on analogous principles are carefully sought; the records of expository jurisprudence are perpetually swelled, and the general maxim comes attended in the books by a host of corroborative instances of its application. Hence the voluminous books of reports, from which the inquirer is to seek his principles, his maxims, his precedents—scarcely

32

more from the cases which have *established*, than from those which have sought to *impeach* them.

Hence too the importance, nay, necessity, as adjudicated cases multiply, of arranging them in classes, and extracting their spirit in treatises. This method subserves a double purpose: it gives the student a comprehensive view of the subject, and collects under his eye the cases from which it has been extracted, to which he may, and often should refer for confirmation or correction. It is true, that while a student has the power to inquire at the fountains themselves; while the amount of collected knowledge is not yet so great but that within the usual legal novitiate, he may himself survey the whole ground, it is all important, for correct and certain knowledge, that he mark, learn, and digest for himself. Such, however, is the vast extent of most of the branches of *legal* science, that such a mode of study would be nearly impossible. But should he pursue this course to the greatest extent, the methodized treatises, especially of our own time, are of infinite use: they give the natural order of inquiry, they show what is to be sought, and where it is to be found—with such aids, if we inquire for ourselves, it is of little importance that our conclusion shall be exactly the same.

33

The common law has in it a feature somewhat peculiar: or at least it has this in a peculiar degree. We find that it has survived many ages, and many revolutions of manners, and has yet been accommodated to them all. Hence, in many cases, it has retained its *form*, while it has altered its *spirit*, and the student, astonished sometimes at the principles, and more frequently at the forms which it presents, can only discover their reason in an antiquated system. It is scarcely necessary to say how valuable is a guide through these mazes of blackletter learning, where so much is dark, some is useless, and some perhaps, even absurd. How, necessary, if not brilliant, the *industry*, which, content to groupe, like a Belzoni among the catacombs, brings from amidst dust, oblivion, and darkness, some scattered but valuable relicks!

These considerations may serve to show the usefulness and true province of a *lecturer*—to collate and select with diligence and discernment—to trace his doctrines from their first germ to their final growth, through all the variations of judicial opinions—to mark the accordance of decided cases with general principles, or the exceptions and deviations—to declare what has been said, not *merely* and *indiscriminately*, but with a view to gen-

?4

eral results, and with an examination of its consistency with legal analogy and reason—and finally, to refute, or fearlessly to combat error, without regard to mere authority, remembering with the philosophick Boyle, that although *authority* be a long-bow, the effect of which generally depends on the strength of the arm which draws it, reason is a cross-bow of equal efficacy in the hands of the dwarf and the giant.

These, I apprehend, are the chief features of such a method of instruction, and thus united, they present the subject in the fullest manner, and most obvious light, stripped at the same time of the too frequent incumbrance of pedantick learning, or of false reasoning. The student, informed of the *sources* of the knowledge which is imparted by the professor, has ample opportunity, in the intervals his instruction, to examine, to reason, and to criticize for himself; and his attention, in the mean while, is directed with particular force to what is presented in condensed form, and becomes therefore the theme of solitary inquiry, or of ardent discussion with other learners. We march more patiently forward, when a pioneer thus opens the way; and we add emulation to patience, when thus accompanied in the march by

35

companions, who are sometimes aids and sometimes competitors.

However we may acknowledge in general the force of habit, we do not always sufficiently weigh its power in selecting, and in the manner of pursuing our avocations. The interests, the topicks of these around us, affect us insensibly, and almost determine the bent of our emulation, whatever abstract opinions we may entertain of the comparative excellence and importance of things. We all remember, and sometimes with a smile, when the immediate excitement is past, the importance which we have attached to successive objects and pursuits—to the feats of boyhood—the scholastic exercises of our *alma mater,*—and even the trifles of the drawing room, or the turf—a feeling, which though it springs in some degree, from the natural changes wrought by years, and the progress of life, is no doubt, prodigiously spread and heightened by sympathy with such as happen to surround us. If, therefore, *similarity of pursuits* did not naturally determine us in the choice of companions, *policy* should lead us to select those, who animated by the same views as ourselves, perpetually start topicks of inquiry akin to our studies, and minister the spirit of emulation.

36

The peculiarity of collegiate manners has been often noticed: The members of such institutions, separated in some degree from every day pursuits, gather topicks, and objects of emulation peculiar to themselves. A metaphysical distinction shall make as obstinate *parties* as ever divided a parliament or a cabinet; and youths naturally become scholars where nothing but scholarship is an object of dictinction—such a spot has been aptly called by a giant scholar *"an atmosphere of learning;"* and it strikes me that, if the habits of our country had not established a different system in this matter, a Law Seminary, would be eminently useful if conducted under a similar discipline, where all that should be seen and heard, all that would interest, and emulate, and distinguish, is connected with an expanded and enlightened study of jurisprudence, where, to vary the phrase, the very *air* should be *legal.*

In the pursuit of studies so harsh as those of law are apt at first to appear, where the mind must be fashioned by habit, and impelled by strong motive, to its daily task, where some stimulus more poignant than the remote and somewhat uncertain prospect of emolument or honour, is required to rouse the flagging attention—the advantage of such an institution may seem ex-

37

tremely obvious. In this country it has been usual to pursue these studies not only without these aids, but amidst a vortex of opposite feelings, and seductive pleasures; for the years, at which young men begin their legal studies are generally those which are most eagerly devoted to society, fashion and pleasure. Separated into groups, over the country, under instructors of every kind (if the busy, and more often inattentive advocates, whose offices they frequent, can be called such)—and having little or no close association with fellow students, or, with an ambition diverted into more agreeable paths than that of arid and fatiguing research; students, thus situated, have on the one hand few incitements from emulation, and that inborn love of eminence which when strongly indicated points to future greatness, and is generally first shown in communion with many; but on the other hand they are strongly solicited by idleness, by pleasure, by a notoriety, pleasing to the inexperienced, and more easy of attainment—by all the amiable seductions, in fine, which attend the first essay in society.

It is, perhaps, a fault in the manners of our country, that the young are introduced too early into the circles of the gay; and it is a question of some consequence in the education of young men,

38

Whether that partial *separation* of them from the world, which obtains at colleges, while they are in pursuit of *philosophy* and the *classicks*, might not be extended with advantage through the period during which they receive the elements of *professional learning*. At all events, if they are at that period to taste of the first allurements of gaiety, they should not be deprived of the advantages of collegiate association: they might still, with benefit, be collected into *studious communities*, where emulation might be propagated from mind to mind, where talents and success in professional acquirements might be the sole reason of distinction, and where the topicks of professional learning, being constantly discussed, might still excite them to inquiry, and urge them forward in the race of competition.

However inadequate the talents which I could bring to the accomplishment of so desirable a scheme, it would be a matter of pride and satisfaction to me to collect around me some portion of the large fund of talent which is annually devoted by the *rising hopes* of the country to the *first profession in it*. Baltimore, in a central position from north to south, is conveniently located for such an object. It is salubrious, populous and refined; its libraries and publick institutions

39

comparatively good; its manners auspicious to strangers; it is near to the seat of the national government; and it already draws annually into its bosom some hundreds of young gentlemen devoted to another of the liberal professions. A Law Seminary established here under such circumstances, beside the direct instructions of the professor, would be fraught, therefore, with numerous indirect advantages. Its members, as I have just said, would form a kind of *studious republick*, employed in the same subjects, and animated by the same emulation; the spirit of research would be kindled and increased among members; friendships would be formed (at years more mature than those which are usually spent at colleges) which while fraught with as much advantage as pleasure to individuals, would foster the *esprit du corps* among the members of a profession which largely contributes its talent to the most conspicuous stations of the government. The mind of the student amidst such a nursery of scientifick curiosity and spirit, would be withdrawn, in some measure, from the influence of pleasure and dissipation. It matters little to the gratification of the mind, what is the object of interest, while it is of much moment to its profit to fasten that interest on pursuits of grave and substantial benefit. These reflections will receive

40

some weight from the recollection how long, even in the thoughtlessness of boyhood, the notions and sentiments abide by us, which have grown up in the scholastic retirement of colleges and universities. I would add to this the advantage (and in time it may become an important one) of prosecuting your *legal* studies under the auspices of a university, and of obtaining from it the honours awarded to those who have complied with its requisitions. These will be stated to you at another time.

I forbear to say any thing of what benefit may be derived to you from the lectures I am about to pronounce, or from those which will be *annually added*, until my course is complete—except, that so far as much zeal and industry in a pursuit, which has ever been with me a very favourite one, can give assurance, I feel that I have not been wanting to myself or to you.

The Syllabus, which has been submitted to you, presents the outline of a very extensive course of legal instruction. This has been with me, and will continue to be, our mutual guide,— with no deviations, except those which will lead to a deeper research into particular topicks, than was originally intended. The whole course, when finished, will embrace three hundred and one

41

lectures, and will occupy at least eighteen months, and more probably two years in the delivery. As the whole scheme, however, is divided into thirteen titles, students may commence their attendance at any of them, as they may be more or less advanced in their studies. By a lecture, however, is not meant that portion which may be delivered at a particular time, but the *integral* portions or divisions of my subject. Thus, on some occasions, perhaps two lectures will be delivered on the same day; and at others, a lecture may occupy, in its delivery, the allotted time of two or more days. Those which I am about to commence will demand of us at least an hour, generally more, four times a week, during four months. The first title, as it is the *prolegomina* of a course which is designed to treat the principal topicks, not only of local but universal law, of censorial, no less than of expository jurisprudence, may be found to occupy more of our time than is indicated by the Syllabus. Some may also be inclined to the opinion, that as the instruction embraced in this first division of my subject is initiatory to a scheme so much more extensive than what is *at once* to be entered on, it will be found disproportioned to that which is immediately to follow. This, indeed, is true: but it is to be remembered

42

that this course is to be regularly augmented, until the whole design be complete, which will certainly be the case should life and health be allowed me: and farther, the objection loses all weight, if the course now to be delivered be valuable in itself.—The subjects themselves are obviously so; nor could any other plan be consistently adopted. I shall, therefore, proceed in my undertaking, without any material deflexion from the outline which I have prescribed to myself.

The ensuing course of lectures, then, will be introduced with various *metaphysical* and *ethical* dissertations; with discussions on most of the interesting topicks of natural jurisprudence, and the philosophy of legislation; with the elements of political law, and with occasional biographical and bibliographical information, as it may be suggested by the subjects under consideration. I have commenced the course with the metaphysicks and ethicks of the law, from a profound conviction of their particular serviceableness to the lawyer, as well in disciplining his mind to logical accuracy, as in opening to him the foundations of all municipal law. Metaphysical science is invaluable to him to whom habits of abstract thought, of accuracy, of subtlety, of scrupulous precision of language, are among the first requisites to success,

43

whether in acquiring the learning, or conducting the argumentative war of his profession.

It may be laid down as a fundamental truth, that all sound legislation must have relation both to the moral and physical nature and condition of man. Such is the intimate relation between *mind* and *matter* as to render it impossible to proceed far in the philosophy of natural and political jurisprudence, without some acquaintance even with man's physical nature, and certainly with the phenomena of mental philosophy. Hence was it that the great German metaphysicians, Leibnitz and Kant, were not content to study the georgicks of the mind—they cultivated the laws of *matter* with equal zeal—so Descartes, Clarke, Cudworth, Locke, Reid, Stewart, and others, have acknowledged the intimate connexion between physicks and metaphysicks, on the one hand, and ethicks and jurisprudence, on the other. The judicious remarks of Dugald Stewart on the aid which metaphysicks have lent to inquirers into sciences, seemingly remote from its pursuits, have a particular force as regards the jurisprudent. To the lawyer the ready perception of distinctions, the scrupulous and determined definition of terms, the analytical powers, and the habit of sifting the combinations established in the fancy, and the

44

casual associations which warp *common* understandings, are of utility every day, and must be made *habits* of the mind, because their exercise is for the most part extemporary.—"The connexion between metaphysicks and ethicks," says Stewart, "is more particularly close, the theory of morals having furnished several of the most abstruse questions which have been agitated concerning the general principles (both intellectual and active) of the human frame,"—and, we may add, what is ethicks, moral philosophy, and natural jurisprudence, but different *names* for essentially the same system of rules, all dependent on the laws of the human mind? But, without pressing further this alliance between the laws of matter and of mind, and the close connexion between Ethicks and Natural Law, it must be admitted that ethical and political considerations are nearly akin to the proper studies of the accomplished lawyer. Even municipal law (in its most restricted signification) is not a system of merely positive and arbitrary rules. It has its deep foundations in the universal laws of our moral nature, and, all its positive enactments, proceeding on these, must receive their just interpretation with a reference to them. Would it be possible (for instance) to interpret justly a law, or explain a contract, with-

45

out knowledge of the general principles on which they are promulgated or entered into? Whence proceeds the rule that laws should not be retrospective, but from the principle of natural law, or ethicks, that associations are bound only by rules to which they may be supposed to have consented? What are the rules of evidence, but metaphysical and ethical modes of investigating truth on the one hand, and limiting our deductions by a regard to human rights and feelings, and to our moral constitution, on the other? How else is the great point of expatriation (on which there have been so many positive enactments) to be settled but by reference to the universal principles on which political association at first arose? In these and infinite other cases, nay, in all modifications of positive institutions, there can be no just design on the part of legislators, nor correct interpretation on those who administer their provisions, without knowledge of the true principles of moral and political philosophy. Nay, the very obedience of the governed proceeds, doubtless, from an apprehension, however imperfect, of the great and obvious principles of moral justice. As in the construction of the most elaborate machine, no law of physical nature can possibly be transgressed, so in the great scheme of government,

46

provisions seemingly the most arbitrary, and the most connected with an artifical state of society, cannot violate, with impunity, the great moral law—and therefore, whether as legislators or expounders of legislative institutions, you must be sure that you understand justly their true principles. Metaphysicks, ethicks, and politicks, then, are the appropriate studies of the jurisprudent—on these repose, as solid foundations, all sound legislative enactments; and, as these apply to the conduct of a being composed of body, as well as soul or mind, the physical and moral nature of this being should be known to those who presume to minister, in any way, in the temple of justice. I have deemed these observations proper for those (should there be any such) who may erroneously incline to regard with indifference the ethicks and metaphysicks of the law, and would wish to vindicate the propriety of bestowing much attention on these too much neglected portions of our science.

After we have dwelt, somewhat in detail, on the important doctrines to which we have just alluded, we shall conclude the *first title* of our subject with an inquiry into the elementary and constitutional principles of the *municipal* law, and shall investigate, with some minuteness, the origin, progress,

47

and influence of that remarkable polity which, during many centuries, pervaded Europe; affected all her political and civil institutions; diminished the lustre even of the imperial law; impressed on the international law of Europe some bold and enduring features, which the refinements even of the present age have not entirely obliterated; and, finally, which by reason of its universality has been denominated the *Jus Gentium* of the western world, but is known to us all, under the more appropriate name of the *Feudal Law*. No one can study the history, language, or jurisprudence of England, without at once perceiving their miscellaneous character. The history of that country shows the mixed and even discordant materials which compose its population: the *language* is Celtic, Teutonic, Greek, and Latin: the *laws* are British, Saxon, Feudal, Roman—but nearly every portion of this vast system of jurisprudence is somewhat tinctured with feudalism, and the laws affecting *real* property in particular, have their foundations deeply laid in the rules, customs, and principles of the dark and feudal ages.

In order, therefore, to acquire a comprehensive view of the laws of our parent country, we must study her history, and that of Europe generally—we must explore feudal institutions and laws,

48.

which are the very sources and springs whence our jurisprudence originated. Should this be neglected, what student can repose with confidence on the certainty, or fixity of his legal attainments? Whose memory will be adequate to retain the numerous refined distinctions which appear so arbitrary and even absurd, without this key to their true import? How numerous are the rules of this description, which perplex students, who have not previously laid a sure foundation in the learning of the feudists? The operation of *common law conveyances*, so called, in contradistinction to those deriving their efficacy from the statute of uses, and which were introduced with no other design than to supplant the more rigid and subtle doctrines of the feudal law—most of the rules affecting *remainders,* whether vested or contingent—nearly all of the rules or canons of *descent;* the learning of *Conditions,* of *Entails*—the doctrines of *Abeyance,* of *Merger,* of *Forfeiture,* of *Rents,* properly so called—of *Releases,* of *Warranty,* and of the well known **Rule in Shelly's Case,** are all essentially of feudal origin, and of feudal modification; and never can be comprehended to any useful extent, without a competent acquaintance with that extraordinary code, which for a time maintained *divisum imperium*

49

with the Roman Civil Law, but which finally gained a decided ascendancy.

Passing from these topicks, we shall then proceed to the *second* division of our subject—the extensive and important learning of the *Realty*. This we shall delight to dwell on, as, we trust, before we leave it, we shall redeem this portion of our jurisprudence from the unmerited charge of exhaustive abstruseness, of unphilosophical arrangement, and of useless subtleties. We hope to show that, of all the branches of the vast and multifarious system of Common Law, none is entitled to more of your admiration, and respect, and studious attention, than this, whether we regard its own intrinsic excellence and importance, the numerous useful analogies furnished by it, or the happy influence which it exercises in fashioning the mind to close and systematick investigation.

Having thus briefly stated to you, gentlemen, an outline of the ensuing *commencement* of my professorial engagement—there are some auxiliary modes of instruction, to which I now claim your attention; as they enter into the views of that scheme of legal education, which I have selected, and which, whilst they confirm you in the knowledge derived from *books*, will serve to illustrate and familiarize the *practice* of a profession, so

50

often beset with difficulties to the young practitioner, and which, not unfrequently, are the cause of much anxiety, and even despondency, to those who have studied the science with no little care and industry. The auxiliaries, to which I allude, are the organization of a tribunal for the argument of supposed cases, brought before it with a strict regard to *all the forms of good Pleading*, and the rules of *Evidence*, and prosecuted with a rigid attention to all the decorums of forensick disputation. This tribunal will have the name of *Moot Court*, the history and nature of which I shall presently explain.

There is also much advantage to be received from the discussion of such general doctrines (of a legal nature) as cannot well be introduced through the ordinary forms of judicature. Such points will be argued in a distinct association, denominated *The Rota*. In regard to the "Rota," I would merely observe that it is an appellation derived from the celebrated Harrington, whose debating society, under that name, is too well known to need further mention, in order to justify our adoption of the word. Added to these, (which we trust will prove themselves powerful provocatives to the acquisition of legal learning) we shall propose annually four topicks, for prize essays,

51

not to exceed sixty, or to fall short of thirty printed pages. For the two best essays, (the merit of which will be decided on by the Faculty of Law) a golden medal will be awarded to each author—and for the successful candidates for the remaining two, a silver medal will be adjudged, in the same manner. These written discussions will be open to all of the members of the Law Institute, the Moot Court, the Rota, and those who attend lectures, if they be students of law. There is still another auxiliary to which we would direct your attention. Too little regard, we think, has been paid, in all countries, to the comfort and convenience of those engaged in the toils of a long and arduous course of study. The law student, in common with those of divinity and medicine, cannot be too strongly invited to constancy in his pursuits; and this can hardly be expected, unless the *locus studiorum* be in itself inviting. When the numerous days and nights, perhaps, of many years, are to be spent in intellectual toil, it is fit that some attention be paid to physical comfort; and likewise that students should have at hand, all that may be requisite to facilitate their progress. With this design an establishment has been opened, which we have named the Law Institute. In this a limited number of students, of

52

industrious habits, and who are actuated by the honourable ambition of becoming enlightened lawyers, are admitted. The advantages of this institution are, in brief, a *course of methodical study: colloquial examinations: union of practical, with theoretical knowledge: oral and written discussions of legal subjects: frequent presentation of questiones vexatæ: and resort to an extensive library, in every department of legal science.* Under the auspices of these several means of facilitating your studies, we cherish a hope of your certain, speedy, and solid advancement in the knowledge of your profession.

It can scarcely be necessary to dwell on the advantages of instruction by *lectures,* over any other mode: for though it be not indispensable in the *moral,* as it certainly is, in most *physical* sciences, where reasoning requires the aid of *experiment,* or other occular demonstration, yet it cannot be questioned that law, perhaps, more than any other moral science, may be most beneficially communicated by lectures orally delivered. The prominent advantages of this mode are, first, the *greater liveliness* with which knowledge may be impressed by oral instruction, than by the silent and retired labours of the closet; secondly, the *compendious views* which may be given by

53

lectures, after researches which were found by the student, either difficult or unprofitable; thirdly, the familiarity of example, and the illustration, in which they are allowed to indulge; which cannot be exercised by an author in his printed works, lest they should be too voluminous, and perhaps, too colloquial; fourthly, the opportunity which is afforded of solving, by private study, doubts which have arisen during the lectures; fifthly, the necessity students are under, of daily adding to their store of legal knowledge; sixthly, the advantage they possess in receiving this knowledge simultaneously through the medium of two, and in some degree, three of the senses, (if we are to trust the notions of metaphysicians on this point) viz. in hearing the professor; seeing the motion of his lips, and the other natural and impressive actions of his body; and lastly, through the touch or feeling consequent on noting down the substance of the lectures as they are delivered; all of which circumstances, no doubt, add strength and vividness to those impressions which are made by the subject alone. To these we may add, the advantages students have in the discourses of a lecturer, whose constant aim is to study, and anticipate their various doubts and perplexities; to offer a simple solution of them;

54

and to encourage students, in their moments of despondency, by some appropriate history of the triumph of industry and method over the most appaling combination of difficulties. These advantages are certainly too manifest to require illustration: the most important, however, is, that the professor can give greater latitude to his illustrations and examples, and can present his subject in a greater variety of aspects than is consistent with the condensed language of books—and besides this advantage, (which will be much valued by those who have pursued their law studies, unaided and solitary,) the lecturer can combine, in one view, points and principles which can be sought only in many books, and which are mingled with much matter, that is either useless in itself, or darkly and barbarously set forth.

This mode of instruction is particularly convenient, nay necessary, to *American* students. The laws of **England**, with some exceptions, are to be studied as much in detail by them, as by English students; to which must be added the laws of the United States; those of the state in which they design to practice; and also, such of the laws of the other states as relate to topicks of universal concern. If they would keep pace, too, with the growth of the science, as it is measured by the numerous volumes which emanate from English and American presses, they must have some acquaintance with a mass of books, which they have neither time to study, nor, perhaps, the means of procuring; for, scarcely a week passes, which does not usher to light some new treatise of law, or a former one, with such amendments and additions, as render the old one of little utility. A complete law library, at present, consists of many thousand volumes, requiring nearly a fortune to procure them, in addition to the judgment and time necessary for their selection. In this point of view, the utility of lecturing is strongly displayed, as thereby most of the difficulties would be solved, and most of what is valuable in these voluminous works, advantageously set forth.

That law is a proper subject for university instruction, through the medium of lectures, appears to have been the opinion of jurists and publicists as early as the first reduction of law into a systematick science. As far back as history gives us any knowledge of a regular code, we find jurisprudence taught, as one of the most important branches of learning, in publick seminaries, colleges, and universities. In Egypt, Rome, Constantinople, Berytus, Bagdad, Bologna, Cæsarea,

56

Laodicea, Carthage, and more recently in most of the European countries, law has been taught by lectures; and in many of them degrees have been conferred in this, as in other departments of knowledge.

Irnerius, Bartolus, Cujacius, Baldus, Voetius, Accursius, Heineccius, Gentilis, Gothofrede, Lampredi, Buddœus, Gravina, Imola, Zouch, Pothier, Blackstone, Wooddeson, Brown, and *Sullivan,* all members of universities, are great and imposing names, as professors in this august science: and the reasons which have made it to be thus taught, are of yet greater weight in this country, whose fundamental principles of government invite all, without distinction of rank, to the participation of political power, and to the administration of its laws.

The advantages of *social* over *solitary* study have been in no way, perhaps, more strikingly manifested than in the history of the *Inns of Court,* and of *Chancery,* those seminaries of common law, established in England many centuries since; to whose influence the judicious Spelman attributes most of what is regular, scientifick and excellent in English jurisprudence. A short examination into the origin and designs of these institutions, will not (we trust) be deemed digres-

57

sive; as it will be found confirmatory of the views we have endeavoured to inculcate, in regard to the benefits we would hope from assembling in our own country the dispersed students, or *apprentitii ad legem*, and forming them into an associated body, incited and stimulated by the noble ambition of continually honouring, and being honoured by a profession, whose aim is the preservation of every valuable right of nations, no less than of ndividuals.

We are to date the establishment of these *Inns of Court*, and of *Chancery* from the reign of the third Henry. Prior to that period the courts of judicature were ambulatory; and were holden in such of the king's palaces, as the royal personage happened to reside in. It is obvious, and so history informs us, that the professors and students of law would not be likely to have a *fixed* abode, or to assemble in such numbers as to accomplish any useful design of self-improvement, or of the melioration of a science, then extremely rude and chaotic. When it was ordained however, by *magna charta*, that the "Common Pleas should no longer follow the king's court, but be held in some certain place," the fixation of this important tribunal in Westminster, at once induced those learned in the *common* law, to assemble in London.

58

Students at law, from all parts of the kingdom, attracted by this talent and knowledge, also convened.—A little republick was almost immediately formed; they all addicted themselves to closer, and more methodical study; and finally they constituted themselves into a collegiate body, no less beneficial to the experienced or learned, than to students; who previous to this, had been used to no guide whatever, amidst the barren mazes of the then common law. The extensive dwelling houses of several noblemen, then called *Inns,* (meaning the same as the French word *Hotel,*) were purchased, and fitted up for their reception. They were organized as colleges for instruction in the *common law*—the universities of Oxford and Cambridge having adopted the Roman civil law as the basis of their lecturing.

The colleges thus established were of two kinds, one denominated Inns of Court, the other Inns of Chancery.

Inns of *Court* are for a higher order of instruction, and are supposed to have derived the *adjunct* name, from the necessity their students were under of attending the *courts* of judicature; or, as some contend, because, on their first establishment, these students were chiefly the sons of noblemen qualified to serve the king in his court.

59

Inns of *Chancery* derive their adjunct name from the fact that their students were mainly employed in the study of the forms of the various writs emanating from Chancery. These Inns were preparatory colleges for younger students, prior to their admission into the Inns of Court. Very little, however, is known of any of these Inns during the reign of Henry III. In that of Edward II. four of them were established; viz: *Johnson's, Fetter's, Pater Noster,* and *Lincoln's* Inns. Several others were established in the reign of Edward III. viz: *Thaive's, Gray's, Clifford's* and *The New Temple;* some of which were Inns of Court, and others of Chancery. But it was during the reign of the sixth Henry, that these law societies most flourished. There were then not less than ten Inns of Chancery, for elementary studies, and particularly, as we have stated, for instruction in the *forms* of original and judicial writs; which in those days was esteemed the very *substratum* of a good legal education. There were also four Inns of Court. We are informed by Fortescue, that these various Inns accommodated no less than two thousand students of law; that "*in them all vice was discouraged and banished, and every thing good and virtuous taught.*" He further states, that "*in addition to* LAW, *musick,*

60

singing, dancing, history, (sacred and profane,) were taught; and divers other accomplishments."

These juridical universities, as my Lord Coke denominates them, received the royal protection; by all persons being inhibited from teaching law, except members of the Inns of Court and Chancery.

The *exercises* established in these Inns, were various, and admirably adapted to promote emulation, and to advance the student in the practical as well as theoretick knowledge of his profession. After a long novitiate, and many ordeals, students were admitted to the honours of these grave institutions. Degrees were conferred on them in the common law, similar to those conferred in the more ancient universities, in the canon and civil law. The degrees were those of *Barrister*, equivalent to Bachelor of Law; and *Sergeant*, which corresponds to that of Doctor in the Civil and Canon Law. These barristers were styled Apprentices; now more usually Counsellors at Law. They may be called, by the king's mandate, to the degree of Sergeant at Law, after they have been of sixteen years standing as Barristers. The ceremonies, used in the creation of these dignified law officers, were very curious, and conducted with much expensive pomp and festivity. Ser-

61

geants at law, however, are of greater antiquity than the institution of these Inns, and are supposed, by Dugdale and others, to have been known even prior to the Conquest; certain it is, that this dignity existed in the reign of the first Edward.

Formerly, students were obliged to study in these Inns eight years, prior to their admission to the degree of Barrister—it is now, however, reduced to five years. The gentlemen of the Inns of Court are of three degrees, viz. 1. *No Utter Barristers,* or Students, properly so called; 2. *Utter* or *Outer Barristers,* and 3. *Inner Barristers,* or *Benchers.* These three compose the company of what are called *Masters* Commons. There is still, however, a class of inferior, or rather, junior students, who compose the company of *Clerks* Commons. This is formed of students during their two first years of standing; or rather, until they are called to the society of the *Masters* Commons.

The degrees of progression, from the commencement of a student's course, to that of his taking the coif, appear to have been eight, viz.

1st. *Admission into the Clerks Commons,* in which students generally continued two years, or

62

until admitted members of the company of *Masters* Commons.

2d. *No Utter Barrister*, or Students, properly so called, when first admitted into fellowship with the Masters Commons. They generally continued such three or four years.

3d. *Utter Barristers*, who had been of five or six years standing, that is, about two years as Clerks, and three or four as No Utter Barristers. They were then called on to argue at the mootings; they wore a bar-gown, and practised their profession after a certain number of mootings.

4th. *Cupboard Men*, who were such Utter Barristers, as had taken the oath of supremacy at the cupboard, and had performed certain moots, and given an expensive feast, declaring their intention of accepting the duties of Reader, should they be appointed to that station.

5th. *Inner Barristers*, or *Benchers*, who had been in these Inns fourteen or fifteen years, having passed through the previous degrees.

6th. *Readers*, chosen from the Benchers, to read or expound the law openly to the society and Students in the Inns of Chancery. Benchers were generally chosen Readers after they had been Cupboard Men two years. When appointed

63

a second time, they were called Double Readers, which was regarded a high honour.

7th. *New Sergeants,* those, who having been called to this honourable degree, had not yet taken the coif.

8th, and lastly. *Coifed* or *perfect Sergeants* at law, who had then assigned to them chambers in the Sergeant's Inn. They took a formal and solemn leave of the Inn of Court, on which occasion the treasurer of the Inn presented each with a purse of gold, value ten pounds, as a present from the whole society.

The internal regulations of these institutions were often very minute, and we are inclined to believe, sometimes equally absurd. Were it not too particular, we might here notice the silly regulations in regard to the *costume* of their members; who, among other things, were not allowed to wear cut or pansied hosen, or pansied doublets, on pain of expulsion; and the sin of wearing *long beards,* could be expiated by nothing less than being excommoned, or by what we now understand, being put in coventry, or under the ban. But these Inns not being corporations, had no judicial power over their members—all was conventional—the laws were preserved and enforced by no other sanction than an honourable *esprit du*

64

corps—a sacred respect for a plight given by students on their admission. If the rules were violated, the offenders were, by universal acclamation, either excommoned, that is, not permitted to eat or commune in any way with the rest; or their chambers were closed. This being notified, comity excluded them from admission into any of the other Inns.

The various and continued learned exercises in these institutions, could not fail to produce the happiest results. We find, accordingly, that most of the enlightened jurists of that country received in them their legal education.

The great commentator on Littleton owed, in great part, his rapid promotion, to the solid learning, and merited honours, which he had received in the *Inner Temple.* Lord Chancellor Audly, Sir Heneage Finch, Manwood, and Anderson—all students, and subsequently Benchers and Readers in this Inn of Court—are names too well known, in the common law, to need further mention.

To the *Middle Temple* are we indebted for the names of Plowden, Dyer, Doddridge; the Lord Chancellors, Rich, Yorke, Cowper, and Eldon; Lord Chief Justice Kenyon, Mr. Justice Blackstone, and numerous others.

65

From *Gray's Inn* we hear of the illustrious Bacon, and the Lord Keeper, Nicholas Bacon; and *Lincoln's Inn* is honoured by the names of Fortescue, Sir Thomas More, Spelman, Sir Matthew Hale—a splendid constellation, on which every student must delight to gaze.

In fine, nearly all who have been eminent, and learned, and virtuous in this most distinguished profession, had their morals, their studies, and their habits fashioned, and established in these illustrious seminaries of the common law.

The Inns of Court at present existing, are four, viz. the Inner Temple, and Middle Temple, Lincoln's Inn, and Gray's Inn. The two Temples are so called, from their being anciently the dwelling houses of the Knights Templars, and by them leased, in the reign of the third Edward, to certain professors, who established Inns of Court. In the reign of Henry VIII. these Temples (on the dissolution of the religious houses) fell to the crown, and were granted by King James I. in fee simple, to these collegiate bodies, for the reception of the professors and students of the common law.

Lincoln's Inn, and Gray's Inn, were so called

66

from the Earls of those names, in the reigns of Edward II. and III. when they were founded.

The Inns of Chancery existing at present, are nine; viz. *Clifford's* and *Thavie's*, established in the reign of Edward III.; *Clement's* and *Furnival's*, in the reign of Henry IV.; *Staple's* and *Lyon's*, in the reign of Henry V.; *Bernard's*, in that of Henry VI. and *New Inn*, in the reign of Henry VIII.

These Inns of Chancery belong to, or are attached to the four Inns of Court; viz. to the *Inner Temple*, Clifford's, Clement's, and Lyon's Inns are subordinate. To the *Middle Temple*, New Inn. To *Lincoln's Inn*, are attached Furnival's and Thavie's Inns; and to *Gray's Inn*, belong Staple's and Bernard's Inns. These Inns of Chancery, however, can now scarcely be considered in their former light, as students are no longer entered in them, with a view of subsequent admission into the Inns of Court; and these Inns of Court do not regard the time spent in the Inns of Chancery as a portion of the student's legal novitiate.

Having (tediously we are apprehensive) explained the origin, organization, and general views of these Inns of Court and of Chancery; and alluded to the very beneficial influence exerted by them, in forming accomplished scholars in the

67

law, and thereby adding dignity and lustre to the science; we shall now explain more particularly, the *means* adopted by them for the advancement of students in their legal education. We trust that this inquiry will strongly evince the probable utility of the several auxiliaries which we (in humble imitation) have already proposed.

The exercises practised by students of law in these Inns, were principally in attending the various *readings,* and in arguing *moot cases* before the Benchers, and also among themselves.

The *readings* consisted of lectures on any subject of the common law, delivered by Benchers, specially appointed as Readers. These Benchers were such as had been *Utter* Barristers for many years, and having been made *Inner* Barristers, or Benchers, were, occasionally appointed Readers, to treat and expound any statute or doctrine to the students of the Inns of Chancery, or to their society at large.

Whilst their appointment lasted they were called Readers, but when it terminated, they again took the name of Bencher. "During the time of his readings," says Stowe, (which lasted nearly two months in the year) "the Reader kept a constant and splendid table, feasting the nobil-

68

ity, judges, bishops, and sometimes the king himself, at a cost of about one thousand pounds."

There were two great periods assigned for these readings, called the *grand vacations;* one during Lent, the other late in summer. During these "Learnings," as they were also called, the elementary students, or No Utter Barristers, were obliged to attend every reading, under the penalty of twenty shillings for each default.

When the vacation readings were closed, the students attended their Reader with great state to his residence, and invited him at night, to partake of a sumptuous repast, at their own charge.

Readings were also given, during what was called Term time; when each of the Inns of Court sent two Readers to each of the Inns of Chancery. Students were also employed in various other exercises during these vacations and term time.

The most important of them all was that of mooting. The word *moot* is supposed, by some, to be derived from the French *mot*, (word) and by others, with more likelihood, from the Saxon *metan, gemetan,* or *gemot,* (meeting,) because at appointed meetings or assemblings of students, questions, fit for grave disputation, were argued by them, and determined by the Benchers. This deduction is highly probable, as there are many

69

compound words with similar termination, which are universally allowed to import an *assemblage*. As for example; *reevemote, shiremote, folkmote, wettena-gemot*, which last means an assembly of wise men. Be this, however, as it may, the points argued by students in the Inns of Court and Chancery, were called moot cases; the students who argued them, moot men; the place where they convened, moot hall; the disputations, mootings; and the Benchers, before whom they usually argued, a moot court. Students who thus argued, were the Utter or Outer Barristers; in contradistinction to those, on the one hand, whose inexperience ordinarily excluded them from these exercises; and who, as I have already stated, were called No Utter Barristers, Tyros, or Elementary Students; and to the Benchers, on the other hand, who, from superior knowledge, were raised from Utter to the degree of Inner Barristers; and, as such, entitled to sit as Judges at these mootings.

These Benchers annually appointed an officer, called the Bailiff, or *Surveyor of the Moots;* whose duty it was, to keep an accurate account of all matters argued; by whom discussed; and all other proceedings in these mock forensick encounters. These mootings were of two kinds, *grand* and *petty*. The former occurred during

70

the grand vacations, of which I have spoken; that is, during the Readings. When the Reading had terminated, any Utter Barrister was at liberty to oppose some point advanced by the Reader; and thus was the grand mooting commenced. At these vacations, the elementary students, also, were entitled to open points, before three of the Benchers; they were then followed by the Utter Barristers; and the case was decided by the Benchers. All this was done in that barbarous dialect, the Law French, of which Sir Henry Spelman so feelingly complains, when sent by his mother to commence his studies in the common law, at Lincoln's Inn.

"*Emisit me mater Londinum,*" (says he) "*juris nostri capessendi gratia; cujus cum vestibulum salutassem, reperissemque linguam peregrinam, dialectum barbarum, methodum inconcinnam, molem non ingentem solum, sed perpetuis humeris sustinendam, excedit mihi fateor animus.*"

The *petty mootings* were those which occurred in term time before the Readers, or Benchers of the respective Inns. There were also other mootings, called *mean vacation* moots, or chapel moots: these were performed by the younger students after the term, and grand vacations were over. There

71

were likewise *private* mootings, which are thus described by one of the black-letter law writers:

"Furthermore, after dynner and supper, the students and lerners in the house sit together, by *three* and *three* in a company; and one of the three putteth forth some doubtful question in the law, to the other two of his company; and they reason and argue unto it in English; and at last, he that putteth forth the question declaryth his own minde, also showing unto them the judgment, or better opinion of his boke, where he had the same question—and this do the students observe every day through the yere, except *festivall* days."

It is reasonable to suppose that these various exercises, publick and private, must have been attended with the most salutary consequences; and that they largely contributed to the ascendency of the Common over the Civil Law, which for ages had maintained an angry jealousy between their numerous professors and retainers.

The detail, which I have now brought to a close, I fear has been too minute, and proved tedious to my auditors. But we had, in this investigation, several objects to gratify; otherwise we should not have introduced it, as it has been one of no easy accomplishment, amidst the many dark

72

and conflicting statements of various dull and dusty authors. We supposed, that a minute account of what has been done for students, in the land whence we have derived most of our law; together with an exposition of the admirable results, could not fail to stimulate the young jurisprudents of this country, favourably to receive and foster an attempt to introduce among us, not the *same*, but *similar* institutions, adapted to the more refined state of our manners and jurisprudence.

From what has been stated, we perceive how important it has been deemed in England, not only that students of law should be *assembled*, and *associated* in their studies, but that they should be disciplined in regular and methodical exercises.

Were this matter, however, open to doubt, after the example we have just furnished; and, indeed, were it not obvious in itself, we might appeal to the views and practice of the ancient Romans, among whom similar methodical studies were deemed essential; and students were assembled from all parts of the empire, to receive instruction at appointed places. We are informed that in their law schools, over which the *Antecessor*, or professor presided, students were divided

73

into five classes; viz—*Dupondii, Edictales, Papinianistæ, Lytæ,* and *Prolytæ.* Four years were occupied by them before they were expected to engage in the study of the Code, or Imperial Constitutions.

The *Dupondii* were such elementary students as were engaged during the first year of their novitiate, in the study of the Institutes, and the first four books of the Digests. They were called *dupondii*, or students of small consideration, from the most common coin known in the Roman empire, about the value of a penny sterling, and as they were then admitted only "*ad limina legitimæ scientiæ.*" The emperor Justinian, however, whose parental regard for students induced him to attend even to such small matters, changed the name of this first class, to *Justinianei novi*; this being a more flattering designation.

The *Edictales* occupied the second year, in the study of the Digests, from the fifth to the twentieth book, inclusive; which contain the *Edicta Magistratuum.*

The *Papinianistæ* were such students, as during the third year, were employed in reading the Digests, from the twenty-first to the twenty-eighth book, inclusive; which contain the opinions of Papinian, justly styled the "living voice, and oracle

74

of Roman jurisprudence"—arriving at this stage of their studious career, they were regarded as having accomplished more than the passage of the *pons assinorum*. *"Quo nomine, Papinianistæ,"* says Heinecceus, *"adeo sibi placebant, ut diem quo ejus doctrinâ primum fuerant initiati, festum solennemque haberent."* And this rejoicing, and festivity are not to be considered as mere juvenile gaiety—for it was a festival not only countenanced but instituted, by imperial authority, evincive of the deep respect for the learning, virtues and talents of one of the most accomplished of Roman jurists.

The *Lytæ* finished the Digests during the fourth year; and were then regarded as competent to the solution of the most difficult points. But still, those *"qui juris nodos, legumque ænigmata solvunt,"* were then put to the study of the Code, and other works, *ad libitum:* at this time they assumed the name of *Prolytæ*, and usually completed their studies at the end of the fifth year.

The quinquennial term of study appears to have obtained in most ages. In the reign of Queen Mary, a famous civilian styled himself *"Magister Artium, et Prolyta juris,"*—and in most of the universities of the continent, this

75

period has been adopted as the time of legal study. By a statute of the University of Oxford, it is provided, *"Quodque per* BIENNIUM *in Academiâ, Dialecticæ, Morali Philosophiæ et Politicæ aliisque Humanioribus Literis incumbat, priusquam* QUINQUENNIUM *in studio juris ponere incipiat;"* and the statute of Cambridge ordains, that "a *year* be devoted by students in their chambers, to the study of the institutes, after which they shall hear, during *five years,* the publick prælector of law."

The provisions made at various times by the Roman Emperors, were admirably adapted to produce enlightened lawyers; and to repress those ignorant pretenders in the science, those *leguleii,* whom Cicero so much censures and ridicules, as being versed only in numerous unmeaning forms, and an unceasing flow of forensick jargon. We might here detail the wise institutions of the Emperor Valentinian, in his celebrated constitution, *"De Studiis,"* &c. We might dwell on the discipline and studies of the ancient seminaries of learning—a topick full of interest and profit; to this we might add, an inquiry into many important regulations in various modern universities, in regard to law students—but these would demand a further call on your time—already too freely occupied.

76

In conclusion—May we not emphatically ask, are not like institutions and regulations essential in *this country?* Is it not of first importance, that American students of law should have *prescribed studies* and *stated exercises;* and, in order to incite a suitable emulation, that they should be brought, as far as may be practicable, to *associate* in their studies? Is there any system of law, of any age or country, more various, complicated, and extensive than our own? We admit there are in our, as in other professions, degrees of knowledge suited to different capacities, and fitted to the particular, ultimate views of individuals. But those who are ambitious of fame, and an elevated standing in their profession; those who would honour and be honoured by their vocation; and, in fine, those who desire to minister as high priests at the altar, and give their opinions as oracular, must regard the study of the law, as the assiduous and methodized labour of *a life*—full of toils, but likewise full of encouragements and auspicious promises—ever realized to the truly zealous and persevering.

I would embrace the present occasion, to correct a misapprehension, which has partially prevailed, that the engagements into which I am about entering, may interfere, in some degree, with my avocations as Counsellor and Attorney. No impression can be more unjust, as the studies in which the prosecution of these lectures will engage me, would have been pursued, had the present enterprise never been attempted—and as my scheme thus far, has been prosecuted only in leisure hours. I therefore desire to state, emphatically, that my duties here, can never, in any way, be permitted to interfere with those due to my Clients—but, on the contrary, that I do not contemplate the relinquishment of any portion either of my professional zeal, or of my practice.

An Address

To Students of Law, 1824

(CIRCULAR.)

AN

Address

TO

STUDENTS OF LAW

IN THE

UNITED STATES.

Baltimore:
PRINTED BY JOHN D TOY,
Corner of St. Paul's lane and Market street.
JULY, 1824.

CIRCULAR

TO

STUDENTS OF LAW.

I SOMETIME since announced to students of law that I had established in this city a Law Institute, and had commenced the delivery of a Publick Course of Lectures. The frequent applications which are made to me from a distance for information in regard to these enterprises, (although I had set forth my views in the preface to my "Syllabus," and in an Introductory Lecture recently published) induce me to advert again at this time to the objects which I propose, and to the plans by which I aim to attain them. The publications in which this has already been done in part, were too bulky to be distributed with convenience as extensively as I could wish; and, at all events, I am desirous to furnish every information in regard to plans on which I have bestowed much labour, which are already in more

4

than partial operation, and in whose entire success, I honestly own, I feel a very great interest.

It must be obvious that this concern is neither pecuniary, nor even in a great degree personal. The labour and the time which I have expended on the Lectures, whose outline I have given to the publick, had brought me, perhaps, if otherwise employed, more of that for which men too frequently toil, than I shall probably ever reap from the maturity of all my designs. But the scheme has long been the favourite of my mind; my professional studies necessarily subserved it, and as every one would contribute his share of usefulness to society, and reap his portion of honest reputation, my wishes in respect to both seemed naturally connected with a profession of which I am a member, and for which I cherish a high veneration. I have therefore persevered, through some toil, and a few sacrifices, cheered however, I am happy to say, by the good wishes and encouragement of some of the most eminent persons that adorn the bench and bar of this country.

The Regents of the University of Maryland, impressed with the propriety of making jurisprudence a part of university education, established in the year 1816 a Professorship of Law, and did

5

me the honour to name me to that chair. In most of the European nations this formed an important part of the studies of universities; and even in England, the inattention of the two great national universities to this point of education, was in a considerable degree compensated by the establishment of the Inns of Court and Chancery, in the vicinity of the great courts of Westminster. In America alone, the student of the most learned and abstruse profession, was left to his own insulated and unassisted efforts; law learning seldom formed a part of college education, and there was no institution, with the exception only of the Litchfield school, where even the *institutes* were taught. In the hope of supplying what I deemed an important deficiency in the education of our country, I have since my appointment to the law chair, applied myself, with more or less diligence, during the intervals of professional engagements, in preparing a course of lectures; and, as my views insensibly expanded, I sketched the plan laid before the publick in my Syllabus, which embraces every title known to the great body of law, viz. Ethicks, Common, Statute, National, Roman, Admiralty, Mercantile, and Constitutional law, and which exceeds in variety and extent any scheme of lectures hitherto attempted. Very

6

early in the prosecution of this design, and when I came to refer to numerous and very different works in treating even of a single subject, I was struck not more with the undigested character of the works themselves, than with the immethodical order in which they were usually read by students. Various and mixed as is the learning of the common law, it has its natural connexions and dependencies; and in proportion, indeed, to the multifariousness of its topicks, is their *just order* to be consulted by the student—to exhibit this, and to point out the best sources of information, I prepared the "Course of Legal Study," which, I presume, was the first manual ever arranged for law students either in England or this country. If I may trust the representations of my friends, it has not been without its use to the tyros of the profession—not only by displaying that natural sequence and coherence of their studies, (which, though real and serviceable, is not, at first sight, very obvious) but by collecting under proper divisions the authoritative law on every branch of jurisprudence.

In pursuing one object of that work, namely, to point out where the learning of each particular doctrine was to be found, I felt at every step how desirable was a digest of every great branch of

7

the law, which should orderly display, not only the elementary *philosophy*, but the material *learning* of each subject. Most of the works on the institutes of legal science, are necessarily barren of minute learning, whilst on the other hand the digests are often replete with learning, but deficient in elementary instruction. Of the usefulness of this plan of condensing and methodizing, so as at the same time, to preserve an institutionary character, no one perhaps is better entitled to pass an opinion than he who has been engaged in the task. Not to speak of the innumerable interesting points worthy to be known, though they might not repay to every individual the labour of research, it is evident how much even in the ordinary points of a lawyer's education, his labours might be lightened by system, and by finding educed and described the general principles and outlines of the entire science, combined with all of its more important learning. The student soon becomes aware that the doctrines of our law have been the growth of successive ages, and are scattered through thousands of reports of adjudicated cases, crude digests, and every sized treatises, of extremely unequal merit. In the present state of legal bibliography, it is no less costly to the purse to collect, than to the mind

8

to search the bulky and innumerable *tomes* in which the *Law* lies scattered—and in the absence of some general digest, such as I have described, made by *legislative* authority, the importance of those which are the labour of *individual minds*, becomes every day more apparent. I have, however, in the publications before alluded to, said enough of this topick, and also of the propriety of imparting legal instruction through the medium of lectures.

I certainly cannot flatter myself that either my life, or my talents will endure to the completion of my plan, with any considerable degree of excellence. If the former should be spared me, the *entire course* will certainly be accomplished at no very distant day, which will require two years in its delivery, allowing a daily lecture for ten months in each year.

To aid the student in every part of his career, to adopt in all the branches of the law that plan of digesting and arranging principles, of which I have spoken; to illustrate doctrines by the cases which decided them, and particularly by those in which former adjudications have been compared, reconciled, confirmed, or repudiated; to show wherein the common law has been modified by statutory provisions; to trace the history of a

9

legal principle through various times and circumstances, down to its actual modifications; and sometimes to point out what I consider inconsistencies in our excellent body of law—these, with other matters principally of curiosity, which students have often neither time nor books to investigate with precision, have been my objects in the lectures which I have commenced delivering, and those which are to follow. The course to be commenced in the fall, will occupy one or two hours of, perhaps, every day during four months, commencing with the first Monday in October; the course will be annually added to, until the scheme is completed; and though a great part of the materials of the whole course are prepared, the completion of a plan demanding so much labour, will not be hurried by me, until it is ascertained in what degree I am to depend on the support of those destined to the profession, especially in the southern and western states, to which my institution is more immediately contiguous. Thus far I have had nothing to discourage my expectations. Under any circumstances whatever, I shall annually add to my lectures, and cannot but cherish the hope, that I shall witness the completion of my design. which can only be retarded by the want of that encouragement which all enterprises, however zealously pursued, must have. Such is the progress I have made in one part of my plan.

Presuming it highly probable that a course of publick lectures, particularly one of such vast extent as that in which I am engaged, would require various auxiliaries to insure its eventual success, I opened an establishment which I denominated the *Maryland Law Institute*. Too little regard, we think, has been paid in all countries to the comforts and convenience of those engaged in the toils of a long and arduous course of study. Students of law, in common with those of divinity and medicine, cannot be too strongly invited to constancy in their pursuits, and this can hardly be expected, unless their studies are directed, their doubts relieved, and the *locus studiorum* be in itself inviting. When the numerous days and nights, perhaps of many years, are to be spent in intellectual toils, it is fit that some attention be paid even to physical comfort. With this design the establishment has been opened in a spacious and commodious building in South, near Market street, in this city, the apartments of which have been handsomely fitted up, and arranged in every respect for the accommodation of students. The advantages of this institution are,

11

in brief, *a course of methodical study adapted to the students' progress, and their separate views in regard to the place in which they design to practise their profession; colloquial examinations; union of practical with theoretical knowledge; oral and written discussions of legal subjects; frequent presentation of questiones vexatæ, and resort to an extensive library in every department of legal science and general knowledge.*

In regard to the *discipline* of the institute, it is hoped that little more is necessary, than for students to bear in mind the great importance of their pursuit, and that, at a distance from home, with advantages of comparatively brief duration, no moment of time should be recklessly thrown away. A strict attention, however, will be required to the rules in regard to the hours of study, the *silence* to be observed in the chambers, their *undivided* attention to *legal* subjects during the prescribed hours, the mode of using the library, and the other few but essential regulations which have been introduced, as well for the comfort and advancement of the students, as for the convenience of the professor.

The next auxiliary, to which I have alluded, as a means of ultimately establishing my main

12

design, is the organization of a tribunal for the argument of supposed cases, brought before it with a strict regard to *all the forms of good pleading and the rules of evidence,* and prosecuted with a rigid attention to all the forms of forensick disputation. This tribunal will have the name of *Moot Court.*—In this, regular dockets will be opened, adapted to the State Courts, and those of the United States, and fictitious suits will be instituted of such a character as to suggest important questions of law, the niceties of pleading, and the forms of practice. Experience is decisive as to the practicability of suggesting by this plan even the subtleties of pleading, that logick of the law, and those niceties of practice, which seeming often arbitrary and trivial, involve however, true distinctions of things, and correspond to the just principles of the science. There are several other minor auxiliary modes of advancing the student which have heretofore been adverted to by me, and which need not be repeated.

I am conscious that in such as are absolutely careless of learning, all external aids are insufficient to produce the fruits of sound knowledge. But to those who would pursue an entensive, various and noble science with a corresponding zeal, I flatter myself that the course and scheme of

13

instruction presented to them in the various departments of the Law Institute, offer advantages too obvious to require insisting on.

The recent exertions which are making in several of the states in advancement of the point I have so long had at heart—viz. the methodical study, and scientifick teaching of our most excellent and noble profession, is truly gratifying to me. Professorships are established in Kentucky, Pennsylvania, Massachusetts, New-York, and perhaps elsewhere; which, united to the aid furnished by the Law Academy of Philadelphia, under the guidance of those distinguished jurists. P. S. Du Ponceau and Thomas Sergeant, Esqs. and the establishment at Northampton, in Massachusetts, by Messrs. Howe and Mills, cannot fail greatly to promote these desirable objects.

The City of *Baltimore* is happily situated for the perfect execution of the plans I have set forth.

It is central; contiguous to the seat of national government; and presents every advantage of salubrity, agreeableness, economy in living, and lectures on many of the most important departments of learning. The spirit of letters is diffusing itself among its people, and numerous literary and scientifick institutions are rising up. To such as aim only at a studious life, it offers every

14

facility of study, and by those who, reading law as one of the liberal studies, desire to unite to it the benefit of a few years' residence in a city, it will be found to possess every facility for the acquisition of polite and solid knowledge.

There is an infinite advantage in the association of many liberal minds in a common pursuit. It is highly important at that age when emulation is in its first vigour, to give it an impulse in the direction of its future objects. We flag in the race when we do not hear the tread of our competitors near at hand; and the very same principle of imitation which excites us to enterprise among our own brotherhood, divests our efforts when among those of different aims and interests. If on this principle the learned collect themselves into societies, students into colleges, and members of the same craft into fraternities and companies, there is equal, perhaps superior reason for the law student, (who would invigorate his honest ambition, and learn to love that atmosphere of competition in which he is destined to spend his life) to emerge from that studious solitude in which hitherto it has been the fashion to attain the laborious learning of his profession.

In conclusion, it is proper to say a word in regard to the *terms* of the Institute and Public Lectures. They are established as follows:

15

1. *Law Institute.*—This comprehends office accommodations, use of an extensive Law and Miscellaneous Library, direction of studies, private examinations, occasional private readings, and publick lectures, which commence on the first Monday in October of every year, and will be delivered five times a week for at least four months, but to be annually increased until the entire course is completed. *Fee* (always to remain the same) *per annum.* $100

2. *Law Institute.*—For those who enter during the period of publick lecturing. Fee (changes every year) now, for the four months, - - - - - $50

3. *Public Lectures alone, for Law Students.* Fee (changes annually) now - $30

4. *Same.*—For Professional Gentlemen and others, (now) - - - - $15

5. *Moot Court.*—Fee, unchangeable, $20

6. *Moot Court and Lectures.*—Fee (now) $40

The student can under no circumstance be charged more than $120, including the *Moot Court,* which, however, is optional with the student.

DAVID HOFFMAN.

Balt. July, 1824.

A Lecture

Being the Second of a Series of Lectures, Introductory to a Course of Lectures Now Delivering in the University of Maryland, 1825

A

LECTURE

BEING THE SECOND OF A

Series of Lectures,

INTRODUCTORY TO A

COURSE OF LECTURES

NOW DELIVERING IN THE

UNIVERSITY OF MARYLAND.

BY DAVID HOFFMAN.

PUBLISHED AT THE REQUEST OF THE FACULTY OF LAW.

Baltimore:
PRINTED BY JOHN D. TOY,
Corner of St. Paul and Market streets.
June, 1825.

SECOND

INTRODUCTORY LECTURE.

IN my first Introductory Discourse, delivered in this place, besides the general topicks suggested by the enterprize in which I am engaged, I endeavoured to show you the essential connexion between the various subjects embraced in the First and Second Titles of the Syllabus of these Lectures; these titles comprehending first, *Metaphysicks*, *Ethicks*, and *Natural Law;*—secondly, the learning of the *Feudists*, and what has been technically called the *Doctrine of the Realty*. In pointing your attention to the *first* class of subjects, I aimed to impress on your minds their great importance, and how intimately akin they are to the proper studies of the accomplished lawyer. In that lecture I endeavoured to illustrate their utility; the links by which they are associated; and the necessity of proceeding in your studies methodically, from the contemplation of

4

the foundations of *moral obligation,* in the original structure of the mind, to the view of these obligations as they are contemplated or modified in *society,* whether of *individuals* or of *nations.* Your attention was then carried to that peculiar organization of civil society, called the Feudal System, from which the government and laws of modern communities have taken a permanent tincture; and I endeavoured, in the last place, to indicate more particularly the pervading connexion between the general feudal law, and that refined system of the English Law which affects *landed* property;—a system the whole of whose parts demonstrate its origin and structure to have been feudal; and which is consequently very unintelligible without the aid of feudal learning.

In the present discourse we shall present you with some observations on the connexion of the various subjects embraced under the *Third* Title of the Syllabus; viz. the Law of *Personal Rights, and Personal Remedies;* and as I shall in my succeeding introductory discourses pursue the same plan in regard to the successive titles of the course, they will form a Series of Essays on the general features, leading relations, excellencies, and defects of each of the grand divisions of the law.

5

This third title or branch of our subject, gentlemen, embraces *first*, personal *rights*, and *secondly*, the means or *remedies* established by law for their assertion; together with a variety of incidental matters, which will be presently mentioned.

Personal *rights* may be considered 1st, in regard to the *individual* or person; 2dly, as they are affected by his *relations* in society; which may be those of husband and wife, parent and child, master and servant, guardian and ward, governor and governed. The *remedies* adopted for the enforcement of these rights, are also susceptible of a great variety of divisions; involving the several topicks of *Courts* and their organization; *Officers* of courts, their duties and powers; the *forms* of action and procedure, denominated *pleading* and *practice;* after which follow, in succession, the modes of *trial;* the requisite *evidence* to sustain them; the *errours* in these proceedings, with the redress by *appeal* &c. to superior tribunals; and lastly, the means of enforcing decisions of courts by *execution*, which is favoured in the law, as it is *fructus, finis et effectus legis,*—the very *life, aim,* and *effect* of the law.

The gradual evolution of these subjects, in the order of their natural connexion, is essential to their right understanding, and their easy attain-

6

ment. If the ties associating these apparently dissimilar subjects, be not properly regarded, we lose much of the spirit and philosophy which really appertain to them; and we pursue our studies with as little interest as one who travels a labyrinth, ignorant that its numerous windings are in any way connected, or that they all tend to one desired goal. May we not, indeed, attribute much of the *ennui* which even pleasing subjects sometimes occasion, to the limited view we take of their important divisions, to that view which confines the mental eye to the *parts* of a great whole, leaving blanks in the vision at the points of their connexion.

It will be my endeavour, when I come to treat of these topicks, to show with some minuteness these points of association: all that we shall at present attempt, is to exhibit their general relations to each other; and to remove, if possible, some popular grounds of cavil in regard to them.

I would remark in the outset, what is emphatically true in regard to the *lex mercatoria*, and some other branches of English jurisprudence, that the learning of *personal rights and remedies* is much less tinged with feudal principles, and the technicalities growing out of them,—and proceeds much more on the general grounds of *obligation* and *morals*, than does that of the *realty*. Hence

7

its conclusions are less remote from our ordinary comprehension, and its reasoning more within the compass of a mind unfashioned to the contemplation of subtilties.

It is true, indeed, that feudalism did exercise no small portion of influence even on this branch of English jurisprudence: as, for example, in the doctrine of guardian and ward, particularly before the statutory modification of that law; and, in some degree, in the various forms of real and personal actions; and even in pleading, practice, and the modes of trial. But in general it will be found that the feudal spirit is most visible in all that concerns lands, tenements, and hereditaments, which are coextensive with the entire doctrine of the realty.

I have already remarked, gentlemen, that the learning of the *personal* law is extremely various; it may hence occur as a question to the student, by what *general* bond of connexion is it that topicks so dissimilar are united under one general division of personal law. With what justice, it may be asked, has the term *"personal rights"* been adopted; and, when adopted in compliance with established usage, how are their boundaries distinguished from those of *real rights?* It may be justly observed that, in point of metaphysical

8

truth, all *rights* being inherent, (not in things, which are incapable of rights,) but in persons, are *personal* rights: the phrase *"real rights,"* therefore, seems to be a solecism adopted in order to avoid a periphrasis, namely, *"personal rights as they are connected with the realty."*—This point, however, has been canvassed by me elsewhere; and it is rather the object of the present remarks to show how it comes to pass, that so large a body of topicks, many of which do undoubtedly concern the realty, as well as personalty, are nevertheless usually treated under the general head of *"personal law."*

A philosophical, and, at the same time, a practical analysis of the laws of England, is a task of no easy accomplishment. It is certainly desirable that every integral portion of the system should be found in the analysis in its proper place. "The scheme should be so comprehensive as that every title might be reduced under some one or other of its general heads, which the student might pursue to any degree of minuteness; and, at the same time, so contracted that he might, with tolerable application, contemplate and understand the whole."

With this view Lord Hale prepared his celebrated analysis. Several anonymous productions

9

of a similar kind, subsequently appeared, and finally Mr. Justice Blackstone, and Mr. Nolan published their analyses. They all, however, have adopted nearly the same division of their subject, and almost exactly the same phraseology. The fact is, that the laws of the realty and personalty are, in some instances, so intimately blended, that separation is impossible; and in others the personalty is so much the more important, that it gives the *name* or character to the title, although under it is also to be found much that equally appertains to the realty. Thus, for example, students will find in the Syllabus I have presented to them, that various subjects are placed by me exclusively under the head of the personalty, when, in truth, several of these topicks embrace much that concern real rights, and real remedies. This arises either from the fact, that these branches more *generally* relate to the personalty than to the realty; or that, although *land* may be the object, the *remedy* is not *in rem*, but *in personam;* or, finally, from some other cause which gives to the personalty a preponderating influence, entitling it to give the subject a place under its auspices, rather than those of the realty. As for example: You will find in the Syllabus, under the title of the Personalty, the subject of

10

legacies, though legacies are often charged on lands. The extensive subject of contracts and agreements, many of which also concern the realty, and may require a specifick performance, are, nevertheless, found under the same head. So fraud and duress, which are as likely to occur in agreements concerning the realty as personalty, are yet treated generally under the latter head. So likewise execution, with its incidents, may affect *lands*, as well as *chattels* or the *person;* yet the nature and various kinds of execution operating on *lands*, are treated under the cardinal division of personal law. *Courts*, also, exercise as large a jurisdiction over territorial rights, as they do over mere personal interests, and, nevertheless, courts and their powers you will find under the same general head. In fine, evidence and pleading, which equally apply to contracts and injuries affecting *lands, tenements*, and *hereditaments*, are still assigned exclusively to this division of our subject. The truth is, that this arrangement, though convenient and generally understood, is technical. All rights, as I have said, are personal; but being differently modified, according to the different *subjects* on which they operate, or to the different *relations* in which we stand to each other, they take different names:

11

the *real* law is, therefore, that branch of the rights of persons which operates on *real property*, with its own peculiar rules arising from its subject-matter—LAND; in the same way that the *lex mercatoria* is a branch of the personal law, with peculiarities arising from *its* subject-matter—MERCHANDISE. We must, therefore, bear in mind, as in other things, that what does not fall under the *exceptions*, will be found to be embraced by the class; so that in the law, what is not referrible to any special division, belongs to the great body of the law of *personal rights* and *personal remedies*. There is another reason, arising from the general principle of classification, which operates to throw the consideration of a very large number of topicks under this third title of our course. The assertion of all rights must necessarily be made through the intervention of *persons,* either of *courts,* which are a kind of artificial or political persons, or of their *officers:* And the powers with which the law invests them for this end, cannot in any way be so conveniently considered as by bringing them all together, and arranging them in distinct titles, under the general head of personal law. Thus, we have seen that courts have powers which directly affect lands, and that execution may be levied on the realty,

3

12

and yet that both these subjects naturally and philosophically fall under the general head; so that the division of the *jura personarum* will be found to comprehend *first*, the rights of persons strictly so called, viz. to *life, liberty, reputation*, &c. *secondly*, the various rights flowing from the *relations* of society, as that of parent and child, husband and wife, guardian and ward, &c. &c. It then passes to the consideration of various *positive* relations, which embrace, among others, those who are invested with political and civil magistracy, or those who, though under the protection of society, are disqualified, in some degree, from partaking of its rights: to this head belong the topicks of infancy, idiocy, lunacy, &c.; and finally, those who, though they are not members of the state, are yet under its protection as temporary residents within it, either on their own private concerns, or the business of sovereigns, viz. aliens, ambassadors, consuls, &c. These several sorts of natural persons, with their incidental rights and relations, being considered, we are led next to artificial ones, viz. corporations, which are societies that emanate directly and expressly from the authority of the great political corporation, or body politick, or are sustained by prescription. In connexion with these we find treated the sub-

13

jects of statutes and by-laws.—The rights flowing from the various relations of men during their life being disclosed, we pass on to those consequent on the alienation of property; first, in contemplation of *death;* and herein are treated the law of wills, testaments, intestacy; the duties of executors, administrators, &c.; and secondly, the disposition of property or rights *inter vivos;* which comprehends the more general topicks of contracts and agreements, and the modes by which our interests may be delegated to, and conducted by others, viz. the law of *agency* or *authority;* and this branch of the personal law is concluded by inquiring how far ill faith and illegal compulsion may vitiate the contracts into which parties may be drawn,—which topicks are assigned to the heads of *fraud* and *duress.*

Our natural and adventitious personal rights being considered, we proceed to the *means* provided by law for their enforcement. This involves the consideration of *courts,* their organization and jurisdiction, whether general or special; their *officers* and their *powers.* As the rights which are sought to be vindicated, and the contracts to be enforced in these tribunals, differ very much according to the subjects of them, we proceed to treat in order of all the various *actions* which

14

wisdom and experience have established for these ends. And as these have their boundaries and forms of procedure, we next inquire in what mode courts of justice expect the *allegations* and *defences* of the parties litigant to be set forth: this includes the important and refined doctrines of *pleading* and of *practice*. In close connexion with these we find the extensive learning of *evidence*,—a topick full of interest, and one on which the student must be content to dwell with persevering and unwearied attention, till not only the principles of this sublime philosophy of proofs and probabilities, but their various applications be so identified with his mind, that the law and reason thereof shall instantly present themselves, with scarcely an exertion of the memory.

But inasmuch as mistakes occur in proceedings, and errors infect the wisest tribunals, we, in the next place, unfold the various provisions made for correcting these mistakes, and revising these decisions.—These subjects are discussed under the heads of *bills of exception, writs of error, supersedeas, scire facias, auditâ querelâ,* and *injunction;* and, in the last place, we speak of the mode which the law hath appointed for the fulfilment of its judgments; and herein we treat of the different kinds of execution, varying according to the policy

15

of the state, or the election of the creditor, as he may deem the *person*, the *land*, or the *goods* of his debtor the best security for his claim. In the arrangement of these numerous topicks, I have consulted their natural order and dependence, and hope I have so disposed them as to render each subsequent subject more intelligible from the previous consideration of those which precede it.

I must not here omit to remark, as I have previously intimated, that the student will find in many of the subjects connected with this title, the eminent utility of being well initiated into the fundamental principles of Morals and of Natural Law. In the decisions of courts, interpretative of contracts, the student will find perpetual references to the elementary principles of that science which is embraced in the first title of this course; and whose study I cannot cease to recommend to his especial attention. The rights of persons, in the technical meaning of the phrase, and the laws of contracts, are, notwithstanding all the numerous provisions of particular statutes, founded essentially on those great general maxims common to all countries, and arising out of the very nature of man and of human society. These maxims of natural jurisprudence have assumed the form of a distinct and important science in the works of

16

Plato, Aristotle, Cicero, Seneca, and many other antient worthies; in the wisdom of the civilians of old; in the enlightened pages of Grotius, Puffendorf, Heineccius, Pothier, Bynkershoek, and the whole host of moral writers, whose productions must ever be resplendent in the annals of mental philosophy.—It is in vain for students to urge that all this is but *common sense*, and *"nature methodized,"*—that natural jurisprudence may with safety be left to the conclusions of their own minds; and that the whole system of morals being based on eternal and immutable principles, must readily occur to every well regulated mind. If this be true, then indeed have Wolfius and Heineccius, Hutchinson, Reid, Stewart, Paley, and Rutherforth written in vain. But can this be true? Have those great minds settled no doubtful points in morals? Have not their reasonings, classifications, definitions, pithy rules, and sententious maxims reared a science out of chaos? Take for example the subject of interpretation, or the construction of contracts. How much light has been shed on this topick, and what numerous aids are afforded us in the pages of Grotius, Puffendorf, Locke, Tillotson, Vattel, Rutherforth and others, and yet how apparently simple are these rules, when once ascertained! How often have the enlightened judges of England been obliged to consult the pages of these philosophers unhappily so much neglected by students in this country. The construction of the statute of frauds, to mention a few instances in a thousand, turned on the nature and essence of an agreement, as defined in the volumes of Natural Law. So likewise in the great case of Miller v Taylor, 4 Burr, 2303, in which was discussed with singular learning and ability the question of literary property, we find all the judges perpetually referring to the elementary principles of natural jurisprudence, and their familiarity with the writings of all antient and modern jurists treating this subject, evinces their respect for the learning and for the authority of these writers.

On this topick (thus digressively introduced,) we take great pleasure in fortifying our opinion heretofore often expressed, by that of one of the most distinguished of our own civilians. Speaking of natural jurisprudence, Mr. Duponceau says, "when the principles of that science are sufficiently disseminated, they will fructify; and statutes and judicial decisions will gradually take their colour from them. System will be introduced where it is wanted, sound theories will take

18

place of false ones, and the rules of genuine logick will direct their application to particular cases." "The common law," continues he, "is destined to acquire in this country the highest degree of perfection of which it is susceptible; and which will raise it, in all respects, above every other system of laws, antient or modern. But it will not have fully reached that towering height, until the maxim shall be completely established in practice as well as in theory,—that pure *ethics*, and sound *logic* are also parts of the *common law*."*

But to proceed: In regard to individual rights the law of England and this country, but more especially our own, may claim the just praise of transcending all other systems of law in tenderness to the rights and liberties of the citizen, and in the security of his property from a despotick and irregular control of the government. Nor, when we compare the course of their legal procedure with that of all other countries, do we find such strong grounds for the ordinary complaints of the tardiness and uncertainty of justice. And if some difference in these points be perceptible between the forms of English and American judicature, and other more summary ones, in countries

* Dup. on Juris. 132.

19

more arbitrarily governed, we should before we hasten to blame, reflect whether we should be willing, for the obtainment of more expedition in justice, to sacrifice the correctness of legal decisions, the certainty we obtain of the principles whereon they proceed, and the delicate caution with which the highest tribunals handle the privileges, and determine on the rights of the citizen. In regard to the tardiness of legal proceedings, it must be confessed that our law is obnoxious to some censure; but whilst this is the case, it must also be as fully conceded, that as much, if not more, of the vexatious delays of the law are owing to its ministers, as to the inherent defects in the laws themselves,—and that if courts, and particularly lawyers, were to hasten the march of justice with only half the rapidity assigned to it by the law, no serious grounds of complaint in this respect would remain. In regard to the certainty of justice, this must ever depend on the learning and virtue of those who are called to distribute it. The wisest laws may be misapplied by the vicious; and their clearest provisions be misinterpreted by the ignorant.

The rules of the English law as to the rights and obligations of men in their private relations, are framed with a just regard to their incapacities

20

and weakness on the one hand, and to the wholesome preservation of justice on the other.—This is generally manifest throughout that extensive and varied system. If, for instance, the law, for wise purposes, deems the servant to be under the control of his master, the wife of her husband, the child of its parent; it relaxes this principle in all cases where it is obviously against his own better knowledge, though in obedience to such control, that either of these subjected persons transgresses the injunction of the law. Thus a servant is, indeed, excused for performing his master's command; but not to commit a felony. So also a wife renders her husband responsible for her debts, as for most purposes her legal existence is merged in that of her husband;—but if he be exiled, is banished, or has abjured the realm, the reason ceasing, the rule ceases also, and she is made responsible. So likewise magistrates and officers are protected in the discharge of their functions; but they shall not be allowed, under colour of these, to violate the privileges of the citizen by an extrajudicial or ministerial act. So again, in regard to most of the fictions and intendments of the law, they will be found to have originated in grounds either highly rational or politick. As for example, that a corporation has no soul, and never

21

dies; that the binding efficacy of collateral warranty and of fines and recoveries, is owing to a supposed *excambium,* or recompense in value, in lieu of the lands affected by them; that a bond made beyond sea, may be pleaded to be made at Leghorn, to wit in Baltimore, in the county aforesaid;—that there is no variance in the case of writs taken out in vacation, but bearing teste the last day of the preceding term; that in an action for the seizure of a vessel, a declaration stating that it was done on the *high seas,* videlicet in *Cheapside,* is not incongruous; that in assumpsit, though the promise is expressly stated, none need exist or be proved; that in trover, though it be stated that the defendant found the goods, yet the finding need not be proved; that in ejectment various matters are to be asserted, which in truth never occurred; that a writ which orders the sheriff to have the defendant's body before the court at a certain time and place, still means nothing more than that he must give bail to the action, and often, in our practice, not even this, but that he must employ an attorney to appear for him; that when judgment has been obtained against a defendant who lives in a different county from that in which the venue was laid in the action, the writ of execution against him must state that a writ hath issued to

22

the county of the venue, though this be not the fact; and finally, the whole doctrine of relation: all of these, we say, will be found generally to rest on rules or presumptions adopted by the courts on the strictest reasons of logick, or on the soundest deductions of experience; and have been used mainly to subserve and expedite the ends of justice.

It must be confessed that some of these fictions and intendments have been continued after the reasons in which they originated have ceased; and that some of them also are very refined and innocently absurd.—But on the whole we are inclined to think, that the vehement objections on this subject which have been made by learned and ingenious authors, who have been rather unfriendly to the English common law, savour too much of cavil.—We are free to own, that could an enlightened body of men be invested with the power of lopping some of the excrescences which times and circumstances or ignorance may have generated in this admirable and extraordinary system, perhaps some good might be the result of such an enterprize; but until a re-modelling of that vast system is entrusted to very competent hands, we are sorry to see a spirit of opposition manifesting itself through party pamphlets, inconsiderate orations, and crude legislative speeches.

23

From these remarks we take great pleasure in excepting (and perhaps others might be included,) a very sensible production from the pen of an eminent member of the New York Bar. In the production to which we allude, we find many judicious observations on the evils and absurdities of the practice of the English common law, as adopted generally in this country; with some useful suggestions for their correction.—And although we do not entirely agree with this author, we cannot deny that he has placed most of his subject in a very forcible light. We shall take occasion to call your attention to this subject before we close the present lecture.

In the present state of the English judiciary, when the jurisdiction of the various courts is accurately distinguished and bounded, it presents a beautiful system both for the administration of justice in the first instance, and for the review and correction of their sentences. That arrangement of their courts called familiarly the *Nisi Prius* system, which sends the cause to be tried on the spot where it arose, and reserves general questions springing out of it, for the final decision of the high courts of Westminster Hall, is beyond doubt admirably adapted, *first* for the speedy disposition of causes, and *secondly* for bringing

24

important or doubtful points to be decided where the greatest learning and ability may pass upon them; and *thirdly* for preserving these decisions, as much as may be, uniform and consistent. And I must be permitted to say, without reflecting harshly on many of the judicial systems of this country and of this state in particular, that our plan, however it may have the advantage of bringing home justice, as it is said, more immediately to our own doors, falls in some of the respects I have just alluded to, far below the English system. The station of a judge in either of the high courts of England, is one of such dignity and *eclat*, that it can hardly fail to be filled with the first juridical talents and learning of the country; and as most of the disputed points come naturally before them in the course of judicial procedure, these have the advantage to be settled on the best grounds, and often after argument by all the judges of England. Points not less important come every day, according to the arrangement of our judiciary system, before persons whose learning and ability cannot reasonably be expected to be of the like imposing kind, because neither the emoluments, honours, nor apparent responsibility are the same. When we add to this the vast number of independent tribunals which, reckoning only

25

those of the highest appellate jurisdiction, the form of the American confederacy necessarily invests with the decisions of points growing out of our peculiar jurisprudence, either general or local, we see what room there is for great and daily increasing discordance in their judgments, and how difficult the attainment of a homogeneous system of law must necessarily be.

On the other hand, while the student admires the symmetrical system of the British courts, reduced into order in a long succession of years, and amidst the often conflicting claims of various jurisdictions,—he will find from this very circumstance something to displease our natural love of simplicity and directness, in the various fictions and suppositions by which the different courts of Westminster Hall have come to possess on various points a co-ordinate jurisdiction; and in the minute and intricate forms with which for this cause, with others, their procedure is encumbered. Yet here again it must not be forgotten, that these originated generally in the prudence and wisdom of the British judges, who finding, among other things, the number of actions to be constantly increasing from the extension of trade, and the multiplication of property in moveables, incorporated into law the assumptions of jurisdiction made

26

from time to time by the courts, in matters not originally within the scope of their cognizance. Hence the court of King's Bench now takes cognizance of *all* actions, under the fiction that the defendant has been guilty of a tresspass: The court of Exchequer, under the notion that the plaintiff is a debtor of the king; and that by reason of the defendant's undischarged debts to him, the plaintiff is the less able to pay his duty or debt to the king. I think too it must be acknowledged, that the grounds on which the court of Chancery has claimed jurisdiction in some matters now confessedly within its control, are extremely nice and metaphysical, and more defensible on the plea of high expediency, than on the ground of any directness of deduction, or on the ingenious legal fictions and intendments to which the chancellors resorted. All these, and many other features which will present themselves in the course of your studies, however they may amuse you by an exhibition of the subtile expedients to which courts of justice resorted, may induce, perhaps, a wish that the system of English courts as regards practice, &c. could have been adapted to the exigencies of the times with more naturalness, directness, and good sense than it now exhibits, especially to the uninitiated observer.

27

The philosophick student, however, will not fail to remember, on the one hand, the clumsiness which is inevitable from adapting the forms of procedure framed in reference to one system of circumstances and policy, to the results of progressive and necessary change—and, on the other, the danger and great difficulty of entirely remodelling them, so as to fit them in all points to long established principles and usages. The student, therefore, must contentedly refer these anomalies to the nature of human affairs, which never permits the best adjusted system to endure long in complete fitness to its objects; and instead of complaining of these inelegant but useful devices of judges and courts, be happy to find them explainable by research into the antient foundations of the law, and generally subservient to the great ends of justice betwixt man and man. There is, after all, a good deal of gratification derivable from these inquiries; nor is it uncommon for the student, long engaged in tracing the origin of these fictions, to view them with that species of interest mentioned by Justice Blackstone in his beautiful simile of the feudal castle of the common law, more especially since he finds them to answer the necessities of justice in the modern condition of affairs, at the same time that they retain these antique and ex-

28

traordinary features. Though our admiration of the English common law is great, and we believe well grounded; and though the spirit of innovation is dangerous, as it cannot be restricted to wise heads and pure hearts, and is consequently to be indulged with great caution; yet I would not be understood that the fictions in various departments of the law, and especially the technicalities derived from the peculiar nature of the various actions, are in all instances necessary or convenient, and might not in a great degree be done away with, without injury to the substantial parts of the fabrick. The distinction between *assumpsit* and *tort*, for example, is perhaps not always well founded in the reason of things, when by merely varying the form from one to the other, a man shall succeed in vindicating a claim which he had otherwise failed in; and courts have sometimes been obliged both by policy and justice, to make this formal distinction of actions give way to obvious right and reason.* The forms of Roman actions, the modern bill in chancery, and the libel in courts proceeding on the basis of the Civil Law, show that this technical distinction of actions is not inherent or essential; and consequently that

* 1 E. N. P. Cases, 192. Peake's Cases, 223. S. C. *Sed vide* 8. D. E. 335

29

they may even now in a great degree be dispensed with without detriment, and perhaps with advantage to the ends of justice. How this may be done I will not presume to point out, as these remarks are made not so much with the view of suggesting a reform at this day, as of showing that the peculiar circumstances which have given the present shape to English actions, have not produced the most simple form of presenting claims and defences, nor of always deciding them according to sound justice. It is not that each action is not consistent in it's own principles, but that their variety, complication, and nicety too often expose the client to loss from the want of adequate knowledge in those whose province it is to conduct suits. We have mentioned the simplicity of the forms and proceedings of the civil law; not that we would be understood as intimating either the policy or practicability of reducing ours to the same state, but merely to show that as refinements are not necessary, there would be no danger of impairing rights by a judicious and authorized retrenchment of forms.

In regard to the organization and jurisdiction of courts, also, we might indulge in similar remarks—time however will not serve; we shall therefore only casually notice that peculiar juris-

30

diction which is exercised among us by the chancellor, in contradistinction to the judge. The principles which sustain and limit this jurisdiction, are certainly much better known at present than in former times; but still there is no point on which it is more difficult to convey clear and definite notions to students, than on the true nature and province of a court of equity. In common acceptation equity is moral justice—and the uninformed can scarcely be persuaded that the chancellor's powers are not coextensive with the aims of right reason, and sound ethicks. But the student soon learns that moral equity and legal equity, (if the expressions be allowed) are often not synonymous; and, in process of time, he ascertains that a court of chancery is by no means a tribunal which decides every case on its own individual equity, as opposed to law, without regard to precedent and principle. He finds that it is at last in reality little else than a court of law, differing from other legal tribunals only in its modes of proof, trial, and relief, together with a few matters of exclusive jurisdiction; which however, are regulated by as certain a system of law, as any known to our jurisprudence. This being the case—the student naturally desires to know, why there should exist in the same scheme of jurisprudence two distinct

31

tribunals, so extremely different in the points I have mentioned. If the practice of chancery be the best adapted to the discovery of truth, and the administration of relief, as in many cases it undoubtedly is, why should not courts of law be invested with similar powers, and thus avoid the contradiction of denying justice at one tribunal, and granting it at another which professes to be guided by law and precedent, and not by the particular moral justice of a case? Before we can give any reply to this objection, we would admit that the existence of courts of equity rests on the concession, that the remedies provided in courts of common law are inadequate to render full justice; and that however usage and time may have diminished the inconvenience of this difference in the remedial power of these several tribunals, it certainly detracts from the simplicity, symmetry and reason of the English judicial system. But notwithstanding this concession, we would be the last to sanction either the amalgamation of these several jurisdictions, or the abolition of the known powers of chancery. The truth is, that the origin and necessity of this tribunal, and the answer to the objections I have stated, are to be found in the history of the common law itself. It must be remembered that this common law is the gradual

32

result of exigencies, the progressive accretion of ages;—a system of many parts, having at first no assimilating principle,—no common tie gradually bringing together its discordant materials. Courts of common law were coeval with this crude system; their principles of organization and action were moulded by that system; and it is not surprising when the progress of society demanded a judicial legislation varying from the common system, that distinct tribunals should gradually arise for its administration. This indeed is the historical fact. Courts of equity are comparatively of modern origin, and were introduced from a necessity imposed by the previous existence of tribunals jealous of their own powers, and their own system of judicial administration. Hence we see the origin of the existing anomaly, if it be one, of distinct tribunals in the same country: one often acting on essentially the same system of law, but still invested with powers, and administering a code, but little, if at all known, in the inception of the other. The complaints, therefore, which we often hear of the distinction between law and equity, and their separate administration, appear to us at this time highly unseasonable; first, because it was in its origin the child of necessity, and not of choice; secondly, because, in truth, there is no substantial

33

incongruity in distinct tribunals having different powers, and attaining the ends of justice by means peculiar to each. The fact, indeed, is to be found in a degree in every court: courts of admiralty and maritime jurisdiction, for example, have in some respects concurrent powers with the courts of common law. May it not then be asked, with nearly the same propriety,—why should the admiralty be permitted to adjudicate at all on such subjects, as its modes of trial, proof and relief are so different? If such questions can be made, then all distinction of tribunals must not only be unnecessary but wrong; and all courts must be resolved into one kind; or, in other words, every court must administer justice formally and substantially in the same way. But if we admit for the sake of argument, that it was originally practicable and politic that no such distinction as that which exists between law and equity, should have been introduced, it by no means follows that it can with safety be now abolished. If the power of chancery were stricken out of our scheme of jurisprudence, nearly the entire common law would have to be remodelled before a homogeneous system, commensurate with the aims of justice, could be produced. If, on the other hand, these powers be given to common law tribunals, great inconve-

34

nience would result from the amalgamation of a theory and practice in so many respects variant from those of the common law, whilst it is highly probable also, that equal confusion would be produced in the minds of the judges; and that few, if any, would be found equal to the task of administering both schemes in their primitive purity. A hybridous, and unseemly monster of the law would be generated from such a union, having the comeliness and the virtues of neither parent.

Whilst therefore we admit there is room for improvement, we contend that this can never be effected by individual ridicule, nor by any thing less than an unprejudiced, studious, and cautious exertion of the best legal talents of a nation, called forth by competent authority for that express purpose. Could this be done in each branch of the law under the same circumstances of eminent talent, extensive learning, and indefatigable research that appear in the author of the late projected code of Louisiana, the enterprise might indeed be safely entrusted in individual hands, to the high and permanent improvement of the science. But we zealously protest against that cavilling spirit which collects from the entire system its faults, with a view of producing by their concentration, an inflamed judgment, and of testing the merits

35

of the great whole, by a humorous display of its most prominent defects. This is neither useful nor ingenuous. No system of philosophy or of morals can endure such an ordeal; but with regard to the common law it is peculiarly unhappy, as many of these blemishes are either wholly innocent, or necessarily direct the student's inquiries into a more philosophical examination of the entire system.

If we pass from courts and the actions which they entertain, to the subject of practice, we shall find it, (so far as it is not merely arbitrary, and directed by particular provisions in different points,) to be one of great curiosity to every inquiring legal mind. We have already casually alluded to some of the fictions and intendments resorted to in this branch of the law; and though we found something to condemn in it, we have presumed to discourage the too growing spirit of innovation, which threatens to destroy not only the tares but the wheat also. The more we consider the peculiarities of this system, the more we shall find them to hinge on the recognized principles, and to be connected with the general philosophy of the law, insomuch that a student cannot peruse with understanding a book of practice, without having his mind perpetually recur to

36

leading principles. The complaints which are made of the difficulty of acquiring this kind of technical knowledge, can apply only to that practical skill which in every thing is the result of use only; and not to the understanding of the principles which govern its philosophy. But at the same time, while all these multiplied rules of practice undoubtedly have their foundation in the antient principles of law, and call up our knowledge on that very account, it cannot be denied by the most zealous admirer of the common law, that many of these rules proceed on suppositions which are no longer true in point of fact, if they ever were; and that while they may exercise the ingenuity of the learned jurisprudent, they are extremely puzzling to young practitioners, and confounding to the *lay gents*, who are altogether innocent of this antiquated learning.

Thus, for example, the commencement of a suit in the court of King's Bench, when the defendant is not in Middlesex where the court sits, is by a *latitat;* which recites that there had previously issued a precept to the sheriff of Middlesex, viz. the Bill of Middlesex. But as there in fact never issues any Bill in such case, and as, when the Bill of Middlesex itself issues, namely, against a defendant residing in Middlesex, there is supposed to have been a previous *Plaint*, with attachment thereon, and a return on the attachment, here are no less than four suppositions or intendments of facts which, in truth, never occurred, to warrant the issuing of the *latitat*. Another singularity is this: inasmuch as the Bill of Middlesex was framed originally as the process only in actions of trespass, the true cause of action is, from a reason familiar to students, never expressed in it, if the debt be under £40; and again, if above £40, the true cause of action is indeed expressed in the *ac etiam* clause, but it is in company with an untrue cause of action. All this is rather a clumsy contrivance, and a fiction, which to be sure deceives nobody, in order to vest jurisdiction in the court of King's Bench. As a further example we may mention, that the *latitat* is tested either on the first day of term, if sued out in term, or on the last day of the preceding one, if sued out in vacation; so that in either case it gives no notice of the real time of issuing the writ; and all this is because *in law* all the term, forsooth, is considered but as one day. Again; in the bailable Bill of Middlesex the sheriff is commanded to have the body of the defendant at Westminster, &c. but instead thereof bail is given to the sheriff for the defendant's appearance, which appearance is not made

38

in person, but in lieu of it an entry is made, and bail above put in, by an attorney. These forms and many others, as for example, the mode of entering what is called *common* bail—the giving of oyer, which is founded on the idea that a party to be affected by a deed, has it read to him in court—the clause in the *venire facias* and *distringas*, which, supposing what never comes to pass, orders the jury to be convened where it is never intended they shall come, and other similar cases present, as we have before stated, a string of fictions and legal intendments very extraordinary and unintelligible in the first instance to the learner. If to these we add the infinite number of entries, rules, motions and notices, some of which seem to have little other intent than to induce delay or to augment fees; and, moreover, the frequent transcripts of the record, the requisition of unnecessary affidavits, &c. we cannot but confess that, even when explained by reverting to old doctrines of the law, and the stubborn inflexibility of antient judicial procedure, much of this matter is not only deficient in simplicity, but is, in not a few instances, far from real utility. I have here alluded to the English practice only, because it is with that mainly that you can now be supposed in any degree acquainted. My remarks, however,

39

will be found not inapplicable to our own modes of practice. In some of the states many salutary improvements have certainly been made; but in others an ignorant spirit of reform, and an overweening hatred of that copious fountain, the common law of England, whence we derived our jurisprudence, have made sad havoc among the soundest principles known to the law of forensick proceedings; and little remains to regulate them but the good sense or folly, as the case may be, of those who preside in courts of justice.

Pleading shares very largely, in the view of the vulgar, in the obloquy attached to *practice*. Yet it is a system most nicely adjusted to the sense and requisitions of the common law; and its faults are those of that system, to which it strictly conforms, not those of its own structure. In the science of pleading (for it is well entitled to that appellation) much more depends on abstract reasoning, and less on arbitrary rules, than in the *practice* of courts. But as all close reasoning in matters removed from ordinary apprehension, seems to the uninformed too refined; and as the very nicety of the science must often produce unskilfulness in its professors; it happens from these two causes, that the refinements of pleading have been complained of as inimical to the inte-

40

rests of justice. That this nicety has sometimes degenerated into subtilty, this syllogistick strictness into formal technicality, I am not disposed to deny; but it is impossible once to understand the true nature and objects of pleading. without coming to the conclusion that it is a practical logick, and proceeds on its nice but infallible rules. Nor is it fair to confound the unskilfulness of practitioners with the science itself; or to conclude that pleading is sophistical or ridiculous, because pleaders are liable, from ignorance, to be both. It were as wise to ridicule reason itself, because there are bad reasoners.

The whole object of pleading is so to arrange the declarations of one party, and the denials of another;—the claims of the plaintiff, and the counter claims, excuses, or assertions of performance, of the defendant, as that, instead of disputing for ever on impertinent points, they shall come at once to issue on some point of fact or of law conclusive of the controversy. In verbal disputes (and pleadings were originally *ore tenus*) it is comparatively easy for the moderator of the argument to recal the combatants when they wander from the point; yet what endless controversies arise from false logick in the ordinary discourse even of intelligent men! But as pleadings are at

41

this day not conducted in the presence of the court, but are reduced into formal writings; and as the court cannot, from the nature of the thing, interfere at the moment to correct an errour, and so prevent other consequent errours; it must be so much the more rigid in the rules established for bringing the parties to a right understanding of what they disagree about,—the exact point on which they are willing to rest the merits of the case. To this end all the rules of good pleading are constructed,—with a strictness truly philosophical; and if the pleaders, from defect of skill, wander into entangled bye-paths, this is no sound objection against the science, as long as it presents in all cases, one broad legitimate road whereby the wanderer may, if he will, travel with expedition and certainty. The *short cuts* which the untechnical would pursue, though they might answer in particular instances, are very apt, in the main, to produce nothing but intricacy and confusion; and in pleading it will often be found, if I may indulge in perhaps a too colloquial phrase, that "the longest road round is the shortest way home."

Is there any thing that is not entirely philosophical and reasonable in requiring, for example, that the declaration shall contain a logical and legal

42

statement of the facts on which the suitor rests his claim;—that he shall not, however, state those which the court must *ex officio* notice; that it shall be made in the name of the parties, and of them only, in whom the law recognizes the right, if any, to exist,—lest property be thus transferred only from one wrong hand to another;—that the plea of the defendant shall be single and certain, in order that the plaintiff may not have to battle two points, when one will determine the controversy, and also that he may understand distinctly what is the nature of that one;—that when, as is sometimes the case, the defendant is allowed to plead two pleas to the same matter, he shall not plead such as are inconsistent, and so deny in one breath what he had asserted in another;—that he shall not traverse what the plaintiff has stated only by way of inducement or introduction;—that the plaintiff in replying shall not be guilty of a departure, or, in other words, induce the defendant to suppose from the declaration one ground of action, and prepare his proof accordingly, and then lead him in chase of another by his replication;— that the parties shall come to issue on something material to, and decisive of the question;—that the defendant shall not plead a plea to the jurisdiction or in abatement after his plea in bar, or (to drop the technical language,) that he shall not first put the court to decide the main topick of controversy, and then go on to deny its power or right to decide it;—that a plea shall answer all the charges of the declaration, lest, after laborious investigation and trial of a point, it shall be discovered that it did not embrace all the merits of the question, and thus it should become necessary to go over the whole ground again? Are not these, and innumerable other rules of pleading, the best calculated to bring the real question to trial, by the mode which is at once the shortest and most correct? They certainly prove that the general foundation of pleading is sound logick and sound sense, and its aim the speedy and just settlement of conflicting claims.

The student will find that the rules I have stated of this admirable science, are at its very foundation. If pleaders mistake the right application of them, or if they wilfully misapply them, this is an accident that may befal the most perfect system, and is a vice inherent, not in the science of pleading, but in human nature itself. To get rid of these difficulties we must reform the human understanding, and eradicate baseness and the love of chicane from its morals. I am aware that the science of practice and pleading has its preten-

44.

ders—its charlatans—those who departing from its philosophy and its justice, study its quirks and its quibbles, to entangle justice in the net of forms, and under the mask of shrewdness and skilful practice, to work every species of wrong. It is sometimes the case also, that the vulgar and the vicious applaud this as admirable; whilst the same vulgar, (with matchless inconsistency,) condemn the entire science and all its votaries, with the severest reprobation. But those who mistake the artful subtilties of some practitioners for skilful practice, are not further from the truth, than those who reprobate the science for the sins of a few of its unworthy retainers. The railers at our honourable science of the law, forget that it is impossible to establish general rules without seeing them misapplied; they forget that it is impossible to entrust discretion with the judges, lest it should be abused; and that it is equally impracticable to determine every case on its own equitable merits, lest all principle and precedent be lost, and confusion and an arbitrary will alone constitute law.

We should speedily, in such case, hear complaints of a quite opposite, and indeed more reasonable nature; viz. that all *precedent* was lost, all general principles neglected; and that law, instead of being a general, and therefore certain

45

rule, had become a something undefined and undefinable, resting in the discretion of various degrees of understanding and, what were worse, of honesty.

As, therefore, the rules of pleading are founded in logick, or, when technical, spring out of the principles of the common law, it is obvious that they are capable of being referred to a scientifick system, and explained upon it. This is manifest in every treatise of pleading, and the reader of Chitty finds it any thing but a dry, unphilosophical digest of arbitrary rules, without reason or mutual dependence. It were to be wished, however, that some able hand would undertake to explain in a more familiar and less technical manner than is usual, the connexion of pleading with the philosophy of logick on the one hand, and with the principles arising out of the nature of the English law on the other. The philosophy of pleading is a rich and ample field that has been but little trodden. The *bibliotheca legum* affords but a single essay on this interesting subject. I allude to Hammond's "Analysis of the Principles of Pleading"—a work which must be recommended in the absence of a better. it being too general, and quite too brief, to develope the nice connexions of plead-

46

ing, and its pervading consistency with common sense, and the common law.* Some of the rules of pleading appear arbitrary and inconvenient, only because we do not extend our consideration of them to their general operation, and to that mutual dependence of which I have just spoken. Thus, for instance, the student finds that on a covenant with *two* for the benefit of *one* of them, who dies, the interest goes to the representative of the person benefited, and the right of action to the surviving covenantee, because the action, for many good reasons, must follow the nature of the legal interest. Again, he will find that when a contract is made with several, if the interest is joint, the action *ex contractû* must be joint, although the covenant were in terms joint and several; because a court could not know, if all could sue separately, for whom to give judgment. So also, a proviso in mere defeazance of a contract, need not be stated in declaring on the contract; but if it form a con-

---

* Since this lecture was delivered, a still more elementary and scientifick treatise of pleading has appeared from the pen of Mr. Stephen. This production should be in the hands of every student of law; and, in the commencement of this branch of his studies, it should be his *vade mecum*. It has certainly supplied many of the *desiderata* of which we have been speaking.

47

dition precedent, it must, because it may be that the contract, from the non-performance of the condition, never took existence at all. Likewise the student finds that time and place must be stated, and often the true time and place: The first, that the defendant may know what particular contract he is to disprove, and the court, that it arose before action brought; the second, to inform the sheriff from what neighbourhood to summon the triers: and so as to innumerable other rules, the seeming arbitrariness will be found to arise, not from the defect of the science, but from our ignorance of it. Even the curious and subtile doctrine of *colour* in pleading, is not deficient in philosophy and utility. It is based on the necessity which the pleaders conceived there was, of preserving in its integrity, not only the substance, but the forms of systematick pleading. This giving of colour, moreover, could be productive of no evil, but rather of good; inasmuch as the matter suggested by way of colour, was known to be fictitious, and therefore not to be traversable; while, at the same time, it reminded all concerned in it, of the necessity of preserving a harmonious operation of the rules of pleading, which, in the absence of colour, would have made an issue triable by a jury; whereas the

48

party by giving colour effected his object of transferring the issue to the decision of the court. In fine, it appears to me, that the great object of all good pleading is to produce a material, simple, and certain issue of law or of fact, and that this shall be effected with the least possible delay, prolixity, or obscurity. And although the primary rules of pleading may sometimes operate with severity, yet, like all other legislation, they are to be judged of, not by the partial evil they may sometimes occasion, but by the good which they most generally produce. We may extend the same remarks to the rules of *evidence*, respecting which the careful student will probably arrive at the conclusion of Mr. M'Kinnon, viz. "that the law of evidence, as found in the books, is founded on correct logick, applied to a profound knowledge of human nature, and the diversified concerns of human life." And here let me observe, that one of the greatest among legal *desiderata,* is a familiar exposition of the philosophy of evidence; a topick which has, perhaps, never been written on, with the exception of the very unsatisfactory essay of Mr. M'Kinnon, and the scattered remarks of Mr. Kirwan.

In concluding this address, gentlemen, I would only remark, that the carpers against our doctrine of evidence seem to forget, that it is only with disputed and complicated points that lawyers have to do; and that these had never been brought into question, if they had not either been involved in doubt by their own intrinsick difficulty, or their true merits purposely concealed by interest and fraud. They who are thus perpetually traversing, as it were, a region of defiles, can neither be expected to reach their point with the same facility, nor to pursue the same modes of travelling, as those who have a plainer and less embarrassed path. In the infinite number of ill-worded agreements, who, with all the helps of art, shall extract with perfect certainty the true meaning of parties, whom fraud renders unwilling, or ignorance or death incapable to express it themselves? Who, in the imperfection of language, shall adjust the exact meaning to an ambiguous but material word? Who can contrive always, even by the most skilful investigation of all parts of a story, to discover the latent inconsistency and deceit? Who shall apportion the just degree of credit to be given to or withdrawn from various degrees of capacity, interest, competence, and favour? In fact, in the practical application of this important branch of the law, the advocate requires high and rare endowments of the

50

human mind;—metaphysical knowledge well founded and well applied; a historical acquaintance with the play and scope of human passions; a close observance of actual life; and a power of impartial consideration. I must say, as but just to the profession to which we belong, that I wonder much less at what it has failed to accomplish, than at the beautiful, extensive, useful, and ingenious structure which in successive ages has risen beneath its hands.

BALTIMORE, *October 6th,* 1824.

A LECTURE

Being the Third of a Series of Lectures, Introductory to a Course of Lectures Now Delivering in the University of Maryland, 1826

A LECTURE

BEING THE THIRD OF A

Series of Lectures,

INTRODUCTORY TO A

COURSE OF LECTURES

NOW DELIVERING IN THE

UNIVERSITY OF MARYLAND.

BY DAVID HOFFMAN.

PUBLISHED AT THE REQUEST OF THE FACULTY OF LAW.

Baltimore:
PRINTED BY J. D. TOY,
Corner of St. Paul and Market streets.
April, 1826.

THIRD

INTRODUCTORY LECTURE.

The annual duty assigned me of delivering in this Institution a publick discourse, has been twice, zealously, but perhaps, imperfectly performed.

Had I availed myself of the privilege allowed me of selecting, without reserve, any topick which might prove interesting to my audience, so numerous are the themes presented by that sublime and endlessly diffusive science to which we are dedicated, that, although the performance of that duty would have been less irksome, *selection* must have been somewhat difficult.

I have, however, for the sake of eventual utility, preferred to restrict myself in these prelections, to such topicks only as have an immediate relation to the main object of each successive title of the entire course of lectures; designing thereby, in these introductory discourses, not only to sha-

4

dow forth some of the general features and pervading principles of these cardinal divisions of my subject, but also gradually to disclose to the student my views in regard to such auxiliary means of instruction as I have selected, and, in great part, put into execution in the Law Institute, the general designs of which have been already fully explained in my *first* discourse. In my second introductory lecture we spoke, somewhat at large, of the connexion of the various subjects embraced under the third title of my Syllabus "*Personal Rights and Personal Remedies*," and we then pointed out some of the prominent defects, both in the theory and practice, of this branch of our favourite science: we endeavoured to vindicate it from a few of the popular grounds of cavil, which traditional ignorance, or wilful blindness has raised against it, especially as regards Practice, Pleading, and Evidence;—admitting, however, that there is much room for improvement, but questioning the utility of the abuse which has been so lavishly, and, we think, indiscriminately cast upon it, mainly by those who not only desire great changes in the Law, but thorough revolutions in many other things that concern the happiness of nations, no less than of individuals. We avoided, however,

5

the discussion of the delicate question of the transplantation to these favoured shores of the English Common Law;—of the practicability of remodelling it, and of reducing the whole of our vast science into a written code, which should speak a language so clear and palpable as almost to exclude the possibility of judicial legislation, or of even judicial interpretation. This, indeed, would have been a topick of much interest, and by no means misplaced; but, as we shall have a more fit occasion to call your attention to this subject in our introductory discourse to the tenth title, we have passed it by; and would, at this time, only observe that, whilst we should be among the last to do ought that might lessen our veneration for the English Common Law, and the very last to countenance an exclusively *written* Code, we cannot doubt but that there are in the philosophy of Codification, many wholesome, and practical principles, which it would be wisdom in us to adopt, and to enforce. Whilst, therefore, we greatly respect many of the views and opinions of the continental jurists on this subject; and find much good sense in the writings of Mr. Bentham and his admirers; we are persuaded that the *entire* jurisprudence of no country can be reduced to a written code. Still, we feel no alarm

6

whatever, for the enduring strength and vigour of the common law in this country, from the application, to either our statute or unwritten law, of many of the principles of that very ingenious, though too zealous, writer; or from resorting to those views which originated the Roman Digests, the Codes of the French empire, that of Louisiana, or the more recent, and we believe, truly philosophical enterprize, in which the state of New York is at this time engaged. But, to pass on with our subject.—Our attention was also directed, in the preceding introductory discourse, to pointing out that general bond which associates, under one head, the various topicks comprehended by the title "Personal Rights and Personal Remedies."—As that title is not only extremely various, but embraces those subjects which generally become of the most *practical* importance to the young lawyer; and as *Pleading*, *Practice* and *Evidence* do not belong exclusively to *personal law*, but pervade, in their principles at least, all the other titles, we shall be excused if we mainly devote the present lecture to an explanation of what we believe would prove an effectual means of acquiring a familiar acquaintance with the various stages of an *action*, and remove those difficulties, of which students and young

7

practitioners are most wont to complain, in regard to the practical application of their knowledge derived from books. It is, indeed, somewhat unfortunate for the young lawyer, that while the difficulty of learning the minute points of *practice* is confessed, on all sides, and skilfulness therein is the result of long experience only,—this, for the most part, embraces subjects on which he is very early called to exercise his ingenuity.

A student is often pretty well versed in abstruse legal learning, and well qualified to make an argument both solid and ingenious, who stumbles at some point of practice, which experience has made familiar to much inferior understandings. We, of course, here use the word *practice* in its most comprehensive sense, as embracing the four periods of an action, viz. *process, pleading, trial,* and *execution.* We would briefly premise that by an *action* we mean a *legally defined* mode of *ascertaining* and *enforcing*, through the medium of *Judicature,* a *right,* which may be *legally* due to any person.

A legal *right* is that *power* which is given to one, by law, over certain *persons* or *things.*

By *judicature* we mean tribunals, constituted by *law,* which are authorised to ascertain and enforce legal rights.

8

Process embraces all those legal measures which may be taken by the *actor* or plaintiff in a suit, to compel the *reus* or defendant therein, to appear in judicature, and answer his demand,—and such measures, likewise, as the defendant is sometimes permitted to take against the actor.

Pleading is a system of rules and forms prescribed by law to the actor and reus, whereby they are enabled exactly to ascertain and define the point in dispute between them; and that point is denominated an Issue,—which is either of *fact*, or of *law*.

Trial comprehends the examination of the issue, by the tribunal (whether court, or, court and jury;) also, the nature of the *evidence* to sustain, or disprove the allegations and denials involved in an issue of fact; and lastly, the *decision* given on an issue, whether of law or of fact.

Execution, which is the last stage of an action, embraces all those *direct* means taken by a court to enforce its judgment.

In the preceding lecture we made a few remarks on each of the periods of an action, and dwelt, somewhat on *Process;* we shall now, again advert, though very cursorily, to the other three stages of a suit.

9

In studying the doctrine of *Pleading*, in common with all other sciences, we are to investigate its *constituent* parts, that is, those parts only which are adapted to attain the object of its institution. Now, the design of all pleadings is to obtain an answer, from the court or jury, on a defined point in controversy. But these constituent parts are themselves either *essential*, or *accidental;* in other words,—those are the constituent, *essential* parts of pleading which occur in the regular course of the second stage of a suit, and which are productive, not only of a final issue, but a state of readiness for trial: and those are the constituent *accidental* parts which contingently happen, but which are either auxiliary to, or do not directly tend to produce a final issue. Thus for example, the essential parts are 1, *A Declaration,* (with one or more counts.) 2. *Defence,* (of several kinds.) 3, *Plea,* (general or special.) 4, *Replication,* (general or special.) 5, *Rejoinder.* 6, *Surrejoinder.* 7, *Rebutter.* 8, *Surrebutter.* 9, *Tender of issue.* 10, *Joinder of issue.* 11, *Demurrer,* (general or special.) 12, *Joinder in demurrer.* 13, *Issue in fact.* 14, *Issue in law.* 15, *General issue.* 16, *Special issue.* 17, *Simple general issue.** 18, *Sim-*

---

* Consequent, for example, on the plea of *non cul:* or *nil debet.*

10

ple special issue.* 19, *Compound general issue.* 20, *Compound special issue,* 21, *Continuance.*

The accidental parts of pleading are, 1, Plea in *abatement.* 2, Plea of *parol demurrer.* 3, *Imparlance,* of several kinds. 4, *Profert,* (only of deeds, or letters testamentary, and of administration. 5, *Oyer,* and *Counter plea* of same. 6, *Prayer of enrolment,* and *counter plea* of same. 7, *Prayer of aid,* and *counter plea* of same. 8, *Voucher* (single, double, &c.) and *counter plea* of same. 9, *Summons and severance.* 10, *New Assignment.* 11, Plea *puis darrein continuance.* 12, *Retraxit.* 13, *Nonsuit.* 14, *Abridgment of Plaint.* 15, *Claim of Conusance.* A philosophical and elementary explanation of these subjects has been until very recently, *a desideratum;* but Mr. Stephen, and Mr. Hammond in their late works† have vindicated the eulogiums of Lord Mansfield, who says,

* Consequent, for example, (after the statement of *special* matter) on the pleas of *et sic non cul:* or *et sic nil debet:* or *et sic non est factum.*

† Vide Stephen's Treatise on the Principles of Pleading in Civil Actions, comprising a summary view of the whole Proceeding in a suit of Law. Hammond's Treatise on the Law of Nisi Prius; and Hammond's Analysis of the Principles of Pleading, or Idea of a Study of that Science.

11

"the substantial rules of pleading are founded in strong sense, and in the soundest and closest logick,"—of Sir William Jones, who informs us "that the science of pleading is founded in the most exquisite logick,"—and of Mr. Bell of Scotland, who tells his countrymen, that the English "system of pleading is, to those who understand it, beautiful in the perfection of its rules, and in the correct and complete way in which it produces issues of fact and of law."

We are entirely persuaded that the great complaints which are made of the expense, vexatious delay, and absurd refinements in the English, and in some of the American courts, are just,—but that the artifices of chicane, the desire of lucre, and the contracted views of *mere* special pleaders, have very much spoiled a most ingenious, beautiful and wonderful system;—a system entitled, when well comprehended, honestly practised, and reduced to its real elements, to rank with the sciences most worthy of being studied. It is against the excrescences of pleading (the gradual accretion of time, and of the want of judicious legislation in pruning them) that we should utter our invectives; and not against the science itself—which has no inherent tendency to abuse, or corruption, but just the contrary. Indeed, very

12

many of the odious features in the system of English practice, have been either never adopted by our courts, or have been remedied by the legislature; and we are daily perfecting our scheme of pleading (based as it is on the solid foundation of the common law) by progressively getting rid of the adscititious refinements which sully its philosophy, occasion endless delay, and insupportable expense,—and introducing, in their stead, such of the equitable doctrines of the Roman law as sufficiently harmonise with the primitive English pleading,—so that we may in time produce a coherent whole;—one that will possess the peculiar excellences of each code, and be obnoxious to none of the merited censures, at present cast on this important portion of our jurisprudence.

We think, however, that most of those who have attempted to expose the defects of English and American pleading have been a little visionary, and have written as if they saw the entire scheme through a glass darkly. We surely never can agree with those who are inclined to restore *oral* pleading; we are compelled to regard most of the arguments against the fictions of the law,—as, for example, that they mislead and deceive,—that they tend to encourage mendacity, and wholly to pervert truth, &c. &c. as extremely futile,

13

and wholly unworthy of the dignity of the subject. We also but little respect most of the arguments urged against the various counts in a declaration,—the proceedings in ejectment,—the formula of a nar: in trover,—the inflamed statements, so usual in declarations, &c. &c. because we think they are either entirely innocent, or, what is still better, most of them may be *legally* avoided; so that it is not the science which should be so strongly animadverted on, but its unworthy *practitioners.* If a lawyer (being entitled to charge for every word written by him) will be so unprincipled as to insert at length, four hundred and eighty counts in one declaration, when, perhaps, four would have answered quite as well;* and if he will *write out* eight or ten of the general counts, when it has been decided that a more summary form is equally good; it is the fault of the courts and their officers, and not of the science itself, if the *formula* are prolix, tedious, and vexatiously expensive.— On the whole, we entertain no doubt that a very few simple regulations in regard to pleading, would remove all the solid objections which have been raised against it. We may sufficiently illustrate our views on this subject by a few examples.

* Vide Tidd's Prac. 618.

14

1. We would abolish all taxation of costs—lawyers should not be permitted to *create* business, and then charge for it, though the charges be regulated by *law*. Much of the grievous expense of English judicature has proceeded from this cause, and is wholly unnecessary, as is proved in many of the states of the union.

2. The writ should cite the defendant to *appear* at a fixed time and place, in person, or by *counsel*, and to give *bail*, if then required.

3. All *rules* to compel either party to proceed should be abolished, as it ought to be the duty of each party to proceed at *stated* times, at his peril. This would avoid the endless delay and expense to which parties are often subjected under the English practice.

4. The *plaintiff* should be responsible, in the first instance, for all costs, to abide the final decision of the cause;—whereas by the English rule, no defendant is *permitted to plead* until he has paid for the *plaintiff*'s declaration,—which, in that country, is often very onerous, and sometimes a total denial of justice.

5. A Bill of particulars should be furnished at the defendant's instance, but it should be auxiliary to, and not in avoidance of the declaration: so

15

that whatever can be proved, may be recovered, if found in the one or the other.

6. The general counts might all be summary, that is, containing the mere substance of each, as for example, for goods bargained and sold, goods sold and delivered, money lent, money paid, money received to plaintiff's use, work performed, &c. &c. there can be no necessity to write them at length.

7. In ejectment the *first* declaration should be *adopted* by the tenant on his admission, and not be, as it always is, *copied;* or, indeed, the whole fiction, as to parties, might be abolished, though we confess we have never been able to perceive the evils complained of, except those which are consequent on a too tenacious adherence to the fiction; as, in the instance mentioned, of copying the whole of the first declaration, when there is no other variance between the two than in the name of the real defendant.

It is unnecessary to pursue the subject farther.

The Pleadings being closed, the parties then proceed to trial. This introduces the important doctrine of *Evidence.* There are certainly many anomalies in the law of Evidence, as administered in England and this country; but it is liable to fewer objections than what obtain against plead-

16

ing. We shall not tax your patience, in a preliminary discourse, even with an enumeration of the anomalies to which we allude, but leave you to extract them, by a careful study of the late works on the subject of evidence, by Mr. Phillips, and Mr. Starkie. It has been a common fault with writers on English law, that too little recourse is had to the general principles of human action,—to the pervading truths which essentially appertain to a given subject,—and to that enlarged philosophy which belongs to most topicks, abstractly considered, or which grows out of the vast mass of experience of other nations, and other times. Our law treatises are too English, too technical, too much based on our own experience, and legal notions. Sir William Jones has shown us, in his admirable outline of the law of Bailments, what may be done by bringing to a portion of English jurisprudence, an untechnical mind, a pure and expanded intelligence, and all the riches of a deep and varied research into other codes. Mr. Stephen, in his Treatise of Pleading, and Mr. Hammond, in his late work on Actions, as also Mr. Phillips and Mr. Starkie, in their recent works on Evidence, have caught a considerable portion of the spirit to which we refer: and we think we can perceive, in the jurists of our day, a growing

17.

sense of the necessity of appealing to general experience, and general principles, instead of restricting themselves to the narrow limits of our own common law. The philosophy of the law of English evidence has been much impaired by a too strict adherence to the analogies of the common law, and by an almost total neglect of the writings of the civilians, and of the continental jurists. The science of evidence should be founded on the closest observation of man's moral, and intellectual nature, and should suffer no control from technical, or arbitrary rules, instituted for the sake of conformity to supposed analogies, or at least those which might be safely departed from.

The doctrine of our Evidence is, without doubt, the most important branch of a student's course; we would therefore recommend to him, in addition to the English treatises on Evidence and Proof (which are often drily expository) such works as manifest the great and pervading truths of the science,—evince its general philosophy,—and teach the experience of other ages, and other nations;* and more especially such works, or

* Such, for example, as Farinacius "*De Testibus.*" Menochius "*De Præsumptionibus.*" Everhardus "*De Fide Instrumentorum.*" Domat's Civil Law. Chap. "*Of*

18

parts of the same, as are freely censorial, pointing out what the law of evidence, in many instances, *ought* to be, rather than what it really is.

Proofs and Presumptions." De Moivre's *"Doctrine of Chances."* Kirwan's Logick, Vol. I. Part 3, p. 169—304. Vol. II. p. 305—350; part 4, chap. 2, 3, p. 551—622. Rees' Cyclop. *"Chance." "Probability."* Locke on the Hum. Under. Book iv. chap. 1, 2, 3, 4, 15, 16, 17. Butler's Analogy. Lord Littleton's *Conversion of St. Paul.* Gibbon's Inquiry concerning the *Man with the iron Mask.* Dr. Gregory's Pamphlet in reply to Dr. James Hamilton, Jr. Edinb. 1793. Paley's *"Horæ Paulinæ"* (a work of pure logick.) Pothier on Oblig. Part. iv. chap. 1, 2, 3. Van Leeuwen's Roman-Dutch Law, Book v. chap. xx. xxi. xxii. Ruth. Insti. Vol. 2, ch. vii.

Reid on the Hum. Mind. Essay 2, 3, 6, 7. Buffier's *First Truths.* Steuart's Phil. Hum. Mind, 2 vols. c. 1, 2.

Quintil. Insti. Orat. Book V. Bentham's Princip. Mor. and Legis. chap. 7. Select cases in *"Causes Célébres."* Arguments in the case of the Representatives of *Gen. Stanwix and his Daughter.* Fearne's Posth. Works, p. 37. The controversies relative to the *Letters of Junius,* the authenticity of *Ossian's Poems, Rowley's Poems,* the existence of *Troy,* &c. &c. Camp. Philo. Rhet. Book I. chap. 5. Beattie's Essay on Truth, Part 1, ch. 2. *et passim.* Sir Tho. Brown's *Inquiry into Vulgar Errors.* Bacon's *Novum Organum,* lib. 1. *De Aug. Sci.* lib. 5. ca. 4. Paley's Evidences of Christianity. Soame Jenyns' Evid. of ditto. Warb. Div. Leg. of Moses. Paris and Foublanque on "Medical Jurisprudence" *passim.* Cooper's Med. Jurip. *passim.* Dr. Campbell's Dissertation on Miracles. Hume's Essay on Hum. Under. § iv. v. vi. Hume's Essay on Miracles; and M. Le Cat's Essay on the Senses. The philosophy of Evidence relates to intrinsick, and extrinsick proofs: the former may result from what is

19

The effect to be allowed to intrinsick evidence, or that educed from a combination of circumstances, has been but little explored by the legal philosophers of any country. There *are* materials extant both of principle and fact, which if collected with due care, and amplified, and fashioned by a vigorous, discriminating, and embellished mind, would supply one of the most important among the legal *desiderata*. But, this is a task to be assigned to no man; it is one of those great works which, if performed at all, will be conferred on the world, unexpectedly, by some preeminent genius,—a philosopher of a century, who having conceived a passion for the enterprise, devoted to it a life of toil, research, and reflection. But, to pass on to another topick.

The last stage of an action is *Execution*. Some difficulties arise in this branch of law, from certain distinctions known to our system, as 1, of le-

called circumstantial, or presumptive evidence, and also from the judicious application of the laws of construction or interpretation. Hence the entire subject seems to embrace 1, direct testimony; 2, circumstantial testimony; 3, inferences deduced from sound interpretation. We have recommended, therefore, not only such works as display the various sources of *errour*, but such as show the *true* grounds of belief, from testimony, direct and circumstantial, and also from construction. We think these subjects are inseparably allied.

4

20

gal and equitable interests; 2, of real and personal estate; 3, of choses in possession, and choses in action; 4, of mere possibilities, and contingent interests; 5, of liens at law, and liens in equity; 6, of docketted and undocketted judgments; 7, of execution against the person, or property of the debtor; 8, as it may be against an executor, or the property of his testator; 9, as to property *extra jurisdictionem* of the tribunal which pronounced the sentence; 10, when the judgment has become prescribed, and the execution thereon is a nullity. These, and many others, some of intrinsick difficulty, have never been satisfactorily treated; and the law of the entire subject of Execution is no where to be found in a concentrated form: it is to be sought for in the *nisi prius* law generally,—in treatises on mortgages,—on the law of executors,—of sheriffs,—in the books of reports, and abridgments,—and finally, in almost any, and every volume, in the lawyer's collection.

The foregoing are, indeed, very brief remarks on the general nature, and objects of **Practice**, as it comprehends the cardinal divisions of a suit, civil, or criminal, at law, or in equity. The doctrines are all of them of the greatest importance, and pervade the entire system of our jurispru-

21

dence; but still they will be found to appertain, more particularly, to the topicks embraced under the *Third Title* of our Course, to which the preceding, with the present lecture, are designed to be preliminary.

We shall now, as promised, advert to the principal object of the present discourse, viz. the utility, and organization of a Moot Court.

In claiming your attention to the plan of what we trust may prove a powerful auxiliary in the acquisition of legal knowledge, which I propose to my junior professional brethren, in common with students of law, I feel assured that my motives will be duly valued, should I even fail in imparting to you as deep a sense of its importance, as that which rests on my own mind.

The Lord Chancellor Fortescue, in his admirable little manual, *De laudibus legum Angliæ*, excites his illustrious pupil to diligent study by a number of arguments in praise of the Laws of England. The force of these was felt, but the Prince (as many students, and even lawyers of our day are) was dismayed at the boundless extent of the science; and, with despondent feelings, said; "There is one thing which agitates my mind in such a manner, that, like a vessel tossed in the tumultuous ocean, I know not how to direct my

22

course;—it is, that when I recollect the number of years, which students of law employ, before they acquire a sufficient degree of knowledge, I am apprehensive lest, in studies of this nature, I should consume the *whole of my youth.*"

The apprehensions of the young prince were very natural, but his fears were easily subdued by the amiable preceptor; for the laws of England, in those days, were not, as they now are, "the collected wisdom of ages, combining the principles of original justice with the endless variety of human concerns." The jurisprudence of our day is vastly more extensive; it has kept equal pace with the growth of knowledge generally; and even those sages of the law, my Lords Coke, and Bacon, before they could attain "unto the depths of the learning" of our times, would have to become severe *students* of law for many years. The prince, moreover, had no occasion to *master* the science even as it then stood; hence the Chancellor informed his pupil that "it will not be necessary for him, at a great expense of his time, to scrutinize curious and intricate points of discussion;" *principles alone* would be sufficient for those who are not actually to minister in the temples of justice.—Thus were the prince's apprehensions allayed. But those who are to be

23

counsellors, or judges, if they duly appreciate the nature of their high calling, have just and greater reason now to entertain the fears expressed by the young prince to his distinguished preceptor: they must even go much further than he apprehended, and consume, not only the whole of their *youth*, but the whole of their *life;* and this too, with a zeal and devotion unremitting, and a steadiness of purpose, which allows of no compromise.

If this be, as it certainly is, the case, is it not reasonable that students, and junior lawyers should, with great alacrity, avail themselves of every facility, which the enlarged spirit of our times may suggest for their advancement? It must be confessed, that whilst the boundaries of our science have been greatly enlarged, the means of a philosophical and methodical study of the science have been, also, much increased: but, we think, not in a just proportion; and even those which have been tendered, have not always been as generously and zealously availed of, as might be expected from those who were cultivating a pursuit so honourable, laudable, and profitable.

I have addressed myself to a portion of my professional brethren. In so doing, it may be necessary to offer a special explanation, lest I may possibly be misunderstood, and, by some, be

24

even accused of vanity, where nothing but kindness and a moderate and just sense of my own capabilities have actuated me. My notions of the august science which we are endeavouring to attain, lead me to the firmest conviction that its study is the assiduous and methodized *labour of a life,* full of toils, but I confess, full of encouragements, and auspicious promises to those who truly persevere.

If there be then any of my brethren who may be inclined to the opinion that the proposed exercises of a moot court are suited for *students* only, and, that on coming to the Bar, they have assumed the *toga verilis* of their profession,—my brief reply to them is, that all past experience has shewn that those alone have become eminently learned in the law, who have been *students* throughout their life; that in this science, alone, we find there are no *masters,* but all are *pupils;*—that its truest votaries have been those who have been content never to cast off the *prætexta,* for the *toga;* and, in fine, that all liberal and expanded minds, ardent in the pursuit, have chosen to find no *resting place,* but have, "with ever growing, new delight" gained one horizon, only to find another of equal extent.

25

We think it is impossible for any one to take, even a superficial view, of the vast body of the law which must be familiar to an American jurisprudent, without agreeing with me that it demands an undivided heart and mind, and a feeling of thankfulness to those who have removed impediments, and urged us on without despondency. To those who, with folded arms, can rest content with moderate attainments, we presume to offer no attractions. We are only ambitious to rouse the energies of those who respect the *science*, and desire its *highest honours*. We tender no inducement to such as believe there is a short and "royal road" by which all may be attained with but little labour. My Lord Mansfield never saw the setting sun of that day which had not added to his generous store of knowledge; and, perhaps, that day never dawned on him, which was not accompanied by a fresh desire for a further insight into the *arcana* of his profession,—of which, indeed, he was "the living voice and oracle."—Those truly great and expanded minds, also, which now preside in the supreme tribunal of our country, and which have been devoted for very many years to the acquisition of legal knowledge, modestly, and patiently, and eagerly listen to all that may be imparted to them; and, not

26

unfrequently, decline a decision until a whole year has passed round,—and this, too, on points, which a young practitioner might perhaps dispose of in a much more summary manner. If minds, then, of the highest order, and the richest cultivation, find in this science the task of a well spent life, I have no doubt, I shall be excused, if I invite a portion of my professional brethren to unite with me in a scheme of reciprocal advantage,—in a plan that will greatly facilitate them in their profession,—and, in time, redound to their honour,—their happiness, and eventually, we trust, to their emolument in that which, we think, is too often considered the *chief good of life*.

The proper study of our science has been with me a favourite theme for many years past. As this is a land peculiarly dedicated to liberty, it should be the desire of every American that the science of law may be thoroughly cultivated, since rational liberty can only be sustained and perpetuated, by a wise administration of legal justice. As far as an humble individual can aid the diffusion of law knowledge,—assist the aspiring student,—and stimulate the young practitioner, I confess, it is my ambition to be useful. The sacrifices I have been thus far subjected to, must be obvious to all, but I trust my zeal has not abated, though I have had, from my brethren, so little to enliven and encourage me: all that I desire from the profession generally is a persevering endeavour, on their part, to raise the standard of professional excellence, and never to rest satisfied, whilst any thing remains to be accomplished;— and from that portion of the bar, whom narrow views, and false shame will not prevent from uniting in a laudable and useful enterprize, I solicit time and indulgence for myself, and a hearty cooperation, on their part, without which nothing very effectual can be done.

To most *students* of law the anticipation of the period which is to terminate their novitiate; to bring them into contact with clients, and place them in the presence of courts of justice, and their professional brethren, is accompanied with feelings rather of anxiety, and even despondency, than of pleasure, and of hope. They may know themselves to be well grounded in *principles;* but they doubt their familiarity with the *sources of minute knowledge.* They may have cultivated a *legal mind,* but they still doubt the readiness and faithfulness of their memory, on a sudden emergency. They may heretofore have *written* able law arguments, but they have not cultivated the *ars loquendi;* and they perceive that the logic,

28

eloquence, and knowledge of the bar must often come unsolicited, and be the spontaneous and instant growth of a deep and richly improved soil.—The details of practice present them with a thousand minute doubts and inquiries never before thought of;—and difficult, if not impossible to be found in the books. In this state of the mind their judgment often becomes bewildered; difficulties are magnified—the courts become surrounded with an air of mystery, exciting awe, despondency, and even disgust—judges, lawyers, jurymen, and even the uninitiated and ignorant crowd of spectators, become invested, in the young practitioner's disturbed imagination, with a character for learning, and a disposition to examine with severity, which further acquaintance often dissipates, or, at least, greatly diminishes.

To remedy, as far as may be practicable, this disadvantage, students of law have frequently resorted to *Debating Societies*. These, though highly useful, are by no means as effectual a remedy for the evils we have intimated, as *Moot Courts*, where fictitious law proceedings, and supposed cases are brought and prosecuted with a strict regard to the forms of pleading, the rules of evidence, and all the decorums of forensick disputation.

29

We shall first briefly state our views in regard to Debating Societies, and then proceed to exhibit an outline for the organization, and conduct of a Moot Court—a tribunal which, if we can bring it into effectual operation, according to our enlarged views on the subject, cannot fail to prove a great auxiliary in forming almost veteran practitioners out of timid, doubting, and sciolous students.

The utility of these Debating Societies has been questioned by some; but what point is so simple as not to be disputed, or misunderstood? It would be thought, we imagine, very strange entirely to proscribe *conversation* on the score of the many sophisms advanced in it, the many unprofitable arguments it occasions, the improper passions it excites, and the thousand wrong opinions it gives birth to—the sole arguments usually adduced in opposition to debating, which however, is little more than conversation conducted in a more regular form and adjusted by stricter rules of argumentation.

We admit, indeed, that Debating Societies may prove, not only useless, but prejudicial, when conducted as they sometimes are: still their utility, when composed of such as love truth, and enter into debate as one avenue of approach to it, is equally certain.

30

While therefore, it appears to us thus absurd wholly to condemn these juvenile associations, because of some incidental evils, we acknowledge how unprofitable they frequently are, from the idle speculation, the absence of control and method, the captiousness, and even violence which occasionally prevail in them.

There is in science so large a body of truths whose right understanding is of great practical utility, that it is at best but serious idleness to throw away time in the discussion of topicks useless in themselves, and more so from the improbability of ever arriving at any certain conclusions concerning them. Even in the sciences least subtile and abstruse, there is so much unavoidable errour, so much involuntary sophism, so much difficulty in demonstrating even substantial truth, that there can be no need of the assumption of false positions, or the support of ingenious sophistry to sharpen the wits of disputants, and to exercise them in the arts of logical offence and defence. A judicious selection, therefore, of useful subjects, and moderation, candour, and patience in their investigation, and oral discussion (qualities without which formal controversy is no less than conversation and writing, utterly unconducive to truth) are certainly necessary to render such associations

31

what they are capable of becoming—very profitable schools to those who deem worth attainment, not only the *possession* of knowledge, but the art of agreeably and successfully *imparting* it.

The man of books must sooner or later emerge into the world; must find even his most cherished theories controverted; contend often and long in support of opinions he had looked on as almost self evident; demonstrate many errours whose very manifestness renders demonstration irksome, and difficult; and encounter many false views of life, no less than of science, which his own sincere love of truth prevented ever occurring to his mind. There are few retired students, who, on coming into society, and the active pursuits of life, have not experienced something of this—if there be even a partial remedy for this, it should be sought, and improved.—Debating Societies, while they accustom him to opposition, may instruct him, at the same time, in the arts, and means of countervailing it: they may teach much of that rapid recollection, that quickness of penetration, that felicity of illustration, and, above all, that facility in arranging and methodizing a various subject, so useful in the ordinary intercourse of life, and so essential in the sudden and extemporaneous contests of the bar. The study of the *practical pro-*

32

ceedings of courts of justice; of that "sure oracle of the law"—*good pleading*,—and of that searcher into the diversified concerns of human life,—the *doctrine of evidence*,—we say the *study* of these subjects, though it may require vigorous comprehension, and habits of patient thinking, demands, however, no very peculiar modification of talent. Whoever can be made to understand with facility, may soon comprehend the philosophy of each; whoever can think minutely, may soon be made master of their niceties; but as to the *practical use* of these doctrines, it is considerably otherwise. Men who in solitude think correctly, and reason clearly, are sometimes in publick, masters neither of their thoughts, nor their words. The happy exposition of a subject, the ingenious illucidation of difficulties, the fluency of utterance, the rapidity and skill of forensick evolutions are impracticable to themselves, and irresistible in others. Some minds too are of a temperament too irrascible to endure the triumph of an adversary, the detection of their own errours, or, even opposition to their opinions. On such tempers, we have been asked, if these assemblages for disputation did not exert an unhappy influence? In both the cases we have adduced, if the *want of readiness*, in the first, be not so great as to be in-

33

capable of improvement, and the *warmth of temper*, in the second, such as to be hopeless of remedy, we believe Debating Societies are perhaps the best schools of discipline to impart, by dint of habit, *promptness* in the one case, and *self-restraint* in the other; if the reverse, failure is certainly less painful here, than in more publick and responsible situations. Some cases there undoubtedly are, where these faults of talent or temper are so glaring, that we should dissuade those who are so unfortunate as to possess them, from ever connecting themselves with a society of disputants; but then we should go further, and advise them to detach themselves altogether from a profession, whose pursuits would continually expose them to similar situations of embarrassment and vexation.

Our recommendation of Debating Societies must not be understood, however, of those promiscuous assemblages of young men which chance, idleness, and whim, sometimes collect together.

In the common intercourse of society we studiously avoid the litigious, the sophistical, the vain, the arrogant, and the ignorant;—and no little congeniality of mind is requisite even among those who only meet to be intellectual antagonists. Students, therefore, in establishing these societies, should aim to associate with themselves only those

34

who are engaged in the same pursuits, animated with the same ardour of study, and possessed of the same general views and dispositions;—in the presence of these circumstances, and under judicious regulation, these societies cannot fail, we think, to prove eminently advantageous.

The biographies of distinguished statesmen and lawyers are replete with examples of the beneficial effects of these associations; and, in some instances, their destiny in life appears to have been somewhat controlled by impressions and habits contracted in them. Burke's fondness for the pursuits of a statesman, if not first acquired in debating societies, was certainly first manifested, and greatly augmented in them. It is stated of that able politician that the acquaintance with history which marked his future life, and which tended to the development of much of his political wisdom, was fostered by occasional meetings of the Incipient Historical Society,—"an institution," says the biographer of Curran, "which, as a school of eloquence, was unrivalled, and has given to the bar, and the senate some of their brightest ornaments."

It is recorded of that most estimable lawyer, Sir Samuel Romily, that although his extreme diffidence had been considerably lessened by his associating with his young friends in their debates, yet that when he came to the bar, his apprehensions were almost painful and overwhelming. It is highly probable that had not the keen edge of his constitutional diffidence been somewhat blunted, by his occasional discussions before a debating society, the world might have been deprived of one of the most splendid geniuses, and the bar of its brightest ornament. Had the young lawyer yielded to his embarrassment, such were his sensibilities, that total failure must have ensued, and he might have shrunk into retirement, from which nothing could have urged him.

Lord Mansfield, also, furnishes another example of the salutary effect of these associations. Mr. Butler, in his Reminiscences, relates, that while a student of the Temple, young Murray, with some other students, had regular meetings to discuss legal questions; that they prepared their arguments with great care, and that his lordship afterwards found many of these juvenile exercitations useful to him, not only at the bar, but upon the bench. Numerous other instances might be presented to you, were it necessary. We will only add, that it is related of one of the most profound of our own lawyers, that his astonishing talents were first disclosed in a debating society

36

established by the young physicians of this city.—His eloquence, ingenuity, and zeal in debate were so commanding as to attract the attention of a distinguished judge, who induced the young orator to abandon the worship of Esculapius, for the more animating, wide, and ambitious exercises of the forum:—how fortunate the change has been, no one can doubt who has witnessed the eloquence of Mr. Pinkney.

But if the aid to be derived from such combinations be manifest, how much greater to the law student must these advantages be, when the association assumes all the regularity, the complete organization, and the duties of a court of judicature! The origin and history of moot courts in England were briefly, but sufficiently set forth in my first introductory discourse. Neither in that, nor in this country have they ever, to my knowledge, been so organized as to afford the student most of the advantages of a court; and, indeed, in this country, though they have assumed the name of moot court, they have generally differed but little, if at all, from the ordinary debating society —Our views contemplate something far different. We desire to have the practice, in this mock tribunal, to conform, in every essential respect, to the rules, modes of procedure, and argumentation adopted in the best regulated courts of our country.

Practice in a moot court thus constituted, affords the student, and young lawyer many advantages wholly unknown to the mere debating society: it brings him, on the easiest terms, into a gradual, but certain acquaintance with the *modus operandi* of the various courts of judicature: it familiarises him with the mode of applying legal principles: it renders him not only acquainted with the sources of knowledge, and the art of tracing out a point of law, from its first crude and undefined dawning, to its full establishment, but it instructs him in the means of presenting his claim or defence in a lawyer-like manner, and according to the most approved precedents of pleading: it unfolds to him the practical application of many rules of evidence founded on the soundest logick, which had hitherto rested in his mind only as so many abstract principles: it teaches him, if we may use, in part, the language of Sir William Jones, the mode of extracting from the pleadings, like the roots of an equation, the true points in dispute, and of so analysing a cause as to refer these points, with all imaginable simplicity to the court or jury; further, it enables him to test his memory and judgment, and to ascertain the *cer-*

38

tainty of his knowledge: it dispels that despondency which had haunted him in regard to the details of practice, and the difficulties of *ex tempore* argumentation, by shewing him the true meaning of the former, and by convincing him that the art of speaking eloquently, and logically, is not difficult when based on solid acquirements, and undertaken, in every instance, with appropriate zeal: and lastly, practice in a moot court would seem to possess, at once, all the advantages ascribed by Lord Bacon to *reading, writing,* and *conversation;* the first making a *full* man, the second an *exact* man, and the last a *ready* man.

It is, indeed, surprising that in England, where these advantages have been experienced in a considerable degree, the Inns of Court, and of Chancery should no longer afford the means of legal instruction of any kind,—enrolment in them being at this time, wholly nominal. The young student in that country, is left entirely to himself, and the antient mootings, readings, and other exercises of their once renowned schools for legal education, are now altogether unknown. Even the *Term Lectures* have been abandoned for more than a half century, and the Vinerian professorship, so distinguished by the names of Blackstone and Wooddeson, and which would more than have

39

supplied the loss of the facilities of the Inns of Court and Chancery, terminated with the labours of the latter gentleman, without even an effort to continue, or to revive it. The high expectations, also, which were subsequently raised by the eloquent, and learned political lecturer of Lincoln's Inn Hall, were suffered to expire, after but little more than the splendid and very able Prælection of Sir James Mackintosh.

We have already had occasion to observe that, except some positive rules (introduced merely with a view to a rule of some sort, the number of which is indeed but very few) the principles of practice depend on those of the law itself, and are derived naturally, and necessarily from it. The difficulty, therefore, consists, not so much in ascertaining the relation of these rules to the principles of law, when they are once explained, as in apprehending, readily, and *ex tempore* the application of these rules of practice to the circumstances of a particular case. This is a difficulty common to the apprentices of all sciences, having a practical application to affairs: it is an incapacity which, in all minds, is remedied only by the frequent exercise of this comparison between principles and facts, and the repeated observation of the *relation* between them. Hence

40

we see that the true point to be gained is not so much the actual knowledge of a certain amount of points of practice, as it is a certain *habit of mind* by which the principles acquired in the *study* of the science are readily and certainly applied to individual cases. New points will perpetually arise, and can therefore be solved, as they present themselves, only by holding the clue in the shape of these legal principles.

This being granted (and we presume it is sufficiently clear) it would seem immaterial to the acquisition of this much desired promptness of mind,—this skill in reverting to principles, and instantly applying them as a solvent in our practical difficulties,—I say, it must be immaterial whether the *facts* which we have to deal with be *real,* or *fictitious,*—whether we are quadrating with the rules of our science an *existing*, or a *supposed* case,—or, finally, whether we prepare for trial and argument the cause of a *client,* or an imaginary case stated for discussion in a mock tribunal. Indeed there exists, in these *supposed* cases, an advantage, not necessarily belonging to one of actual occurrence, since they may be designedly so complicated as to present a variety of aspects, and a great number of principles; or, on the other hand, they may be as simple and ele-

41

mentary as we please, so as to adapt them to every stage of a student's progress; and further, they may sometimes be cases already decided in the books, and celebrated for the very complication to which I have just alluded.—Or, they may be cases pending in courts, or such as are probable to be there discussed—or they may be points in which the student has taken a particular and lively interest, but in which his doubts could never be solved by his own exertions: or, lastly, these points may be made to increase in difficulty, so as to keep suitable proportion with the expansion of his knowledge, and his powers of investigation.—Thus is it that this system of factitious practice may be rendered completely institutionary, and methodical. Actual practice, on the other hand, is, from its nature, the reverse;—it may present *early* what can be solved with facility only *late* in the practitioner's course, and the contrary.—In this case, as in some others, fiction may be called the essence of truth.

It may, perhaps, be admitted that knowledge thus acquired in a moot court, will not be so diligently sought, or so distinctly remembered as that which is gained in the actual practice of courts. To this is attached all that zeal which springs from either expected reputation, or contemplated

42

profit—motives to action which in the nature of the mind cannot be supplied by any others. But if the whole object cannot be attained, this should be no reason for neglecting the acquisition of part, especially when it must be conceded that the mock procedure has also its own peculiar advantages. It should likewise be borne in mind that the practitioner is to perfect, in the actual transaction of business, the lesson which he has already conned in these theatres of mooting and preparation. The soldiers of antiquity were certainly not the worse warriors for the sports and games which mimicked the movements and the hurry of the fight; nor were the champions of the tournaments, and mock encounters of more recent times, without their reward, as the tact there acquired served them in stead, on more serious and perilous occasions.

There may undoubtedly arise habits in the mind, as well as in the body; and as the artificer, or the practiser of certain accomplishments, as musick, for example, arrives, after long practice, at a rapidity and delicacy of touch almost inconceivable to the unskilled, so the professor of any practical science learns the ready, and almost intuitive application of principles, which for years he has been wont to compare with facts and circumstances.

43

From this power of habit arises also the difference between speculative students, and practical actors in business. The last is always hastened in the operation of his mind by the pressure and impulse of immediate exigency; whereas the former by this very circumstance often becomes confused, and nearly incapable of proceeding; and having generally had leisure to weigh, and to compare, acquires, indeed, a certain method, but at the same time, slowness of reflexion, which unfits him for extemporary efforts. The practice of a moot court, we think, is admirably calculated, not only to impart much practical knowledge, but in a great degree to confer on students those habits of business, and that collectedness, and well founded confidence, so essential in the argument of causes, whether in the senate, or the forum.

If, therefore, we cannot in the mock proceedings of a moot court, supply those motives to the zealous and industrious acquisition of knowledge, and habits of business, which the appetite for fame or lucre administers, we can at least teach the student and the young lawyer, in some degree, to draw forth from their minds the principles which slumber there, and to learn their relations to certain modes of circumstance; we can teach him readiness, and adroitness, promptitude of resource,

44

self-possession, and what is not the least, the habit of clothing his conceptions in appropriate language.

It is not the most uncommon fault of the solitary speculatist, that conceiving his subject with clearness in his own mind, and having mastered the chain of deduction by which he has reached his conclusion, he forgets that others are not in possession of the same clue, and require to be led to the inference by the same chain by which he himself has attained it, and the links of which he has almost forgotten. The art of popular speaking is, in fact, the art of addressing to hearers, for the most part unskilled in examining the action of their own minds, a plain and familiar series of arguments, each obvious in itself, and adapted to the ordinary range of understanding. True *tact* in this is the fruit of successive experiments only. It is long before the advocate can persuade himself in what degree those reasonings must be simplified for his hearers, which to himself already seem so simple, and analysed to the last degree of plainness. We, of course, here allude chiefly to discussions before a jury, in which, as a general rule, the utmost simplicity should be observed, without the tedious and idle exposition of the obvious. This plain and elementary, but yet solid mode of

45

argumentation is sure to command attention; and, from its perspicuity, cannot fail, if it be entitled so to do, to persuade, or convince. And a portion of this masculine simplicity, and elementary investigation may be carried with great advantage, into the most learned discussions of law points, before courts ever so enlightened. The proper medium, indeed, between triteness, on the one hand, and obscurity, on the other, is, we confess, extremely difficult to be attained;—but in this, we can suggest no other guide than the *good sense* of the speaker. The foregoing observations apply with peculiar force to all discussions before the mock tribunal we are now desirous to see fully established.

In regard to these associations for improvement in the science, and art of the law, whether they be debating societies, or moot courts, no one can justly hesitate as to their utility who will observe, for a moment, the natural propensity of those to *associate,* who have a *community* of pursuit, whether scientifick, or mechanick. This principle of association can justly be referred to nothing else but that natural inclination which men have to speak of what concerns them to such, as a common interest makes attentive listeners, or skill and experience useful instructors. If, therefore, the

46

natural desire thus to interchange thoughts binds men together, and strikes out improvement, whilst it begets emulation, can there be any reason why this kind of association should prove less useful when regulated by method, determined to particular objects, and kindled up by that fire of rivalry which springs up in men whenever a common aim is proposed? Let us not disdain, therefore, in the acquisition of a vast and multifarious science, an aid to which men so naturally betake themselves in the most simple and the most ordinary objects of pursuit; nor, to borrow a simile from a mock encounter of a more warlike nature, disdain the use of the lance because in the keener and closer engagement of the combatants, it must be abandoned for the sword, or the dagger.

We would not conceal however, that a tribunal of this sort, though eminently useful, is a very different field of contention from that of actual business. Apart from the differences to which we have already adverted, another is to be found in the different degrees of excitement which the latter administers to the more *interested* passions of our nature. An actual point of advantage to be gained, begets in the antagonists more obstinacy, more craft, more ungenerous sophistry, and instigates to less candid methods of litigation, than a

47

supposed case, or a mere speculative point. To meet *these* require more civick courage, and presence of mind than are to be easily, if at all, acquired in these schools of more generous disceptation; and those who have engaged warmly and eagerly in the exercises of the last, often shrink from the dishonest arts, and petty subtilities of daily business.—The young practitioner, moreover, will sometimes have to encounter the uncandid praises, the galling irony, the unfeeling sarcasm, and the disingenuous replies of a haughty antagonist, who reposing, with the utmost complacency, on an expansive reputation, and forgetting the days of his own youthful ambition, and modest, but ardent hopes of distinction, feels, or affects to feel, towards the reasoning of his young opponent, the utmost indifference;—lavisehs upon him, without measure, a flood of insult, in the shape of flattery;—and overwhelms his arguments with a mass of good natured satire. At other times the young practitioner must expect to meet in the conflicts of the bar, with those who will not, or who cannot follow him through the mass of learning, which his own familiarity with the books, and his deep and zealous study of his cause has enabled him to present to the court. He will find that his learning, however necessary, and appropriate it may

48

be, and kindly received by the court, will be treated by his opponents, either with total neglect,—a pregnant sneer,—or a bold assertion that the whole is impertinent to the issue, and flowed *ex abundanti doctrina, non apte disposita*. The experience and the courage to meet these must therefore be left to be acquired in their proper school,— the school of the world. In the *fictitious* forum he may be taught to draw readily on his resources; to embody his thoughts in just diction; to arrange his forces with method and science for the combat; but his courage and equanimity in the *real* one, and most of the other moral qualities which enter into the composition of forensick ability, he must draw from actual contact with the rudeness and perplexities which embarrass the course of practical affairs. The true utility of every thing is best seen, and best applied to our purposes, when its defects and incapacities are also stated;—when we know precisely, what an agent will do, and what it will not.

I have been thus plain in exhibiting what I conceive to be the real and comparative advantages of debating societies, and courts of mock procedure, because expecting from them more than is just, we allow them less merit than is actually their due. We would only further remark

49

that in regard to either species of association, almost every thing that is to insure complete success depends mainly on the *student's own* zealous, persevering, and decorous conduct.—The best regulations are in vain, if the students themselves do not sustain to the utmost, the great objects in view; and, in the success of the proposed tribunal, all other means are useless, when its practitioners cease to feel a lively, growing interest,—or to support with their utmost ability, the individual who presides over its business.—In respect to debating societies we would, in conclusion, remark that their failure has sometimes arisen from the character of those who compose them: the young are apt to be dazzled with the subtilities of logick;—with false eloquence, and general declamation: their subjects, also, are often chosen in conformity with these prevalent tastes;—their debates are not regulated by *authority*, and by those who might prune the declaimer's wings, and recal the wanderers in debate. Habits of considering a topick are thus contracted, which, joined to the causes already indicated, sufficiently show why the hero of a debating club may disappoint expectation, and fails in the true and just business of life. At the same time these defects are not altogether inevitable, and incurable. In a moot

50

court, by the plan which in part I propose now to submit to you, I hope they may be in a degree, and perhaps, entirely avoided.

What has been said has sufficiently disclosed my general designs. It is now time to state to you the fundamental regulations which have occurred to me as fit to be adopted in the organization of the proposed court.

1. The number of its practitioners should be adequate to conduct the business of the court with perfect ease, so as not to call, too largely, on their time, or to interrupt the progress of their prescribed studies or professional engagements.

2. Business should be so apportioned, and conducted, that each member may have an equal chance of learning all the details of business, so that there be no monopoly either of the practical matters of the court, or of the debating of questions.

3. The moot court will exercise the jurisdiction, and strictly pursue the practice observed in the following courts:—

    1. County Court.
    2. Orphans' Court.
    3. Court of Appeals.
    4. Court of Chancery.
    5. District Court of U. S.

51

6. Circuit Court of U. S.

7. Supreme Court of U. S.

4. In order to conform as strictly as possible to the practice of the foregoing courts, there will be seven distinct dockets, in which all the appropriate entries will be made by the clerk of the moot court, whose duty it will also be, to take in charge all papers filed; to prepare records in such important cases only, as the Judge shall deem best calculated to illustrate the practical proceedings of courts; and finally, to perform all the essential duties of the clerks of such courts respectively.

5. The rules existing in the said courts are to be observed by the moot court, with no other variation than what may, from time to time, be found to result from the nature of a court of fictitious jurisdiction.

6. Any member may practice in all of the moot courts, or record his name as a practitioner in any particular court.—It shall be the duty of every member to see that the proper entries are made by the clerk in all of the cases under such member's charge. Counsel shall themselves lay the proper rules, and direct the entries, so that the clerk shall in all cases act ministerially under the direction of the counsel. If, however, the clerk should doubt the correctness of any proposed en-

52

try, he shall make the entry in a rough docket, kept for the occasion, until the court's opinion thereon be ascertained, after which the authorised entry shall be made in the clerk's docket.

7. Such rules for the government of the moot court, sitting as either of the said courts, as are *not* to be found in the existing rules of the courts, whose jurisdiction and practice it professes to pursue, shall be prepared by the Judge of the moot court, aided by a committee of its practitioners; and any member will be at liberty to suggest to the court and bar, any rule which he thinks it would be expedient to adopt.

8. The Judge of the moot court, in relation to the business of the court, the preservation of order, the admission and expulsion of members, &c. shall possess unlimited powers; and in the exercise thereof there shall be no publick comment on, or appeal from his decision. It is supposed that less evil would result from arbitrary power, in such a tribunal, than from the debate and contention that might otherwise arise—*order* being the first law of life, and the surest means of expediting all business.

9. The members of the court shall annually appoint two *vice judges,* whose duty it shall be to hold the courts, only in the absence of the judge.

53

These vice judges shall be called *first* and *second* vice judges, one only of whom shall sit. Should the judge and vice judges be absent, the Bar shall appoint a vice judge *pro tempore.*

10. The vice judges shall be, *ex officio, Readers*, with powers and duties similar to those possessed by Readers in the Inns of Chancery.

11. With the exception of the vice judges, none shall be appointed *Reader*, unless he be a junior lawyer, or a student of three years standing, or upwards.—The judge may appoint annually three Readers, who when once appointed shall forever retain their title, and privileges. It shall be the duty of the vice judges, as well as those specially constituted readers, at least once a year, and not oftener than three times, to *read* and *expound* to the assembled students, and members of the moot court, an essay, or opinion on any question of law he may select; in which case it will be expected that every one shall be present. These readings shall be carefully transcribed by each Reader, or by the clerk, into a book provided for that purpose.

12. The moot court shall be open for business nine months in the year, during which period there shall be three sessions; the *first* to commence on the 15th of October, and continue until the 1st of February: the *second* session to com-

54

mence on the first of April, and terminate the 15th of July. The period intervening between the first of February and April shall be called the *"middle session,"* during which time the vice judges shall alternately, or at their pleasure, hold the court; or, at the election of a majority of the whole bar, the middle session may be wholly omitted, and a debating society may be constructed in lieu thereof, to be called the *Rota,* the name and objects of which have been sufficiently explained in my first introductory lecture.

13. During the two regular sessions the court will meet every Monday, and every other Saturday. No other business shall be done on Saturday than that which is preparatory to the argument of causes,—such as the *call of the dockets; making all proper entries; filing declarations, pleas, &c.; entering and justifying bail; making up issues; filing demurrers, motions, rules on the Sheriff, craving over, references to arbitration,* calling the *judicial* and subpœna dockets, and finally all other collateral matters which constitute the practice of each court, and tend to prepare the cases for argument, on *cases stated, special verdicts, general* and *special demurrers,* &c. &c. The dockets of the different courts

55

to be taken up in such order as may suit the convenience of the judge.

14. Motions, rules on the sheriff, and other incidental questions shall be argued by only one counsel on each side.—And no case whatever shall be argued by more than three counsel on each side.

15. Causes, with *consent of court*, may be docketed on a *case stated;* in which case no declaration, or other proceeding need be filed. All other causes must be instituted, and prosecuted with a strict adherence to legal forms, and the rules of the court.

16. No action shall be brought, or case stated with a view of arguing the same, unless the question has been previously submitted to the court in writing, for approval or rejection.

17. It will be expected that every member will institute at least one suit for argument, or other disposition, once a fortnight, and file the same with the clerk on any day except Monday, that being the day assigned for the argument of causes.

18. All writs will be made returnable on Saturday of every week; and the declaration, short note, or titling may be filed with the clerk on any day, *Saturday, the return day,* and Mondays excepted.

56

19. Monday, in each week, shall be employed in the argument of causes, whether on the merits, or any incidental question. The dockets shall be taken up in such order that a cause in each court may be successively argued, and this too, in the order of the seven dockets as already enumerated.

20. Should an argument not be finished on Monday, it shall be adjourned to the next succeeding Monday. Causes of great intricacy may be continued from time to time, until counsel are prepared; but not longer than sixteen terms, that is during the period of one session,—after which it must be dismissed, unless counsel should peremptorily engage to argue it on the following Monday.

21. Equity causes, those of the Admiralty, the court of Appeals, and the Circuit and Supreme courts of the U. S., when argued in the moot court, under the circumstances hereafter mentioned, shall be argued on the *actual records* of those respective courts, in which case, when practicable, the *printed statements* shall be procured, and used by the counsel and the court; and when not obtainable, the counsel shall prepare similar *written* statements.

22. Equity causes, whether for argument, or decree, shall be prosecuted with a strict adherence

57

to the practice and rules of the High Court of Chancery, or the Circuit Court of the United States, according to the court in which the suit is pending.

23. The original, appellate, and concurrent jurisdiction of the several courts shall be strictly maintained. Proceedings may be stayed by *injunction* from the chancery and circuit court, as the case may require, and all equity causes shall be prosecuted in those courts only.

24. Causes in the moot court may be argued on *records* of cases pending, or formerly pending in any appellate court; but no cause *then pending* shall be argued in the moot court, unless with the *written* consent of all the counsel engaged in such *real* proceeding.

25. The business of an Orphans' Court shall be so conducted in the moot court, as gradually to unfold the practice of that court under the laws of England, and the testamentary system of this state: and as the proceedings of the Orphans' Courts in this state have been generally too loose, and irregular, practitioners in the moot Orphans' Court should consult the most approved *formulæ*, and the purest sources of information on the law, and procedure generally, of ecclesiastical courts.

26. A *punctual* attendance will be expected

58

from all the members, not only that the argument of causes may proceed without any interruption, but that the *practical* details of business may be advanced. Attendance on *Saturdays* will therefore be insisted on, particularly as those who may be familiar with the ordinary routine of practice will be too often inclined to absent themselves on that account,—forgetting that the association imposes a duty on them to impart their knowledge to others, and to look for their compensation at some future period, when their younger brethren shall become more skilled.

27. A strict adherence, in arguing causes, to the point in debate, and a studious avoidance of all personal, or offensive allusions, will be rigidly enjoined, and the severest forensick decorum enforced.

28. Such junior members of the bar as may practice in the moot court for two years, shall be entitled to perpetual membership, provided that during that period they shall have pronounced three *Readings,* or served as vice judges during one session.

29. The court, at its convenience, will deliver a written opinion on all causes of sufficient importance to require it: and should the business of the court justify it, there will be annually published a

59

small volume of the more important decisions, to be entitled *"Reports of Decisions in the Moot Court, attached to the Maryland Law Institute;"* which volume shall be sold at its *prime cost,* the exclusive object of its publication being to serve the purposes of an advertisement of the objects, progress, and utility of the scheme now proposed.

30. If required, *certificates* will be given of the length of time a member has practised in the court; the number of his *Readings,* the time he may have served as vice judge, and any other matter which may be properly inserted.

I have now finished the view proposed to be given of the general design, and the organization of the court which we desire to see fully, and permanently established in this city. Time, and experience would, no doubt, mature it into a better form; but, if suffered to go into operation on the plan we have stated, or even on a basis of much less extent, it cannot fail to prove a very powerful means of advancing students and young lawyers in their profession;—a profession which, of all others, requires a willing adoption of every means for its acquisition; a profession only honourable, when well understood;—a profession profitable and laudable only when sustained by good morals, and good talents industriously cultivated;

60

and finally, a profession the most ennobling, or the most degrading, as its pursuers are virtuous and learned,—or unprincipled and ignorant.

We confess that some apprehensions are entertained that our zeal in this enterprise will be but poorly reciprocated, as well by students as by junior lawyers. This would certainly not be the case were they to take a *coup d'œil* of that ample field which is before them, and consider how much they have to toil and cultivate in it, before they can hope to occupy the foremost ranks in their high vocation. If, indeed, they are content with moderate attainments in the science generally, and even something beyond this, in detached portions, they may pursue the "even tenor of their way," perhaps, without mortification,—but they surely can never hope to reap those delightful gratifications which spring from a thorough knowledge of the vast whole, and from a commensurate and enduring reputation, awarded to those alone who have covetted the science with unabated ardour.

Were the moot court composed of fifty or sixty members, a third of whom should be junior lawyers, its business would be so conducted by them as to render it a source of certain and great improvement; the results of which could not fail to

61

be in time strongly reflected from the *bar,* the *bench,* and the *profession* generally.

With these remarks, explanatory of my views on this subject, which ought to be much more interesting to others than to myself, I shall leave it to them to say whether these plans, in whole or in part, shall be put into execution or not.

Baltimore, Oct. 1825.

N. B. The Moot Court, on the extensive plan delineated in the foregoing lecture, has *not* gone into operation, and probably will not, unless a much more ample zeal, and encouragement on the part of those to whom it was tendered, should be manifested. But a court of less pretension is in operation; and when time and circumstances will justify it, *that one* may, perhaps, mature into the one originally contemplated; though it is not very probable, as students of law (as far as we can perceive) have not generally that zeal for availing themselves of facilities in study, which seem to mark the students of medicine and theology.

Whether the whole of our plans, in regard to the *Law Institute,* and *Scheme of Lectures,* is to be eventually defeated by the want of suitable encouragement, is yet uncertain. We have at all times suspected that it is the lot of one generation to toil for the benefit of the succeeding; and against this we should enter no protest, could we but perceive such indications as would probably encourage others hereafter to engage in a similar enterprise. Our

62

endeavours, however, will be continued in a *moderate* way,—impairing, very materially, neither health, purse, nor *professional business*,—the last of which (with the considerate, and liberal) would be regarded as greatly promoted, and certainly not retarded, by its admixture with other studies, and analogous pursuits.

April, 1826.

To the Trustees

of the University of Maryland in Relation to the Law Chair, 1826

TO THE

Trustees

OF THE

UNIVERSITY OF MARYLAND

IN RELATION TO THE

LAW CHAIR.

Baltimore:
PRINTED BY J. D. TOY,
Corner of Market and St. Paul streets.
1826.

TO THE

TRUSTEES OF THE UNIVERSITY

OF MARYLAND.

Baltimore, November 20th, 1826.

GENTLEMEN,
I take the liberty of addressing you individually in a printed letter, on a matter interesting to you as Trustees of the University of Maryland, and to me of vital importance, as the result of some of the best exertions of my life depends on the prompt decision which shall be made by you. Before I call your attention to the following papers, especially the one marked No. 4, I beg leave to state summarily, that as early as 1811, I bestowed on the then *Medical College* no little of my zeal and industrious exertion. Subsequently, I was strongly instrumental in procuring the organization of the *University* engrafted on the medical department; and in 1814 was appointed Professor of Law. In 1817 and 1818 I rendered some essential pecuniary and other services to the institution, and in June 1819, when the University was oppressed with numerous and heavy debts, and several judgments, and its medical class had sunk to 58 students, I came forward and proposed a thorough re-organization,—procured the election of Professor Pattison,—took charge of all the debts,—advanced between 8 and $10,000,—attended personally, almost daily, at the University, during more than one year,—saw to the erection of a new building,—the complete repair of the then existing ones,—procured most of the furniture, ornaments, &c. of the buildings, and had the pleasure soon to see the class increase to nearly 300 medical students.

In 1822, at the request of the Regents, and the then Faculty of Law, I commenced my duties as Professor of Law, and have constantly since lectured, &c. &c. to a small but increasing class, on a plan of legal instruction perhaps more extensive and complete than had been hitherto adopted any where else. In order to promote the scheme of instruction, and to make

4

it extensively known, I published in succession, a *Course of Legal Study*, a *Syllabus of the Lectures*, a *Circular Letter to Students*, and various *Introductory Lectures*, as they were annually delivered in the institution. The University not being in funds, I procured, at my own expense, all the necessary means of executing my plans, and they were becoming ripened, and fully organized, when some friends, fully aware of my exertions, and the heavy expense I had been put to, and that the Medical Department had *monopolized* all the funds of the institution, applied last winter to the Legislature for a thorough reorganization of the institution. One of the main objects of that organization was to correct the preponderating influence of the Medical Faculty, and to raise the chair of Law, in every respect, as far as pecuniary means could effect that object, on an equally respectable footing with the Medical branch. In connexion with the law which modified the charter, the Legislature enacted a law that the sum of $14,200, out of the next proceeds of the lotteries, should be applied to the purchase of a suitable *building, furniture* and *library* for the Professor of Law. The Trustees met several times, and I was somewhat pained to find, that instead of at all regarding the chair of Law, its deliberations were almost wholly taken up with matters relating to the *Medical* chairs,—and thus a law, which mainly originated in the necessity of getting rid of the too great influence of the Medical department of the University, and of bringing forward the Legal branch of it, appears in its turn to have been primarily used to aid the Medical chairs.

The first monies which came in hand, after the late law which appropriated $14,200 to the chair of Law, "out of the *next* proceeds of the lotteries," have been applied to *Medical* purposes. Perceiving that the Law department could not possibly continue any longer, if not sustained by the University, of which it had been a practical branch ever since October, 1822, but on advances made by myself, I sent a respectful request to the Trustees to examine personally the establishment in which my students were placed, the furniture, library, &c., and the various plans I had adopted for the advancement of the Faculty of Law—this they declined to do—I then requested permission to appear personally before them, so that I might fully explain all that had been done, and the peculiarity of my situation, which so strongly demanded immediate relief. This, also, was permitted to pass unnoticed. I had previously addressed a letter to the *Executive Committee*, erroneously conceiving

5

that it possessed full power to act,—but was simply informed that it possessed no power, and that my application must be made to the Trustees. A committee of three gentlemen was then appointed, whose views appeared to me to be such as must necessarily destroy every hope of success on my part, and which could not fail to compel me at once to abandon all the plans of instruction I had practised for the last four years. This induced me to address a letter to the *Trustees themselves*, which is annexed, marked No. 4. With this letter I also sent a small volume, containing a full outline of the plans I had adopted,—hoping that a hasty glance at this volume would be sufficient to unfold the general organization of my department. This letter and the volume I was much pained to be informed, have never met the eye of the Trustees, who adjourned *sine die;* and, from the day of their last meeting to the present time I have never heard one word concerning my chair, but a general rumor that nothing had been done, except that a resolution had been passed that my *rent* should be paid from June last—but even this resolution has never been notified to me. In this state of things, knowing as I did that upwards of $15,000 were at the command of the Trustees, and that all would be paid in the course of a month or two at furthest, and that my actual expenditure in procuring necessary furniture, and a building, had exceeded my receipts by $2,180, I was compelled to the unpleasant alternative of closing the institution, and of seeing students from various parts of the country disappointed, and returning to their homes. I had sustained the Law department out of my own funds as long as it was prudent for me so to do, and I had the mortification to find that plans which had been maturing for many years, under heavy pecuniary and *professional* sacrifices, were thus at once prostrated, and that a chilling indifference appeared to be manifested towards all that I had done for the University generally, and also for the chair of Law.

It is, however, a duty which I owe to the University and to the scheme which I have digested and published, and which has been so kindly spoken of in most of the states of the Union, except Maryland, that I should not wholly abandon it without one more effort to place my views fully, and in their true light, before your body. All that I ask is an attentive perusal of the following papers. That the law of 1825-6 actually contemplated to furnish the Professor of Law with every essential *from the time he commenced* the discharge of his duties, is to me clear of all doubt; but if a different

6

opinion be entertained by the Trustees, and as the claim is a just one, I have not doubted the aid of the Trustees in procuring from the Legislature at its present session a legislative construction of the law in that respect. In regard, however, to the purchase of a suitable building, furniture and library, as the law is free from all doubt, and the funds are actually in hand, I trust that there will be no hesitation on the part of the Trustees to make the appropriation forthwith, and leave the matter of the small claim which will remain, to be adjusted by the Legislature, or by the Trustees out of funds which may hereafter come in hand, and which are not appropriated by the law to *specific objects*. It is to me a matter of extreme importance that a distinct and speedy decision should be made by the Trustees, as self-protection, and the duty I owe to myself, render it essential that plans so intimately connected with my future *professional* life should either be promptly and wholly abandoned, or at once zealously prosecuted. Without the contemplated aid it is quite impossible for me to proceed,—and it is with the Trustees to say whether the scheme of legal instruction which has been in so great a degree matured, merits success, or must be permitted wholly to fail.

With great respect,
I am, gentlemen,
Your obedient servant,
DAVID HOFFMAN.

☞ Since the foregoing was written, I have been at a loss to account for a part of a communication of the Trustees to the public, bearing date 9th October, 1826. The part to which I allude is as follows.

"In the Faculty of Law the Professor *is furnished* with the amplest accommodations for students in his department, not only for affording the benefit of attending his public course of lectures, but for private studies. His *library* is large and well chosen. His terms vary, according to the privileges enjoyed. The charge for attending the lectures, which extend through ten months in the year, is thirty dollars."

Knowing, as I do, that from 1814 to the present time, I had never received one cent from the University; that I had been left to sustain all the heavy expenses incident to the Faculty of Law, and that I had a capital employed therein exceeding $20,000, and that "the department which is

7

furnished with the amplest accommodations," has been so furnished at my own expense, and that I had in vain appealed to the Trustees to refund those necessary expenses, to pay for that furniture, and to purchase that "large and well chosen library," I felt surprised to find that even the poor merit of *individual enterprise* is denied me by that advertisement, and that the publick generally are left to suppose, and many persons have since so stated it, that all of these accommodations have been actually furnished to me by the University from the commencement of my lecturing, or that they have been recently purchased, in virtue of the law of the last session. This clause of the advertisement I feel persuaded must have been inadvertently written and published, and I only speak of the effect it produces to my prejudice, without the least idea that any such effect could have been intended by any one of the Trustees.

I also called the attention of the Trustees to a small balance yet due to me for money advanced to the University several years since, to pay a judgment then about to be enforced against the institution. This claim has also been in no way noticed that I have heard of.

In conclusion, I beg leave to state that I feel persuaded, that if the Trustees will make themselves fully acquainted with my exertions on behalf of the institution, and particularly in completely organizing the Law Faculty, and discharging its duties to the best of my ability, they will not fail to exert themselves to protect an individual from an actual loss, which loss would be sustained by me as Professor, for advances made necessary by the circumstances in which I was placed, and which I could not for a moment doubt would be refunded; and further, when it is borne in mind that the very law which appropriated a sum for this department contemplated to place the chair of Law on an equal footing with the Medical chairs, *from the time that the Law Professor engaged in the discharge of his duties.* Nor can I bring myself to believe that the chair of Law, organized on the extensive plan I have thus far acted on, can be a matter of indifference to those whom the state hath appointed guardians of the institution, and who have manifested so much zeal on behalf of another portion of that institution, which, from its nature, requires much less support than the department to which I have been assigned.

To you, gentlemen, I leave the means of devising such means as may fully sustain the Law Institute, and make it a powerful medium for the diffusion of legal knowledge, and

8

of building up a regular succession of able lawyers, to enlighten our councils, chasten our jurisprudence, and to hasten the march of political science.
Very respectfully,
Yours, &c.
D. H.

☞ The following letter, addressed by me to the Faculty of Medicine, will show the grounds of complaint against that Body, for having monopolized all the funds of the institution—and which monopoly led to the memorial of the Faculty of Law to the Regents, on behalf of the chair of Law, and finally to the Act of Assembly of last session, which appropriated to that chair a specific sum, which it is now the object of the present communication to call upon the *trustees* to apply in aid of said chair.

No. 1.

Baltimore, January 13, 1824.

GENTLEMEN,

I have purposely delayed replying to your letter of the 9th November, in order to reflect deliberately on its singular contents, and to endeavour, if possible, to ascertain the ground of the offence you have been pleased to take at what you call the "highly exceptionable phraseology" of my letter of the 8th November. I have carefully perused the original letter, of which, at my request, you have been so good as to let me take a copy, and, with a single exception, I cannot find a syllable that the most fastidious person would be justified in considering a departure from the courtesy which should be preserved in such intercourse.

The exception to which I allude, is, I confess, at first view, in some degree exceptionable: but, when the Faculty bear in mind that the fact is, that during a series of years very many unpleasant difficulties have occurred between its several members, and that the writer of that letter had been very often selected as the organ of reconciliation, and was on many occasions made minutely acquainted with all the circumstances relating to these differences, an *allusion* to them might have seemed less exceptionable, by far, in him, than in a total stranger.

But had this allusion been equally or more offensive from me than from a stranger, some allowance was due to the oc-

9

casion. The Faculty should have borne in mind with what readiness I complied with all *their requests* when their views and interests were to be promoted, and that I never suffered any thing to delay my services to them; whereas, when on this and the former occasion, I requested the Medical Faculty to look to *my* interest, I had the mortification to find not only inactivity, but, I must say, indifference, and even *incivility*, inasmuch as my letters and verbal requests obtained no reply whatever, until I insisted on some notice of them, and when it came, it was evasive and wholly unsatisfactory. Another application was made: the funds were at that time very low; and my views and request were, of course, very moderate, more particularly as I had not then actually commenced lecturing, nor organized the plans which are now in operation. To this second request you made a *verbal* reply, that the *Faculty* HAD appropriated $500! With this I was obliged to be content, because my plans did not then so urgently demand more, and because I knew that the means were not so extensive as they have subsequently become; nor could I *at once* be convinced that a body who owed me so much, *could* be indifferent to my views and interests.* In October last, I made a third request of your body. I knew that the Faculty met daily, or could meet, at the Infirmary, without the least inconvenience. After waiting nearly a fortnight, and being informed that no motion even was made towards noticing my application, I addressed you the letter to which you so much object. In your reply to this, you, for the *first time*, come forward with a declaration that you decline acting on my request, and the reason assigned by you is, the offensive phraseology of my letter, and that your body declines to act on any *future* application,—I presume, if ever so respectfully worded.

To this objection I have in part replied; and I have nothing to add except that the Medical Faculty of the University of Maryland, like all other great, enlightened, and powerful bodies, is still liable to be spoken to in the language of *truth* and *candour*. In a spirit of perfect frankness, I informed your Body what were *my* views in regard to the organization of the University on its original principles, and the propriety of a thorough investigation of all that had been done respecting the funds, &c., from the earliest period to the present time. I stated the propriety of the Regents' being fully

---

* But even this $500 was subsequently withheld, because you found some other use for it!

informed, and that the Medical Faculty had, in my opinion, been too long allowed to appropriate every thing to their own use, without accountability, and without the knowledge of any body. I further stated, that matters were now in such a state as imperiously to require that the other faculties should participate in the bounty of the legislature, and that I was doing injustice to myself to permit matters to remain any longer in their present condition. If these truths, thus candidly stated, have given offence, I can truly say I did not *intend* it, nor could I have imagined that your Body was so pre-eminently distinguished for accuracy in business, and zeal for the promotion of the interests of the University generally, as to forbid the imputation of the reverse of either the one or the other. I did suppose that not one of your Body could, in candour, assert, either that the business of the University, (which you had taken into your own hands,) had ever been conducted in a business-like manner, or that it has not been the uniform wish, and almost the avowed policy of your Body, to monopolize all, and to discountenance the organization of the other faculties. My continued intercourse with your Body for several years, and with the individual members of it for many more, constantly impressed and confirmed in me the opinion that your Body never would permit itself seriously to entertain or realize the idea of the organization of the *University*. This reluctance I had many occasions to repel, and I never omitted an opportunity to impress on you the fairness, propriety, and ultimate policy of organizing the entire Institution. But never on any occasion could I obtain a single expression that heartily indicated a concurrence of opinion, and though occasionally some feeble expressions escaped you, favourable to the Law chair, yet even as to this, I never perceived in your Body the hundredth part of the interest for the promotion of *my* views, which I sincerely felt, and efficiently manifested for the promotion of yours.

The *second* ground taken by you for declining to act on my application, is one that at once seems to involve the assertion, that *even yet* not enough has been done for you, and that the Institution is even under obligations to you! I am of opinion that the whole of your views on this subject are radically erroneous. Before I can fully reply to your extraordinary opinions on this subject, I beg leave to extract a part of your letter. You say, "On one point mentioned in your letter of the 8th inst., the Faculty of Physick are desirous of setting you right. They say it is not a fact that the sums expended on *Medical* purposes, cannot fall short of $160,000. The sums expended were for the purpose of erecting *buildings*, that do not *belong* to the Faculty of Physick. Besides, each individual of that Faculty has been paying annually from 5 to 600 dollars out of his own pocket, which must be considered a pretty good rent for the privilege of lecturing in the University buildings." Whether the Faculty have set me right, and convicted me of an errour, now remains to be inquired. Your letter does not deny that the *whole* of the great sums which have been expended, have been exclusively appropriated to the erection of the buildings, the purchase of apparatus, furniture, &c. &c. This being the case, the answer to a single question will decide the matter. Are not all those buildings, apparatus, furniture, &c. exclusively appropriated to the use of your Body, and also, as they now stand, *wholly unfit* for any other purpose? Every candid person must reply, yes! My assertion, therefore, that the *Medical Faculty* had thus far applied to itself the whole means of the University, is, I think, completely vindicated, and I do not perceive what bearing the surprising information contained in your letter, "that these buildings, &c. do not *belong* to the Medical Faculty," has on the case under consideration; since the only inquiry is, whether you enjoy the secure and beneficial use of them. As to the assertion contained in the latter part of the extract I have made from your letter, it appears to me equally untenable. I do not think it could be said, on any principle of calculation, that you are annually paying out of your own pockets, five or six hundred dollars. Property and facilities of various kinds, to the amount of at least $160,000, have been placed in your hands for your sole benefit and use; this property has been the means of accomplishing all your objects, and is now a source of large emolument, which, if properly fostered, must ensure the acquisition of an ample fortune to each. The legislature then loans you $30,000, and seven of your body are bound to pay annually a small interest on that sum. To say that this is a payment of 5 or 600 dollars *per annum* out of your own pockets, is about as accurate as to assert that where a liberal donor had given a *well stocked farm* to a person, on condition of his supplying the donor's family with poultry, this was a tax on the *pocket* of the donee. I cannot think so: if it be, it is certainly one of those personal taxes with which every man who understands his own interest, would be extremely willing to be charged.

3

12

There is only one other part of your letter which it is necessary for me to notice. The following is the passage: "The Faculty of Physick nevertheless *freely* offer to you the use of *any* room in the University buildings, without rent, and they cannot *help thinking*, that a room which is good enough for one of their body to lecture in, is also good enough for the Professor of Law to lecture in." There is a spirit breathing through every line of this part of your letter, which I did not suppose a single member of your Faculty ever had any cause to entertain towards me. Had I acted towards you with uniform hostility, and been habituated for a series of years to mar your views and interests, such a spirit might, perhaps, have been justly manifested. But when I have greatly assisted in raising your Institution from obscurity, confusion, and the prospect of utter dissolution, and have expended much time, precious to me, and when pressing business was often made to give way to your requisitions; and when I reflect that all I have ever done since, of a contrary character, even according to your own admission, is, that I have addressed a letter to the Faculty, some parts of which are, in your opinion, exceptionable, I confess I am astonished that you could be brought to add *mockery* to your *injustice*. If your obligations to me are to be entirely cancelled by a *line*, which, for aught you know, was nothing but the hasty dash of an intemperate pen, and which, when examined, dwindles into nothing; I confess I have no knowledge, and never desire to have, of the human heart. But permit me to examine for a moment the passage I have quoted from your letter. You say "the *Faculty of Physick* will *freely grant* me the use of any of the rooms." I am well aware that your Body has so long indulged the belief and feeling that *all is your own*, that this kind of language has become so natural to you, that you continue to use it without remembering that, in the very preceding sentence of your letter, where you had a *different* object in view, you decline all control over, or property in these buildings, which you now so *freely offer*. You are also pleased to offer me *any room* to *lecture* in, but not to suit it to my purposes. I appeal to you, whether there be one among you who did not well know, and who was not distinctly and emphatically informed by one of your own Body, Professor Pattison, as well as by myself, repeatedly, that the rooms of the present building, (even if they were in the heart of the city,) were in no one respect adapted to my purposes, and that it was essential that *my* rooms should be as completely adapted to

13

my purposes, as your own to yours. Is it then any thing less than sheer mockery, gravely to inform me that the Faculty had come to the resolution freely to offer me the use of a room in the buildings? You further say that "you cannot help thinking that a room which is good enough for one of your Body to lecture in, is also good enough for the Professor of Law." I am not aware that we were ever at issue on this point. The *goodness* of the room is not the matter in controversy, but its *adaption* to our several purposes. I therefore freely admit, (and never did question it for a moment,) that any room which your members lecture in, is good enough, and far better indeed than any I should require. But they are, all and each of them, wholly *unsuited* to my purposes, and, in one respect, *never could be made* suitable: this fact, I am obliged to say, I well know your Body was duly informed of. Your remarks, therefore, on this point, are somewhat extraordinary, and, to one inclined to seek offence, are much more objectionable, both in spirit and language, than any in my letter to you, and which has been so strangely distorted from its manifest import.

I have now replied to every part of your letter which required remark. There are, however, several matters which I avail myself of this occasion to bring to your notice. It has been contended in the discussions of your Faculty, that I am entitled to some credit for my *zeal* on your behalf, but none for my *services*. I did not suppose any one of you could have been rash enough to venture on so bold an assertion. From the year 1811, to the present, I have scarcely alluded, even to my best friends, to the exertions made by me in aid of the views and interests of the Medical Faculty. It was more congenial to my feelings to say nothing on the subject to any one. As I find, however, that you are now willing not only to forget, but to deny these services, I feel justified in fully asserting them, and shall therefore beg leave briefly to bring them to your recollection. Prior to any application being made to the legislature for the establishment of a University, and when the Medical Faculty was denominated the "College of Medicine of Maryland," my services were required in various ways, and often and freely given. When the charter was applied for, I had frequent consultations on its various clauses, and from that time to the present, I have given my professional aid on very many occasions, and so repeatedly as to elude the memory, and which, if charged in the usual way, would afford an undoubted claim to at least the amount of money requested by me. All the title-papers

14

passed under my examination; all the difficulties and doubts in regard to lotteries, were presented to my investigation; and so were the financial concerns of the institution at various times; and various ways and means of raising funds, and appropriating them, were suggested by me. Col. Howard's account, Carey Long's, and the accounts with D. A. Smith, all passed under my examination. I was in the constant habit of consulting with, and being consulted by, the Faculty, and its members. No election took place in which I was not advised with. If unpleasant differences arose between members of your Faculty, I was uniformly consulted. Heavy and urgent debts and judgments hung over the Institution: these were delayed by my constant, zealous exertions. Several times, when *execution* against the University had been applied for, and the very destruction of the Institution was threatened, my persuasions, statements, and promises, avertted the blow. No lottery was ever offered that did not receive considerable aid from my exertions. I wrote letters, and forwarded them in every direction; I wrote a series of newspaper notices of the lotteries, and composed, and had printed, various circulars. I even sold tickets, and made such other exertions in regard to these lotteries, as, I believe, tended strongly to fix the public attention on them in preference to any others. When the University was in its greatest need, and for small sums of money, I procured subscriptions, and (though to a small amount,) yet the members of my own family subscribed as much as the whole city had done, with the exception, I believe, of D. A. Smith. When I had occasion to publish various little productions, I never failed to make the strongest and most honourable mention of the Medical Faculty. Many long pieces were written by me for the newspapers, animating the public mind to an efficient regard for the Institution.

In 1820 the institution was at its lowest ebb. Professor Davidge occupied two chairs: the number of students did not exceed sixty, and there was a heavy debt of $30,000. Executions to the amount of nearly $6,000 were then pending. The buildings, which had never been finished, were in a state of gloomy dilapidation, and a heartlessness and despondency prevailed through the institution to such a degree that Professor De Butts informed me, with much feeling, after we had been visiting the buildings, that it was probable the institution could not last more than another session, unless something could be done to rescue it from its peril. He asked me what could be done. My brief reply

15

was, "go further in debt; get Dr. Davidge to resign one of the chairs; appoint an able Professor to supply the vacancy: repair your buildings, erect a new building for a class-room," &c. &c. It so occurred that Professor Gibson was in the city at this very time, and, no doubt, perceiving the wretched condition of the University, he well knew that it would be for the advantage of the Philadelphia institution that the two chairs should remain united in one individual, and the Maryland University be consequently prevented from looking to Dr. Smith, of Virginia, or Mr. Pattison, late from Glasgow, and then in Philadelphia, from being elected to the chair of Anatomy or Surgery. Several conversations with Professor Gibson induced in me the assurance that this was his feeling. On the very night, therefore, after the abovementioned conversation with Dr. De Butts, I digested the plan of a complete revival of the institution. I requested a meeting of the Medical Faculty at my house, opened to them my views, which were afterwards fully adopted at a meeting held at Professor M'Dowell's. The plan proposed by me was to inquire into the pretensions of Mr. Pattison, and if they were pre-eminent, then to elect him Professor of Anatomy. A difficulty then occurred, which was, to impress Dr. Davidge favourably in regard to the pretensions of Mr. Pattison, and to prevail on him to resign one of the chairs, and, if practicable, that of Anatomy. I was commissioned to wait on Dr. Davidge, whom, after some conversation on the subject, I found *very prompt* in consulting the wishes of the Faculty and the solid interests of the institution. He resigned the chair of Surgery, and Mr. Pattison was elected to it. At the meeting at Professor M'Dowell's, when I first named Mr. Pattison, much despondency was expressed in regard to the debts of the institution, the dilapidated state of the buildings, the necessity of a new building, &c.—and it was fully admitted that the Faculty had no means. I at once offered to provide 5 or $8,000, as it might be wanted,— to examine and audit all the debts of the institution, and to attend to the buildings, repairs, &c. This proposition was received with every mark of thanks, and it was immediately stated, verbally, that I should not encounter any risk, as the new scheme of a lottery, then on the tapis, should be *pledged* to me for my indemnification.* At that time I was too full of zeal for the University, to heed this promise much,

---

* This promise, however, was forgotten as soon as it was made, and the whole lottery was applied to their own purposes.

16

or to see its necessity. I was immediately deputed to visit Philadelphia, see Mr. Pattison, explain matters, and communicate to him his unanimous appointment. This charge I accepted, and a few hours after I was informed that some of the members thought it would be still more complimentary and suitable that Professor De Butts should accompany me, to which proposition I very readily assented. We returned from Philadelphia with an acceptance of the appointment by Mr. Pattison, and I immediately proceeded to employ workmen, and, together with Dr. Howard, was engaged a considerable time, and sometimes till late at night, in making draughts and plans for the contemplated buildings and repairs. For more than a year I attended almost daily at the institution, to see the buildings, repairs, furniture and ornaments finished and displayed to advantage. During this period all the accounts, amounting to several hundred, passed through my hands. All the workmen called at my office, and also creditors of the University, so that my time, during that period, was much more occupied with University matters, than with my own professional duties.

But it has been said that I did not loan the money, but that it was procured on the joint names of myself and the Faculty. This I utterly deny, and state without fear of contradiction, that the money was loaned by me, on my own sole responsibility:—that the Bank loaned me the money, and to no one else, and never would have loaned the Faculty one dollar. I further assert, that the Banks expressly declined permitting the names of the Faculty to be on the note, and did not yield to my request until I urged it on them for my own *security*, not that of the Bank, and even then it was on an express written stipulation required of me, that the $5,000 first obtained should be loaned *to me only*, and the Bank should not be considered as looking to any one but myself. Should a copy of this agreement be requested by your Faculty, it shall be produced. I met with the same requisition from the Mechanicks' Bank: a *certificate* to this effect can also be obtain. I extremely regret the necessity I am under of mentioning these matters, and I never should have done so had I not been urged thereto by verbal, written, and even *printed* declarations that I had never rendered the Faculty any *service*, though my *zeal* was acknowledged to be commendable.

After this I was greatly instrumental in procuring the $30,000 from the Legislature. I decline explaining the whole of this matter; but I do aver that I was much more

17

instrumental in procuring this money than has ever been known, and much more so, even *openly*, than your Body have been willing to admit. In auditing the accounts under the law which granted the $30,000 loan, I spent much time, and my zeal and services never abated, even though I was constantly informed that the Faculty, individually and collectively, affected to disregard them. I perceived that I was no longer invited to attend your Faculty meetings: several of your members passed me with evident coldness; and now that prosperity had not only dawned on you, but seemed near attaining its *noon*, you neither required my future aid, nor recognized my past services; and all this appeared to grow out of your unwillingness to part with power, or to have a *University*. Matters remained in this situation for some time, and until a few months since, when a *golden* opportunity presented itself for realizing all and even more than your lottery privileges had, in remote prospect, ever promised you. This was a delicate matter. Here I was again consulted: we had many meetings, and the final contract between Messrs. Yates and M'Intyre and the Regents was drawn up by me. I could easily, at that time, have stipulated with you for an appropriation of 10 or $15,000 of these monies for the use of the Faculty of Law; but I was too unsuspicious, and had I even been *certain* of what has since occurred, I would have spurned the idea of encumbering my services with any conditions in favour of myself.

I have nothing more, gentlemen, to add, except that I could very easily remind you of much more that I have done in promotion of your views and interests. My simple and old fashioned notions of things compel me to believe that these were *services*, and not merely *unproductive zeal*. I regret that you think differently. I have only to mention that I have said all I ever mean to say to you on this unpleasant subject. I felt it a duty to myself to speak thus plainly and *of myself*, and although I have been most ungenerously treated by you, I am disposed never to think of these matters more. On the contrary, should occasion require my aid, I shall at all times most cheerfully lend it, not only for the promotion of the *general* views of the institution, but of those of the Medical Faculty, and any of its members.

I am, Gentlemen,
Very respectfully,
Your obedient servant,
DAVID HOFFMAN.

18

No. 2.

Memorial of the Faculty of Law to the Regents of the University of Maryland, in October, 1825.

To the Regents of the University of Maryland.

The Faculty of Law of said University beg leave respectfully to represent—

That many years ago application was made to the Legislature of this state for the incorporation of a Body by the name of the "*University of Maryland,*" and its aid was solicited then, and several times since, in the raising of funds to be applied to an institution of *that character.* The Legislature, moved, it is to be presumed, by a desire to foster a *State University,* has accordingly granted its *name* and *aid* for that purpose, and large funds have been collected by these facilities, but applied *exclusively* to the purposes of *one* department of the University. Buildings of a very costly description have been erected, and adapted *altogether* for the accommodation of a Medical School; or, at most, for the teaching of branches auxiliary to that class of science; and large expenditures have been made in the purchase of a splendid apparatus, and various other furniture essential, or convenient to the Medical department. The *Faculty of Law* cannot but feel a lively pleasure in the successful organization of a department of the University so important as the Medical, the more particularly so, as the successful teaching of any great branch of learning cannot fail to operate usefully on all others, and such is the *commune vinculum,* which associates all human knowledge, that, perhaps, a thorough acquaintance with any profession can scarce be attained without some skill in most, if not all of the sciences. This interest which animates the *Faculty of Law,* cannot but be felt in a livelier degree by their *Professor of Law,* as it is well known that a very large portion of his time, labour, and zeal, together with many pecuniary responsibilities and facilities were furnished by him, and which have been the means of rescuing the institution, if not from utter ruin, at least from very great and perilous difficulties. The *Medical* department being now fully established, and the object of the Legislature, and of the Regents of the University, being now obtained, in a degree *quite commensurate,* it is respectfully presumed, with the *relative* importance of that department to *others* comprehended within the scheme of the University, it is suggested by the Faculty of Law to the Regents of

19

the University to apply some part of the funds which have been, and will be raised with the sanction of the Legislature, to the full establishment and effectual support of the chair of Law, it being at this time the only one which has made considerable progress in the fulfilment of its objects, and this too, exclusively through individual exertions, and great professional and other sacrifices.

There are two considerations which will suggest themselves to the Regents of the University, in determining the propriety of this application. The *first* is the *intent* or *motive* of the Legislature in granting the pecuniary facilities required, and obtained of it. The *second* is the *intrinsick importance* of the Law chair, as a member of a *State University;* and *both* of these would seem to require the prompt and grave attention of your Body; which has been constituted, as well to carry faithfully into effect the objects of the Legislature, as to consult the interests of the institution over which you preside, and to see that it is in *reality* as well as in *name*, a *University*, and not a school to promote the interests, exclusively, of *one Faculty*, however important that Faculty may be; but more especially to see that the *whole* of the funds of what ought to be a great and flourishing institution of *general science*, shall not be lavished in securing to *one department*, not only every essential, but also every elegant embellishment which could possibly be expected in one of the most wealthy, and best endowed Universities.

It cannot be doubted that the Legislature of our state, lending its aid to the institution in question, has acted under the impression that it was fostering a State *University*, and has, therefore, granted the pecuniary facilities, under the faith that they would be applied to *that* object, with becoming impartiality; having, it is admitted, a due regard for the *relative importance* of the various branches of knowledge, and also for the sacrifices of time, labour, expense, &c. essential to each. The very *title* and *language* of the various acts passed for the benefit of the "University of Maryland," its *charter*, and numerous other circumstances, leave no doubt on this point. It is also well known that many of the arguments and representations which were addressed to the Legislature, in order to engage its patronage and aid, proceeded on the ground of the importance to the state of a *University;* and most, if not all of the legislative enactments, have been aided and advanced by the exertions, professional and private, of the Professor of Law. It were, therefore, at least a perversion of the intent of the Legisla-

4

20

ture, if not a breach of the confidence reposed in the Regents of this institution, to devote to the particular advancement and edification of *one* of its Faculties, funds which were *intended* for the organization (perhaps *humbly*) of a *University*, comprehending *all* the branches of general and scientific education. While it is allowed, however, that it is within the scope of the authority of the Regents to exercise their *discretion* in applying the funds, according, either to the *relative* importance of the various chairs, or to the *progress* of their different occupants in accomplishing the duties of the same; and while the *Faculty of Law* is fully aware that a preference was due to the Medical Professors, perhaps on both grounds; it is manifest, on the other hand, that the state has a right to expect from the Regents, some steps towards building up the *other* Faculties, and offering such inducements to all of the Professors as will engage them in originating and executing a plan of general instruction. This, at all events, is strongly manifest in regard to the chair of *Law*, whose Professor is now engaged in the delivery of an extensive course of lectures. This enterprise, the Faculty of Law respectfully urges, *ought* not to be permitted for a moment to languish; but without considerable pecuniary aid, it must, not only *languish*, but be wholly *abandoned*, as this Faculty well know that nothing but the heaviest sacrifices, inevitable to such an undertaking, could diminish the zeal of the Professor, and that, after all which can ever be done by your Body to sustain the chair of Law, his sacrifices will ultimately remain *sufficiently heavy*. As regards the relative importance of this chair, it is hardly necessary to say much. It is a subject which, no doubt, the Legislature contemplated with a most favourable eye, and which, in a country of *free* institutions, whose only government is the *law*, is of much greater importance than in those whose institutions are less liberal. Yet even in these countries the *law* is taught from the chairs of *Universities;* and, indeed, forms a very *prominent* part of their course of instruction. A very large portion of the well educated youth of *this country* are bred to the *bar;* and whether we consider them as ministering in the temples of *justice*, or fulfilling a still higher duty, in *framing* the laws of their country, the importance of a liberal scheme of Law education for so large and important a class of the people, is too manifest to be insisted on. Nor will it be contended that the present method of inducting law students into the learning of that science is the best, and needs no change; or, in the present

21

voluminous state of legal learning, great *method*, judicious *condensation*, and other nameless advantages of instruction by lectures, are less essential to them than to other students. Nor is it entirely unworthy of consideration, that the establishment of a permanent course of Law Lectures would cause some of the youths, of the better sort, to resort to *this city*, who, whilst they would greatly stimulate each other in their common pursuit, would form durable attachments to our city, settle among us, and, in time, add greatly to the stock of our *learning, intelligence,* and *usefulness.*

The *Faculty of Law* would for a moment claim the attention of the Regents more particularly to the views of the Law chair. The Professor, it is well known, has been for some time engaged in preparing an extensive course of legal instruction, and is now putting into efficient execution, various *auxiliary* means for the more speedy and certain acquisition of solid legal learning. The scheme of lectures, its *extent*, and the *variety*, must be attended by great labour, and we trust will prove eminently serviceable to the progress of legal science, and ultimately advantageous to the views and interests of this University. But it must be a question of some magnitude to the Professor himself, whether he can bestow the requisite time and labour, with no *other* requital than the prospect of *distant* remuneration; when his more proper professional business offers him the strongest *present* compensation, which must inevitably, be in some degree impaired, by the labour and time which are necessary for the accomplishment of the other. These considerations, the *Faculty of Law* are of opinion, place their Professor's claims to some distinct aid from this University, in a very *strong point of view;* his enterprise is an *experiment;* its success must, for some time, remain problematical; his present sacrifices must be considerable; his success is an object of great interest, we would hope, not only to this University, but to the legal profession generally; and it is with the Regents of this University to relieve the Professor from this dilemma, and ensure his success, by according to him that temporary support which his enterprise demands, and which an honest ambition, and a hope to be useful, render him reluctant to abandon.

From the first establishment of the University, and even prior to that period, the Professor, it is well known, has never ceased to manifest the liveliest interests in the promotion of the views of the Medical department; and, after the annexation to it of the *other* Faculties, it has been his earnest wish

22

to see the University organized, and efficiently in operation. With this view, both his *private* and *professional* aid have been liberally bestowed, and this too, at times when his prospect of deriving from it either reputation or emolument, appeared to be extremely remote; and, indeed, almost *impossible;* and, now that the Medical branch is not only firmly established, but in the possession of *all* that the present means of the University *ought* to allow, consistently with its justice to *other* chairs, the *Faculty of Law* conceives that the *next* object of the Regents' attention should be the *complete* establishment of the chair of Law. Its Professor, having seen that the University has lived through many difficulties, and is now, from its ample funds, likely to attain the objects of its establishment, is naturally desirous to share in its *prosperity*, as he has in its *adversity*. The Faculty of Law beg leave to refer the Regents to the correspondence hereunto annexed, and to the *resolutions* now offered for the purpose of ascertaining the exact condition of the pecuniary means of the University: from the whole of which, the Faculty respectfully submit to the Regents the following resolution.

RESOLUTION.

"Resolved by the Regents of the University of Maryland, that the Treasurer of said Regents do pay to the order of the Dean of the Faculty of Law, the sum of $5,000, on or before the first day of June, 1826, and the further sum of $150, out of each quarterly instalment of $2,500, which is payable by Messrs. Yates and M'Intyre, under their contract for drawing lotteries for the benefit of the University of Maryland; the said monies, when received, to be applied by the Faculty of Law for the support of the Chair of Law, now in operation in this institution."

☞ Note. The object of this memorial was suspended by the State's Lottery Commissioners having applied to the Governor to prevent the further drawing of University Lotteries, and represented to the Legislature in January, 1826, that the University privilege had been exhausted.

This induced the Professor of Law to visit Annapolis, and to explain to the Legislature the mistake of the Commissioners, which finally resulted in the law which con-

23

ferred on the University the privilege of proceeding with their lotteries, to the extent of about $60,000 more, $14,200 of which were appropriated by said act to the chair of Law, and since which time about $15,200 *net* have been raised.

No. 3.

Letter to the Executive Committee of the Trustees of the University of Maryland, 12th July, 1826.

Baltimore, July 12*th,* 1826.

GENTLEMEN,

Permit me to call your attention to the act of the Legislature, passed at its last session, appropriating $14,200 to the Chair of Law, under the direction of the Trustees. The object of my application to the Legislature, was to procure such a portion of the proceeds of the Lotteries, contracted for by Messrs. Yates & M'Intyre, with the University, as would put me on a footing with the other Professors, from October, 1822, when I commenced my public course.

For the history of my connection with the University, since 1814, my services to that Institution, and the many sacrifices I have made on its behalf, I refer you to sundry papers now in the possession of William Frick, Esq., one of your members, and late dean of the Faculty of Law. I also refer you to the report made to the Senate at the last session.

Enclosed, I present a statement of my actual disbursements in establishing the Law Chair, since October, 1822. This statement, though apparently large, falls short of a complete indemnity to me. The outfit for an establishment attractive to students of Law, and the four years since its establishment, will account for the amount I now claim. There are now in the hands of Messrs. Yates & M'Intyre, about $5000, subject to the order of the Trustees. The Lotteries are proceeding on, and the contract with Yates & M'Intyre, is in the hands of Professor De Butts, who will deliver it to your order.

An order from your Committee on Mr. Samuel Scribner, the agent of Messrs. Yates & M'Intyre, in my favour, will be duly honoured.

I am, Gentlemen,
Your most obedient,

To the Executive Committee of the
Trustees of the University of Maryland.

24

No. 4.

Letter addressed by D. Hoffman to the Trustees, September 27th, 1826.

Baltimore, Sept. 27th, 1826.

GENTLEMEN,

Believing that the Trustees cannot place much value on the mere circumstance of handsomely improving the University lot, and concentrating, *in one place*, every accommodation, if those accommodations should be of no real utility to those for whom they are destined, and *knowing* from experience, and mature reflection, that none of the objects of the Chair of Law could possibly succeed, even partially, if I should be restricted to that place, I do not at all despair of convincing the Trustees, that my fixation at the University lot, with the best possible accommodations, would wholly destroy my usefulness, and terminate in a complete failure of plans which I have digested with great care and mature deliberation.

Lectures may be of two kinds—first, Elementary, or what are called popular lectures; and secondly, those which to the *Institutes,* add most of the learning and practical details of the science. It will be found that in all countries the former have failed, (even though sustained by considerable endowments, and by much talent, and eloquence,) whilst the latter have succeeded. The lectures of Blackstone, Woodeson, Sullivan, McIntosh, and Noland, in England; of Wilson, Hare, Cooper, Kent, &c., in this country, endured but a short time; and though the English courses were liberally endowed and sustained by great names, yet they eventually failed, *for want of auditors*, and no one has thought of reviving them. The simple reason of this is, that the Institutes of the Law were only taught, and these were accompanied *by no other facilities.* Students did not find sufficient motives to continue coming from a distance, and both McIntosh and Noland abandoned their enterprise after a few lectures. Students require minute and continued instruction, in the science and practice, otherwise they gradually fall off, and the Professor lectures to empty benches; if this were the case in the times of those distinguished Professors, it is now emphatically more so. The rudiments of the science are now so satisfactorily written on, that mere *lectures* will not suffice, and particularly elementary lectures. On the other hand, the *Inns of Court,* and of *Chancery,* were of a practical nature; they endured for centuries, because young men

25

were brought together permanently under one roof; they were exercised in various solid legal pursuits; they attended lectures and readings, examinations, mootings, &c., and were carried much beyond the rudiments of the science. In this country also, all elementary lectures have been short-lived, and the school of Litchfield has endured for twenty years, merely because the lectures are learned, and the young men are associated in various exercises throughout the year, in a manner similar, but not so extensive and complete as the system I have organized and commenced. Being myself fully persuaded of this fact, I set out with the determination of avoiding the rock on which so many have been wrecked. I have endeavoured to combine in one scheme, all the advantages of the *Inns of Court*, and *Chancery*, and with that view, I opened an establishment on a plan much more attractive than any that has been attempted elsewhere. This was done under the auspices of the Regents, and by the advice of the late General Winder, who was then a Regent. He frequently stated to me his decided opinion, that no other plan could succeed, and that no course of lectures, merely, would ever be permanent, or at all compensate the Professor for his labour and expense. Of the same opinion is Chancellor Kent, who abandoned his attempt for the second time; after having lectured the first time for a very short period, and the second time, wholly abandoned it after the second winter. With his vast reputation, he nevertheless lectured the second winter, to a very small class; and not being willing to model his plan according to his own convictions of what would ensure its success, he gave up his lectures entirely; not less than twenty of the most distinguished lawyers of this country, have expressed to me their conviction that my plan must succeed, and have encouraged me to proceed on with it. Their encouragement has been consoling to me, for I have found but little to stimulate me, in my native state; and all my plans appear to be better known, and excite more interest elsewhere, than in Maryland, and particularly in Baltimore. The only question then appears to me to be, am I to proceed on a well digested, extensive, and laudable plan, which promises well; or am I merely to lecture at the University for a time, and then wholly to fail? Should I lecture there, much time will be daily consumed, (summer and winter,) both by myself and students, in going to and fro, perhaps twice a day. Students, instead of walking from one room to another, will have to relinquish their studies for an hour, to attend a lecture, a quarter of a mile off; my lectures often require me to

26

cite, perhaps, a dozen volumes, and to read from them, and comment; how am I daily to convey my books from my Library to the University? But it is said the Trustees, perhaps, will purchase my Library, and fix it in the University. How then am I to write my lectures, and keep pace with the growth of the science, unless I purchase for myself another library, or settle permanently at the University, day and night. If so, what is to be my compensation? Where is the liberal endowment, or any endowment, to compensate me, or even to secure me from actual loss? All this inconvenience is wholly avoided by the plan I suggest, without the least disadvantage to the University; one plan promises well, the other must end in a ruinous failure. Again, lecturing on Law, in this country, is yet in its infancy; those who have read my plans, have entirely approved of them; I do not doubt their ultimate success. The other, would not only fill me with distrust, but I should commence with the perfect conviction of its ending in the manner I have stated. But even with my own plan, and the best success I could reasonably hope for, it would be a profitless business compared with an exclusive devotion to my professional duties; but I have never so much valued money, as to be unwilling to submit to sacrifices; I expect them, and have already encountered them, and should continue so to do were all my plans matured, and the whole of them under the zealous patronage of the University. How great then must be the injustice that would ask of me a devotion of my time, health, profession, prospects, house, library, furniture, fuel, lights, stationary, &c., as a Professor of the University, for nearly four years, at my *own expense*, and this too, without an immediate certainty, that even the future will promise any thing better? It has been intimated, that all *must now be prospective*, the past was on my private account. This is certainly not the case, I never did any thing, but as a Professor; every lecture I delivered, since October, 1822, was in that character, and no other: and that character was conferred on me by a fully competent authority. All that I now ask, is to be placed on a footing with the other Professors; and on such a foundation, as is the only feasible one to promise success. The Medical Professors, and myself, have raised the institution from nothing, to its present condition. There was a time when it attracted no notice; scarcely any one could be found to regard it in any other light, than as a wild scheme. I started the opposition to the Pennsylvania institution; the whole institution was for several years on my shoulders, and by my exertions, (timely introduced,) and the real talents of several of the Medical Professors; the students at once increased from 60 to upwards of 300. These Professors have had every thing provided for them they could desire—suitable rooms for lectures, museum, library, reading-rooms for students, ample and rich furniture, fuel, lights, a janitor, apparatus, anatomical preparations, infirmary, &c., all to suit the views of the several Medical Professors. They have received for four months' lecturing, from 3 to $5000 per annum, and every expense, for a series of years previous, were refunded to them. Their payment of interest, on the $30,000 loan, is a very nominal matter; it is not out of *their private purse*, as could be most clearly demonstrated, and as I have proved in my letter to the Faculty of Medicine, which, I presume, very few of the present Trustees have seen. I have lectured daily for *six months*, sometimes twice a day—have found every thing—my total receipts, in four years, have only been $3050, and my disbursements, during that time, more than equal to that sum, as I was obliged to establish myself. If my Professorship is to date only from the 1st of June last, or rather the 10th of July last, and the Trustees do not recognize me as such from my original appointment, in 1814, I certainly have no claim, but from July. But I cannot suppose that the letter I sent to the Trustees, in compliance with their requisition, (and which, by some is called *an adhesion*,) is based on the idea that I had been previously *dismissed*, and then re-appointed, or that the Trustees recognize no one who had been appointed by the previously existing authorities. I am very sure this cannot be the idea of the Trustees, though I confess I have been quite at a loss to comprehend the necessity of the note I received from them, or the necessity for any adhesion on my part. I found the Trustees in power, by the law of the land, and that was sufficient for me. I take it for granted, that I continued then a Professor of the University from 1814 to the present day. Some time in 1821, I was requested by the Regents to make a report, as to when I should commence my public lectures—this report was rendered, I think, in October, 1821, as will be found amongst the papers of the Law Faculty, now in the possession of William Frick, Esq., late Dean of that Faculty.

In October, 1822, I commenced my public course; but the institution then had no means; this did not diminish my zeal. I had toiled for many years, and had implicated myself for large sums to sustain the Medical department, and

28

therefore did not hesitate to assist myself, in an enterprize which (perhaps erroneously,) I considered of similar importance; I never for a moment supposed that I should not be ultimately indemnified, and even if the amount I have stated be now paid, I cannot even be indemnified, but am still a considerable loser. In this, however, the University has no concern; but in the other, it does appear to me, that every principle of justice and necessity, urges that this amount should be settled. All of these matters were fully stated at Annapolis, to nearly every member of either house with whom I conversed; my past expenses were most explicitly stated, they considered it a *merit*, and that my claim was far from being *unreasonable*. The very calculation which educed $14,200 as the sum to be appropriated to my chair, was based on the *concessum* that I was to be at once put upon an equality, from the *time I commenced lecturing*, with the Medical Professors; an estimate was made (though a very rude one,) of all past expenses of the University, and one-seventh was to be added, and appropriated to my chair; it was very explicitly stated, that no accommodation whatever, on the University lot, would in any degree advance the objects of the Law chair; and my correspondence with the Medical Faculty, was in Annapolis, more than a month. Hence it was, that the word *"purchase,"* was inserted in the Law. I would also mention, that the first phraseology of the proposed law was, that the appropriation should be under the direction of the Professors; but my sense of propriety induced me to write expressly on this subject, and state, that this ought not to be the case, and that I had perfect confidence, that the Trustees would do me ample justice, and fully indemnify me; that the Law designed what I have just stated, is beyond a doubt; and as it is no more than ordinary justice, I trust, that should there be any difficulty, the Trustees will unite in procuring a Law, at the next session, to place the Chair of Law on the footing I have stated, from October, 1822. The house and accommodations I now have, are, I think, very complete, and quite as good and substantial, and much cheaper, than could be provided by building. And as the University cannot afford endowments, and if it could, I think, ought not, (provided that all other requisites are supplied,) I cannot suppose there will be any serious determination so to appropriate the funds destined for the Law department, as to break it up at once, and render it, I sincerely believe, quite impossible ever to revive it. The Trustees will also bear in mind, that any one who embarks

29

in such an enterprize, when there are new law schools starting up in nearly every state in the union, must not calculate on much success, and must submit to great sacrifices in professional business. I presume, therefore, that the Trustees would not willingly exact from me, those things which would render the evil most certain, and my success much less probable. Should I be obliged to rely mainly on my Professorship, my determination would, of course, be at once fixed; I should be compelled, from necessity, to resign the chair, and dedicate myself wholly to the practice of my profession; but I reasonable supposed that the Trustees would at once perceive, that the Professorship must for ever be a small compensation, in a pecuniary point of view, to one who has ever maintained a large and lucrative practice. I have desired to discharge my duties, zealously, as a Professor, and upon a liberal scale, worthy a University; and without too much self praise, I think I have made such a commencement as deserves success. My course, when finished, will be nearly as extensive as the combined courses of the Medical Professors; I spare no pains, and have submitted to immense sacrifices, but if plans thus matured are to be abandoned, and lecturing only relied on, I am well satisfied, that no talents and industry could sustain the chair, even if endowed to a very liberal extent. Medical lectures, call upon the young men throughout the union, because inducements are offered which private studies cannot procure; hence, I have added to my lectures those inducements, which private studies cannot attain, and these additions form nearly the only attraction which can render a Chair of Law in any degree successful. I now ask of the Trustees (considering me as Professor in this light from 1822,) to pay my rent, fuel, furniture, and other unavoidable disbursements, out of a fund which was designed, in part, for that very purpose, and to permanently promote the necessary objects of the chair—out of a fund procured, in a great degree, by my *personal* exertions—a fund dedicated to the purpose of giving to that chair all the facilities requisite for its success. Some complaint has been intimated to me, that I have presented the claim in the light of a *debt*, I have since reflected upon the mode in which I have presented it, and truly say I am at a loss to conceive the force of the objection; surely the Trustees would not have me present, as a claim on their bounty—it is a debt of justice, because incurred as a Professor in an institution, towards which I have fully discharged my duties for five years, and in the only manner in which it was practicable to discharge them at all. I have charged nothing but what was essential, and by no means, every thing that was essential; but it is intimated that I now have a complete establishment, and can go on, and perhaps my furniture, &c. may hereafter be purchased. What, however, is to sustain me in the mean time? Am I to lecture for four years past, and perhaps two years to come, at my own expense? Am I to pay the University, or the University to pay me? This, in truth, is the fair question to such a suggestion. If I am now, and have been a Professor, why should I sustain any of my necessary expenses? I cannot suppose the Trustees mean this; but I have it intimated to me, that if I am at once supported to the full extent of the law, several other Professorships may be delayed, as there will not be soon money sufficient to give them all accommodations; the law, however, is explicit, and has appropriated, out of the *next proceeds*, every cent that may be raised, to the extent of $14,200, to the Chair of Law. The whole of that sum will, perhaps, permanently accomplish the object, and if, by adding the $2000 granted to the Faculty of Arts, it will not interfere with the $14,200 granted to the Chair of Law, but promote them all exactly to the extent designed by the law, for each. It would then be unreasonable in me to object; but on the other hand, if I am to be delayed, and injured, both as to the past and the future, in order to accommodate other chairs, I then contend that this would be contrary to the spirit and letter of the law; $2000 for the Faculty of Arts, cannot be applied in any way until the whole $14,200 be in hand, for the Chair of Law, also, the further sum of $3800 for the Infirmary, and the $6500 for the chemical apparatus; the Faculty of Arts is the last mentioned object, and even these $2000 are specially designated, not for buildings, but for the "purchase" of an "*apparatus.*" It would be upwards of two years from this time, before the three first mentioned sums could be in hand, and to hasten these chairs to my prejudice, is contrary to the express provisions of the law.

Medicine and law, raised the University from nothing; it is therefore reasonable that they should be first fully established, to the extent mentioned in the law. It has also been intimated, that the Faculty of Arts would not succeed so well, if established at the University—I think so; for past experience has pretty well ascertained, that any lectures out of the regular medical course, cannot succeed at the University; and it has ever been a matter of regret, that even the buildings for medical purposes, is so far out of the way. It

31

has been intimated that, therefore, a building erected in some healthy, but central part of the city, might be put up, so as to accommodate me with as many rooms as I have at present, and at the same time, give the other contemplated loctures an accommodation. This would be wholly free from objection, if I could see money in hand sufficient to accomplish all, or myself sustained in the mean time. But the Trustees will, of course, bear in mind,

1st. That the $2000 for the arts, is merely for the *apparatus*.

2d. That such a *building* alone, could not cost less than $16,200, even if the $2000 could be so applied.

3d. That the law designed fully to sustain the Law Chair, past and to come, with a "*building*," "*library*," and "accommodations," most of which would be defeated, or very long delayed by the plan of a building to accommodate all.

Is then the ultimate views of the Trustees, (however laudable in regard to lectures that may come hereafter,) be such as will unavoidably break up the Chair of Law, and render the establishment of any other Chair of Law a very remote possibility, I trust that the Trustees will not hesitate as to the course they will pursue. It may be well to mention, that when the contract with Yates and M'Intyre was made, nearly the whole of it was dependant on my exertions. I devoted much time to it, and the peculiar circumstances under which the University Lottery schemes then stood, that a word from me of an unfavourable character would have terminated the negotiation. I was then much urged by my friends to stipulate for $30,000 to be applied by the Regents to the Chair of Law, one third of it out of the first proceeds; but I at once refused so to do, stating, that as I was acting with the Medical men, I never would render my services clogged with conditions and stipulations in my own favour. So also when the $30,000 loan was obtained from the state, the University had me implicated, I may say solely and personally, nearly $10,000. This I should have been obliged to provide for *punctually*, had not that fortunate negotiation taken place. I was at that time urged to stipulate for a provision of $5,000 to my Chair; but this also I refused to do, for the same reasons, and I proceeded to use considerable exertions to further that loan, and have since seen every cent of the balance devoted to Medical purposes. The Infirmary, (not then thought of,) rose before my view without a murmur. Every Professor brought in some bill, and these were paid. Professor Pattison subsequently, out of the early proceeds of the contract with Yates and M'Intyre, received $8,000 for his museum. I still was silent. Finding, therefore, that there was not the least *delicacy towards me* on the part of the Medical Gentlemen, and that the Regents promised a good deal, and did nothing for my Chair, I was induced last winter to visit Annapolis, having written many letters against the proposed new Medical School. I there found that both Houses entertained the opinion of the Lottery Commissioners, that the University could draw no more lotteries, as a very clear one; and I found no one who thought differently. I spoke to nearly every member—met several in their rooms—went through the laws with them—and finally convinced them. I was then advised by some of them, to have my views printed. This I did, in a small pamphlet, and in the course of ten days had the satisfaction to find that the law passed with but little opposition. As to the appropriation law, I also could have provided more amply for myself, and it is quite probable it would have passed, as several of the Legislature expressly stated to me, that they should be pleased to see $50,000 appropriated to the Chair of Law, and thought I ought not to hesitate at a future period to press a further aid, so as to procure a library much larger than my own, and every possible means of facilitating my scheme. I believe the $14,200 will nearly accomplish the following—

1st. Secure all the furniture, &c. and indemnify me for every other expenditure from October, 1822.

2d. Purchase the house I now occupy, which is more complete for my purposes than any that could be built for, perhaps, double the amount.

3d. Purchase nearly the whole of my library, which I find consists of about 1600 volumes on law, and one or two subjects immediately connected with the law. ✻ In regard to my library, I confess I have no solicitude to part with it, unless under certain circumstances. I have been nearly 18 years collecting it, with great care, and believe it to be one of the most select law libraries, (though perhaps not the most extensive,) in the country. The reason why I might hesitate to part with my library is in candour this. The late alteration of the charter confers on the Trustees, the unexampled and tremendous power of dismissing Professors *at pleasure;* and though I have the greatest confidence in the Body, as it now exists, yet we all know what may be effected in time. The Body may undergo a total change, even in a short time; strange views may be inculcated by some, and induce others to resign, and various other causes may produce such a change, not only in men, but in opinions, that there may be no safety for permanency of plans, however much approved of at the present time. My library, if once sold at less than its cost, might be wholly taken from me, unless I should accompany it to the University. My nights would thus become useless to me as a time for study, and indeed many other things might be done, which, in self defence, would compel me to purchase another library, and resign my Professorship. I have heard it already very confidently asserted, that new Chairs of Law are to be created; and although I feel no apprehension whatever on this subject, yet times and changes of men, and the mania for new Chairs, might urge some other Body of Trustees to listen to, and finally adopt, propositions which at this time appear absurd; so that there might be as many Professors as there are titles in my entire course. I have felt it my duty to myself to speak thus candidly, without intending the slightest want of confidence, or aught but the greatest and most unfeigned respect for the Trustees. I have honestly stated my grounds of slight apprehension, that no Professor can feel safe whilst the tenure of his trust is dependent on the mere will of any set of men. My only object then in stating my views so plainly, which I fear will be misunderstood, is to manifest to the Trustees how difficult I find it to throw my whole mind and heart perseveringly in plans for the present and future, which may possibly, (if there be no guarantee,) be broken up by those who come into power at some future period. Justice, therefore, to myself, zeal for the interests of the University, (and no want of confidence in the Trustees, to whom I now address myself,) induces me respectfully to suggest the following propositions.

 1st. To appoint a committee of examination to investigate all my necessary and proper expenditures, from October, 1822, to the present time; to indemnify me for the same, and to receive a catalogue of all furniture, &c. included in the same.

 2d. If this be refused, then to countenance an application to the Legislature for the purpose of giving an express construction to the law, so as to place me from October, 1822, on a footing with the Medical Professors, and thus to remove any doubts, if they exist.

 3d. If the first be admitted, then that the Trustees examine for themselves the building, &c. and become fully acquainted with all the plans I have suggested, either publicly

34

or privately, in regard to the object of my Chair and the means of carrying them into effect.

4th. If this be done, then to purchase the same, if they approve of them.

5th. To ascertain the value of the library, and purchase it considerably below its value, with the understanding that it remains in the house in which I lecture, whilst my Professorship endures, to be used by no one out of the *University*.

6th. That if the building I now occupy be not entirely approved of, and another, with like accommodations and in a central situation, be determined on, that my present rent be paid till the new house is ready.

7th. Should none of these propositions be approved of, then that I be permitted to retire from lecturing for four years, so that I may in the mean time have an opportunity to devote myself to other employments—the $14,200 being in the mean time held sacred to the purpose designed by the law; by which time the situation of the entire funds of the institution will be developed, and allowing me, at the same time permission to represent the situation of the Law Chair to the Legislature, without the active concurrence of the Trustees.

I have now stated very fully and without reserve my views. I hope I have done so as to inspire confidence in the Trustees, as to my zeal and the general correctness of my opinions, and not in any manner as to give the slightest outrage, which is the furthest from my thoughts. My attachment to the state and city of my birth would keep me here, though my views are not as kindly received here as elsewhere;—many flattering persuasions have been used by some kind friends to induce me to settle in New York, and by others in Philadelphia, and I have also had a proposition by a western University, which would secure to me for four months lecturing more than two-thirds of the sum I have received in three years in Baltimore. I mention these things merely to impress the Trustees with my conviction as to the soundness of my plans, and that they will ultimately succeed, particularly if zealously sustained by the University. My professional business brought me, from 1818 to 1823, on an average, $9,000 *per annum;* whereas since my public course it has diminished more than *two-thirds;* and though all business has declined, yet I have not the least doubt I have suffered a loss quite equal to $3,000 a year. My business was growing to an immense size, just at the time I commenced my lectures, &c. and though I have used every exertion in

35

my power to counteract the injurious impression, yet it will remain. I merely mention this, also, as another evidence of my zeal on behalf of the University, and that my lectures can never compensate me, even should the University sustain me to the fullest extent that could be required. I embarked in this enterprise willingly, consenting to a considerable sacrifice, but confident at the same time that the University would bear all my necessary expenses. If, however, the plan of establishing the lectures at the University cannot be changed, if I am to be regarded as a Professor only, from June last, and my past exertions must be placed to my own account, I can see no alternative, but I must at once abandon all of my plans which I have as a member of the institution so industriously cultivated, and return to those duties of the bar which for some years past I have in a degree parted from.

     I am, Gentlemen,
      With great respect,
       Your obedient servant,

*To the Trustees
of the University.*

☞ The foregoing papers will fully explain the present situation of the Law Chair. I trust that, as the institution is now amply in funds, a meeting of the Trustees will soon take place, and that the Trustees will inspect the building I now occupy, its furniture and library, and all the facilities offered to students for the acquisition of legal knowledge. Of twenty-two annual students there now remain only ten, and six have declined to enter, as I am obliged to suspend all the facilities heretofore offered, and for the present to close the institution. Those who remain have expressed a desire to continue until it be finally decided that the Law Chair is to proceed as usual, or to be wholly abandoned by me.

I have flattered myself that the difficulty which has occurred has been owing to two circumstances—*first*, the want of full information on the subject, on the part of the Trustees, and *secondly*, a mistake which occurred as to the actual amount due by Yates and M'Intyre on their contract. The

36

object of the present communication is to correct the first, and the second has been corrected by the actual payment by Yates and M'Intyre of more than sufficient to enable the Trustees fully to accomplish the act of 1826.

☞ It need scarce be mentioned, that the foregoing is intended exclusively for the eye of the Trustees.

A Lecture

Being the Ninth of a Series of Lectures, Introductory to a Course of Lectures Now Delivering in the University of Maryland, 1832

A

LECTURE,

BEING THE NINTH OF A

Series of Lectures,

INTRODUCTORY TO A

COURSE OF LECTURES

NOW DELIVERING IN

THE UNIVERSITY OF MARYLAND.

BY DAVID HOFFMAN,
Iur. Utr. Doct. Göttingen.

Baltimore.
PRINTED BY J. D. TOY,
Corner of St. Paul and Market streets.
June, 1832.

NINTH

INTRODUCTORY LECTURE.

THE Prelections delivered by me from this chair, have uniformly been designed to unfold some of the pervading principles, leading characteristics, and prominent utilities of the cardinal division of the scheme of lectures set forth in the syllabus presented to the Regents of this Institution, when I was first honoured with the duties of the professorship

The subject to which I now respectfully ask the indulgent attention of my auditory is, a summary view of the great advantage that students of law, and even the jurists of our country, may derive from a careful study of the *Roman Civil Law*, and the various systems of continental jurisprudence which have been based on it.

Rome, once the mistress of the world, whose empire extended over the greater part of Europe, and large regions of Asia and Africa, perpetuated her renown, and conferred on the world more lasting monuments of her glory and her greatness, by the wisdom and equity of her *laws*, (which we still possess in nearly their original integrity) than by the splendid remnants of her literature, of her philosophy, of her arts, as they have been transmitted to us through the long lapse of ages.

Such is the excellence, the remarkable wisdom and equity of the Roman code, that it has been frequently

4

denominated *systema rationis scripta,* a system of *written reason;** and we are told by St. Austin, in his treatise *De Civitate Dei,* that "Providence made use of the Roman people to subdue the universe by their *arms,* that they might govern it the better by their *laws,* after the utter destruction of their empire." Zonaras thinks that God made choice of the Romans to give to the world a sample of his *justice;* whilst Baldus remarks that in all nations, Roman jurisprudence has the authority which is ever accorded to *pure reason.*

It was, however, at no time the direct policy of the Roman victors to abolish the laws and institutions of the vanquished, though the latter often voluntarily substituted for them those of the victor. In turn, when the vast fabric was assailed and dismembered, by the barbarians of the north, such was the manifest wisdom of the Civil Law, that these victorious barbarians with equal discernment, relinquished their rude codes, and yielded a willing homage and obedience to the majesty of truth and equity, which abounds in those of the eternal City. Hence it was, that when Roman arms, institutions, philosophy, and literature were almost forgotten, and their vestiges could only be found in the cells of the recluse, Roman *laws* were actively diffusing their influence over the world; finally established themselves as the solid foundations of nearly every municipal code of modern Europe; and imparted even to the *jus gentium,* and to the maritime laws of the world, some of their most equitable and valuable principles. During several centuries, however, there was some conflict between the Imperial Code, and that anomalous system denominated the Feudal Law; but the eventual mastery has been gained throughout Europe by

---

* *Quid enim est aliud* (says Gravina) *Ius Romanum, nisi ratio imperans et armata sapientia, sententiæque philosophorum in publica jussa conversæ?* OROTIO DE JURISPRUDENTIA.

5

the former; and though feudalism has certainly left on the jurisprudence of christendom, many deep and lasting impressions, the civil law of Rome is now confessedly the common law of continental Europe; and remains the pure and copious fountain, to which their statesmen, legislators, and jurists perpetually resort, for the solution of doubts, or when their express laws are either silent or defective.

The praises of the Roman law, have been promulgated in the strongest language of eulogy; not by those only who admired its excellence, from ignorance of the merits of other codes; but by philosophers and publicists of the most enlarged views, and of the most extensive knowledge. The profoundly erudite Leibnitz, than whom no higher authority can be named on most subjects which engaged his inquisitive research, is of opinion, that nothing approximates so closely to the method and precision of *geometry*, as the Imperial Code;* and this opinion has been echoed by many German, French, and Scottish civilians. The authority of the German jurists on all subjects relating to the civil law, stands justly pre-eminent, as none have cultivated it with equal ardour, or comparable success, with the exception of Pothier, and the Chancellor D'Aguesseau, of France. The German lawyers regard Roman jurisprudence as an essential part of legal education, for the very reasons which strongly recommend it to our own careful attention. The common law of England, which lies at the foundation of American law, can no more be thoroughly and philosophically comprehended without frequent reference to the civil code, than can be the *Jus Hodiernum* of Germany, a system raised on the basis of that code. The jurisprudence of the United States, is more intimately allied to that of Rome, than is the common law of our parent country; and when

* Opera Leib.—tom. i. 190. tom. iv. 267.

6

closely examined, will be found nearly as dependant on the Roman law, as are the systems of Germany and of several other continental nations. The fact is, that the numerous departures of the American law, which have taken place within the last half century, from the law of our forefathers, have been little else than so many approximations to the Roman Code, and if we desire deeply to understand the principles which we have thus incorporated into our jurisprudence, the illustrations are to be found no where, with certainty, but in the Justinian law; and in the numerous commentaries of former and modern times, to which it has given rise. Dr. Warnkönig, of the University of Liege, has justly remarked, that "*Omnes jurisconsulti eruditi in eo consentiunt, non solum utilissimam sed necessariam adeo esse juris Romani cognitionem, et illud hodie in juris scholis non minori diligentia ac antehac id fieri solebat, esse docendum: nam neminem ad solidiorem juris prudentiam, nisi juris Romani peritum, posse pervenire convenit.*"* If this be the case in Europe, we shall endeavour, presently, to show that it is equally necessary to the American jurisprudent, if he be desirous of thorough accomplishment in the principles of English and American law; both countries being largely indebted to the Roman Code, not merely for occasional rules, but actually for integral portions of their jurisprudence; and the United States, especially, having in numerous particulars, abrogated the strict common law, to receive the milder, more equitable, and more rational doctrines of the civilians.

We have already adverted to the strong terms of praise in which jurists have indulged when speaking of this law, as we find it digested in the Gregorian, Hermogenian Thodosian and Justinian Codes; the last of which, together

---

* *Comment. Juris Romani. tom. i. Introd. xxxviii.*

7

with the Basilika, have nearly superseded reference to the others, and now form, for *many purposes*, a source of *authoritative* law in France, Germany, Spain, Italy, Portugal, Turkey, Holland, Poland, the two Sicilies, Bohemia, Hungary, the Cape of Good Hope, Scotland and England; and, without doubt, in most of the states of this western world; whilst, in other matters, in which they are not *authoritatively* referred to, we still seek for light and ample illustrations, as we do in the volumes of ethics, of political philosophy, and, of what has been denominated, universal jurisprudence.

The remark of an eminent lawyer, that *servatur ubique jus Romanum, non ratione imperii, sed rationis imperio*, or in other words, that the Roman law is every where observed, not by reason of its intrinsic authority, but by the authority of its intrinsic reason, is here perfectly applicable, and illustrates the general nature of its authoritativeness. As to the authority or *quasi* authority of foreign systems of law, in the tribunals of our country, it behooves us to entertain no mistaken ideas. No foreign laws, properly so called, can ever be intrinsically and *per se* authoritative in our courts. If they are ever so regarded, it is because what was once purely of foreign origin, has by legislative or judicial sanction, or by usage and silent acquiescence, become a portion of our general scheme of jurisprudence. The rule on the subject appears to me to be briefly this. Wherever a system, or any integral portion of law, has been confessedly borrowed mainly from a foreign source, and our own laws, decisions, or practice are wholly silent on the particular doctrine of right or of practice which is sought to be established, and for the first time introduced, the courts refer authoritatively to that system, or integral portion of the foreign law; which *pro hac vice*, having been incorporated into our jurisprudence, is to be resorted to with the same respect, but with the same powers of adoption and modi-

8

fication in the particular case, as courts always possess in regard to the system which is domestic, and peculiarly our own. But, when the rule of law or of practice which is sought after, appertains more peculiarly to our own scheme of laws, or to such portions of laws as have not in the main been borrowed from foreign sources, we may then refer to foreign codes merely for light and illustration; the foreign laws, are then only *quasi* authoritative; that is, only to the extent of their own *intrinsic reason*, and perfect adaptation to our wants; and the courts adopt, or reject their principles and practice under the exercise of a sound legal discretion. With this view of the subject, we are not, on the one hand, to permit our admiration of the Roman, or of any other code, to yield a too ready acquiescence to its provisions, either as to our rights or the modes of their enforcement; nor, on the other hand, should we allow a narrow jealousy to exclude from our consideration the wisdom of past or present ages, because of foreign growth. The learned Cujas tells his son, that "no nation *can* be well governed without the help of the Roman law; for without the aid of that divine science, the most prudent, wise, and fortunate man will have but a very imperfect idea of the *rules of equity* and *true justice*." In like manner a French civilian remarks, that "this code is a wonderful collection of the wisdom of many learned men, who did not confine themselves to *particular usages*, but to general justice:" and he further adds, "such laws as were deemed most useful to *mankind*, are there to be found, and they have written the rules of government for all nations, as Solomon did those of divine wisdom." I shall not attempt to trace the origin, progress, and gradual decline of the ignoble prejudice, and sturdy opposition which, for a time, obtained in England in regard to the Roman law; as it is now conceded by their most enlightened lawyers to have been without just cause. We

9

know the fact to be, that English jurisprudence has been copiously supplied from the purest streams of the civil law, though but little, and a very reluctant acknowledgment has ever been made for the heavy debt thus contracted.

It cannot, however, be denied that many of their early writers, as Bracton, Britton, Gilbert de Thornton, the unknown author of Fleta, and many others, have liberally transcribed from the Imperial Code; so much so in the case of Bracton, (whom all the rest have followed) that he has been gravely denied to be an authority in the common law; and when the current set high against the civil law, its enemies endeavoured to repudiate his work, at the very time that the courts, from its superior excellence, were actively enforcing its doctrines.

Though the Roman law has not been extensively studied by the legal scholars of England, there have not been wanting those who perceived the narrow and technical features of the common law, and the expansive and equitable character of its rival. Some, who are now engaged in the laudable exertion of abrogating the rigid and feudal refinements, so unsuited to the present age, and of supplying their place by doctrines found in other codes, have resorted mainly to the writings of the civilians; and even before this, several of their judges, as Hale, Holt, and especially Mansfield, had shown a liberal willingness to appeal authoritatively, in some cases, and with due respect, in others, to the Justinian Code. In these decisions, strengthened by the pure and lustrous wisdom of Roman lawgivers, succeeding judges and lawyers have generally found much to admire, and little to censure. In the Ecclesiastical courts of England also, (whose jurisdiction, in many particulars, is similar to that of our courts of Probate, or Orphan's courts) and in their courts of Admiralty, Exchequer, and Chancery, (the powers of the two

10

former of which, are exercised in this country, by the United States' District and Circuit courts) the law has borrowed copiously from the Roman sources, not merely in matters of right, or general law, but in the *formulæ* and modes of procedure, which, however, have been modified and suited to the changes of the times, to the other exigencies growing out of a miscellaneous system of law, and, in this country, to the primitive habits of our people, which are averse to complex and expensive forms in legal procedures. Whilst, therefore, we are often bound to resort to the law and practice of foreign codes and tribunals, it is rather for *outlines*, than for *authoritative particulars:* and whilst it is manifest that much of the law of legacies, wills, testaments, trusts, uses, executors and administrators, guardian and ward, intestacy, occupancy, accession, confusion, custom, prescription, contracts, bailments, &c. is to be sought in the writings of the civilians, and in the Roman codes, and that much also of the *practical* proceedings of our chancery, ecclesiastical, exchequer and admiralty tribunals, have been in conformity to those of the continental civil law; it cannot be predicated with safety, that we can rely on the correspondent titles of the digest for *our* law of legacies, contracts, bailments, &c. or to the books of practical procedure, such as Clerk's Praxis Curiæ Admiralitatis, for binding and necessarily operative law. Nor can we do this with confidence, even where our own law and practice are silent; since the courts must still exercise their legal discretion, as to what matters of law and of practice are suited to the other pervading features of our jurisprudence. In matters of pure reason, and the eternal principles of justice, as they have been educed by wise heads and sound hearts, we may often rely on the Roman law, and its commentators, with almost unerring confidence. No one can read without admiration, their expositions of the law of contracts, in all

11

its numerous divisions. This is strongly exemplified in the recent very learned Treatise on the doctrine of Bailments, by Mr. Justice Story. We there perceive the riches of a highly cultivated and embellished mind, gratefully returning to the abundant fountain of Roman law, a portion of its borrowed wisdom, and paying the most willing homage to the exalted merits of Justinian, of Pothier, Domat, Vinnius, Heineccius, Ayliff, Wood, Brown, and others. Whilst his learning on the law of bailments, ranges from the year-books, down through all successive ages of the Common law, he illustrates and happily enforces his doctrines by constant references to Roman law, as set forth in the distinguished sources to which I have just alluded. How much more valuable and authoritative he has thereby rendered his work, will be allowed by all, except by those (and there are such) who deem it idle, unprofessional, and even pedantic, to transcend the narrow limits of the Common law, or to pursue our researches into regions, which, to them, are *terræ incognitæ*, and to which, they would apply the carping objection, that the Roman law, if not authoritative, need not be referred to at all, as it would only tend to add to our already unwieldly *bibliotheca legum*, a mass of works accessible only to a few. Lord Holt, however, thought on this subject differently from the sciolists alluded to. In the well known case of Lane against Cotton,* he cites the Civil law with that respect which wisdom knows how to pay to wisdom; and remarks that he has done so, "inasmuch as the laws of all nations are doubtless raised out of the Civil law, as all governments are sprung out of the ruins of the Roman empire; for it must be owned, that the principles of our law are borrowed from the Civil law, therefore, in many things, grounded on the same reason."

* 12 Mod. 482.

12

Dr. Brown, also, very justly observes, that he "scarcely ever met with a point, not connected with the Feudal law, of which, if English law books did not satisfy the doubt, he has failed to find a resolution of the doubt in the Civil law."* Let us pursue this subject somewhat more in detail.

It is conceded on all hands, that Sir Leoline Jenkins, in framing the statute of distributions, 22 and 23 Charles II. had Justinian's 118th Novel distinctly in his view; and that in all cases of intestacy, *personal estates*, under that statute, devolve, with but trivial exceptions, according to the regulations of that celebrated Novel. If so, where shall we seek for the lights of construction, and all the analogies of that statute, with more confidence than in the civil law itself, and in the writings of its expounders? The descent of *real estates* in this country, being generally very similar to the devolution of personal estate, under the statute of Charles, opens to us a still more extensive field of inquiry on this subject, and refers us again to the Novel in question, and to such lights as may have been shed on it by the civilians.

Again: Our doctrine of *Sett Off* is essentially the same as that of *Compensation* in the Digest and Code. In examining the collected view of this subject, as it is presented in M. Pothier's *Pandectæ Justinianeæ*,† we find a digest of those principles which, amplified in judicial opinions, and in the commentaries of English authors, constitute our treatises on the law of set off: and on a further reference to the Code,‡ and to the annotations thereon, we become still more satisfied that these English opinions and treatises, so familiar to us, are but distillations, or rather, reiterations of doctrines which were perfectly well known to the ancient Roman juris-consults; and which

---

*Vide Brown's Civil Law, 13. Note 21.
† Tom. 2. lib. xvi. tit. 2. p. 92.   ‡ Code iv. 3. 1.

13

have become gradually incorporated with our jurisprudence, but with too little acknowledgment, as we think, to the source whence they evidently sprung. Had Mr. Montague, in his treatise of set off, and Mr. Babbington, in his late work on that subject, pursued their explorations beyond the narrow confines of their own Municipal law, and examined any of the numerous volumes of the continental jurists, or the Digest and Code themselves, they would have imparted to their works much additional value.

On the important subject of Contracts, as before stated, the Civil law is peculiarly rich and accurate; and if our limits permitted, it would be no difficult task to point out how greatly, though silently, and almost furtively, is the English law indebted to this *magnus parens* of all modern law: yet, how little express reference is made by Powel, Chitty, and others, to the Roman law! It is impossible to read even the Institutes of Justinian, without perceiving the superiority, not only in classification, but in closeness and accuracy of thought, of the Roman over the English law of contracts; and this conviction cannot fail to be greatly strengthened, after reading in the Digest and Code, the appropriate titles; or the law of contracts, as it has been collected by Pothier, under various heads, in his new arrangement of the Pandects; or, as it is set forth by him in his well known treatise on the law of Obligations· It would be a vain attempt, in the compass of a single prelection, and we might say even of a moderate volume, to state and to illustrate the numerous instances of the close dependence of our law on that of the Roman. We may adopt with perfect truth, the remark of Arthur Duck, when speaking of the authority of the civil law in Scotland; that it obtains here, as there, *"in casibus omissis;"* not, as I have already stated, by reason of any intrinsic power of the Republic, or of the Empire of Rome, to bind all posterity by her laws, but by reason of the essential obli-

14

gation of all posterity, to be guided by that which is absolutely the best and the purest of human legislation, and judicial interpretation.

But the Roman Code, valuable as it certainly is, has, in common with all the labours of man, its blemishes and imperfections. It has some useless learning, and, in parts, breathes a spirit of severity and cruelty, unknown, at least to the practical law of England and of this country. The too great extent of parental power, the severe relations of master and slave, of debtor and creditor; and the penal code and criminal procedure generally, are prominent defects, though it is equally certain that these among the Romans, as is often the case with the laws of most countries, speak a language of more severity, than those which obtained in actual practice, especially in ages long subsequent to their establishment.

We have already made mention of the English hostility to the Roman law. It became visible shortly after the Conquest, and alternately subsided in a degree, and revived with exacerbation, until at length the good sense of all political parties (but only within the last half century) began to perceive that a just detestation of the arbitrary principles to be found in the *jus publicum*, or constitutional law of the Romans, was not inconsistent with the equally just admiration of their *jus privatum*, so replete with wisdom and equity. The folly of condemning *en masse* the civil code, because of a few political or other heresies, abhorent to the free opinions of the people, is now well understood in England. It would be no longer possible in that country, for any future Duke of Exeter to introduce the rack or the *brake*, under the auspices of the Roman law; nor for any future James, for the maintainance of tyrannical prerogative, to repose on the obnoxious declaration, "*Quod principi placuit legis habet vigorem*." Nor will there be, hereafter, any need for a

15

Bracton, a Fleta, or a Thornton, to endeavour to explain away the genuineness of this celebrated passage; nor shall we need a Selden, in turn, to show how vain is such an attempt. The fact is that the *Lex Regia* does contain the arbitrary maxims imputed to it, but if they were greatly more abundant and pervading than they are, they by no means justify the inferences which have been drawn, and certainly not the sarcastic remark of Professor Christian, that they constitute the "Magna Charta of the Civil law." As well might the arbitrary proclamations of the Eighth Henry, be called the Magna Charta of England,—or the wild prerogative rights that have been accorded to many of their kings, be adduced as a reproach against the vast system of British jurisprudence. There were not wanting, at all times, even in Rome, those who openly protested against these imperial declarations. That the English authors, just mentioned, as also the sage Gravina, the learned Heineccius, and the "erudite, rambling, and spirited" Dr. Taylor, should still doubt whether the maxims in question did confer an absolute authority on the prince, seems to us not a little remarkable; and shows very clearly into what strange opinions even the learned may be betrayed, by an overweening admiration of the topics which engage their pen. And although the following constitution of the Theodosian Code, viz: "*Contra jus rescripta non valeant, quocunque modo fuerint impetrata. Quod enim publica jura præscribunt, magis sequi judices debent,*"* seems entirely adverse to despotic power; yet the explicit language of the Digest is very contrary, and would appear to exclude all doubt on the question. We now give the passage, as rendered by Mr. Gibbon. "The *pleasure* of the Emperor has the vigour and effect of *law*, since the Roman people, by the Royal

* Const. 1. Cod. Theod. 1. 2.

16

Law, have transferred to the Prince the full extent of their own power and sovereignty."* This passage, it has been said, was introduced into the Justinian Digest, solely on the high authority of Ulpian; but we do not perceive how this can diminish its force, as it must have been retained, by Tribonian and his coadjutors, *ex industriâ*, being altogether too remarkable to have been introduced *sub silentio*, or under the auspices alone of any name however exalted. Nor is the other theory a more happy one; viz: that although the sin of this passage is not to be imputed to Ulpian, it is to the Emperor Justinian, who is said to have interpolated a confessedly spurious doctrine, under the very eye of his most renowned jurists, in order to give legal countenance to his arbitrary powers. This, however, would seem to be obviously unfounded. The Theodosian Constitution just cited, evidently alludes to arbitrary imperial edicts and rescripts; and though that emperor repudiates, in the Constitution, the power for himself, it still sufficiently, admits the fact of its prior existence. It is quite probable, therefore, that the *writings* of each of the quintumvirate (composed of Caius, Papinian, Paulus, Ulpian, and Modestinus, and which were declared by this same Theodosius to be valid law, and that, in cases of conflict of opinion, plurality should decide,) contained a passage to the like effect with that so long ascribed to Ulpian alone, or to the artifice of Justinian, and his compliant Tribonian: and further, that Theodosius, while he took the merit of rejecting, by his Constitution, the high prerogative of arbitrary power, received it back again through the medium of the writings of those oracles of the law. Be this as it may, the question as to the genuineness of the text, and the probability that it was a doctrine of the *Lex Regia*, long anterior to Justinian, are now conclusively established by the recent happy discovery

---

* Dig. lib. 1. tit. 4. vide also. Pothier's Pandectæ, p. 15. 4to edition.

17

by Niebuhr of the Institutes of Caius, published in 1820, by Prof. Göschen of the Göttingen. This manuscript, of the Institutes of that distinguished Roman jurist, which, like Cicero's treatise De Republicâ, has been brought to light, after its loss has been deplored during so many centuries, reveals the fact that neither Ulpian nor the Emperor Justinian is to be charged with originating this offensive and much spoken of passage; but that, being a known doctrine of the Imperial Law, it, with others of the *jus publicum*, was inserted by the compilers of the Digest, not at the dictation of Justinian, nor on the sole authority of Ulpian, but as previously existing law. The language of Caius is as follows. "Constitutio Principis est, quod Imperator *decreto* vel *edicto*, vel epistolâ, constituit. Nec unquam dubitatum est, quin id legis vicem obtineat, cum ipse Imperator per legem imperium accipiat."* No language can be more explicit; and as Caius lived under the Emperor Marcus Aurelius, nearly four centuries prior to the compilation of the Justinian Code, and more than a century before Ulpian, the despotic declaration is to be ascribed neither to the compilers of the Digest, nor to Ulpian, but must be regarded, as we have already stated, as a recognized doctrine of the Lex Regia.

But parting with this capital defect in the political law of Rome, with which, indeed, we have no concern, as it is not to that portion of the Civil Law that we would direct the student's attention, we proceed to other topics.

* Vide Gaii Institutionum Commentarii iv. Com. 1. §. 5. p. 3. of the Berlin edition of 1824. ☞ The student will perceive that the initial letter of the name is equally G or C. On this M. Pothier remarks "*Modoenim* Caius, *modo* Gaius *scribitur. Rationem Quintilianus Inst. orat. lib.* 1. *cap.* 7. *quia quædam scribuntur aliter quam pronuntiantur. Nam et Gaius littera C. notantur.*" *Vide Pothier's Pandectæ. tom.* 1. *Præfatio,* xxxiv.

3

18

The comparative excellence of the Civil and Common law has been frequently a subject of discussion. It would be vain to decide such a question. Each, without doubt, has its merits and its blemishes; some peculiar, and others common to both. A large portion, even of the *jus publicum*, is full of wisdom and of justice; and when we reflect on the prevailing equitable spirit of the *jus privatum*, and the numerous distinctions contained in it, founded on the most accurate reasoning; when we refer to the Roman law of contracts, legacies, interpretation, evidence, presumptions, the acquisition of property *jure naturæ*, the inartificial division of *things*, and the equally natural rules of succession, in respect to those things; the doctrines as to those who are deemed *sui juris*, or *non sui juris;* the relations of citizens and aliens; the law as to unsolemn wills, the revocation of wills, and the various species of implied emancipation; the formulæ of their legal proceedings; the authority and operation of judicial sentences; and, in fine, to innumerable other topics, we cannot but feel the most unfeigned surprise and regret, that this study should have been so much neglected in England for nearly five centuries; and that, in our own country, it should have made no very sensible impression beyond an extremely small class of individuals; who, with merits of the highest order, have still been deficient in persevering exertion to promote the study of a science so well known to themselves. Were the two systems accurately compared, and the Common law taken *stricto sensu*, we presume the decision of those skilled in both, would be largely in favour of the Imperial Code, as a full, and nearly complete digest of the wisest and most practical principles, both of public and private law. But such an inquiry, however useful, is not likely soon to be made by one at once competent and strictly impartial: and on which ever side the scale might turn, is by no means so

19

important to us, as to the people of England, since, in so many important particulars, we have discarded the evils which grew out of feudalism, and have conformed our jurisprudence in such numerous instances to the Roman models. Be the excellencies and defects, however, of either system, what they may, a sensible mind will not hesitate to seek in each, the former only; and will not, from blind admiration of the one, withhold the tribute of merited praise from the other.

The great imperfections of the Civil Code, as already mentioned, are to be found in the law respecting *persons* rather than of *property*. The *jura rerum* in all of their modifications, were defined with surprising accuracy, simplicity and equity. So, also, the political or constitutional law was in the main, admirably calculated to elevate and glorify the nation, and render the people happy; and though arbitrary maxims are to be occasionally found, and despots sometimes governed, the Romans, from the origin of their city, to the final extinction of their vast and splendid empire, will be found to have enjoyed as great a share of political and civil liberty, as any nation that ever existed, whose history passes through a long succession of ages. That the people are the source of all power, that sovereignty resides essentially in them, and finally, that government is the result of a contract between the people and their rulers, is more distinctly recognised in the laws and history of the Romans, than of any of the ancient nations. This is to be found even in the arbitrary rule of the digest, to which so much has been objected: for though the sentence commences with the declaration, quod *principi* placuit legis habet vigorem, it terminates with the fullest admission, that this was a concession from the people of "their own power and sovereignty," to their prince.

Such, then, is the unrivalled excellence of the Civil Code, to which no eulogium can do justice; a code replete

20

with instruction for the statesman, the lawyer, and the general philosopher. Should it longer be neglected by the American student? Are there not weighty reasons why the learning of this country should be enriched and adorned by the splendid results of the erudition, wisdom and labours of jurists, aided and fostered by imperial munificence? Have we not adopted and amalgamated the doctrines of the civilians to a greater extent than our mother country? What sensible reason, then, can be advanced, why this system should not constitute even a primary branch of the course of an American law student? The *feudal* law is closely studied, and yet, stronger motives can be urged in favour of the study of Roman jurisprudence, than of the learning of the feudalists. We trust, therefore, that students of this country, will perceive the propriety of seeking for the depths, the refinements, and the last polish of their legal knowledge in the abundant wisdom of the corpus juris civilis.

It may be well to state, at this time, that this vast body of law, as reduced by order of the emperor Justinian, embraces, 1st, THE INSTITUTES, in *four* books, each subdivided into titles, and the whole embraced in one volume, comprehending the rudiments or elementary principles of the Roman law. 2d, THE DIGESTS OR PANDECTS, in *fifty* books, subdivided into an unequal number of titles, in all, four hundred and thirty-two. These contain the works and opinions of *forty* of the most distinguished civilians. No less than *two thousand* treatises, containing, as it is said, three millions of lines, were abridged to one hundred and fifty thousand lines, what now constitute the fifty books and the nine thousand one hundred and twenty-three laws, or fragments of laws of the digest. So polished is the style of this work, that it is a common remark, that were all the Roman authors lost, the Latin language might be recovered by aid of these Pandects alone. 3d, THE

21

CODE, in twelve books, and seven hundred and sixty-five titles, comprehending a collection of Imperial constitutions. This *Constitutionum Codex*, a short time after its publication, was augmented and remodelled by the order of Justinian, into its present form; and no remains of the first compilation are now extant, except as they appear in the new work, which passes under the general name of the Code, or *Constitutionum Codex;* and, with those who are particular in such matters, under the more special designation of *Codex Repetitæ Prælectionis*. 4th, THE NOVELS, *Novellæ Constitutiones*, one hundred and sixty-eight in number, being a supplement to the Code. These contain the decrees of various emperors on new questions. The whole of this Justinian compilation was published between the 21st November, 533, and some unknown month, in the year 539; and forms a body of law more extensive and complete in principles, and accurate definitions of legal words, than any that the world has ever known. We have already trespassed too long on the time and attention of the audience, to justify an attempt to give even a rude outline of so extensive a system of jurisprudence, as that transmitted to us by the Romans. There are, however, some select portions of that law to which we invite your attention; and to which the residue of this discourse will be devoted. We propose to take a hasty review of the domestic relations of *Husband and Wife; Parent and Child; Master and Slave;* and to notice incidentally, the doctrines of *Adoption*, as connected with the relation of parent and child; and of *Tutelage* and *Curation*, as allied to that of guardian and ward, and as known in the municipal law of England and this country.

The four primary relations just mentioned, give rise to laws of some kind in even the rudest states of society. Among the Romans they became extremely refined, and were of a very peculiar and anomalous character. A cur-

22

sory view of these relations, would give us no very elevated impressions of the wisdom and purity of their laws, or of the refinement of the nation. Amidst many admirable features, there are great and prominent defects. But in Rome, as in most other countries, the law of these subjects was the gradual accretion of ages, and, in theory, was often very different from what obtained in actual practice; much of the severity of the written law being mitigated in practice by the growing refinements of society.

How many absurdities and severities, for example, do we find in the English system of civil jurisprudence, and how often does her criminal code seem to be written in blood, and dictated by an unrelenting cruelty! If, by that law, a husband, in some cases, may expose his wife for sale at public auction; if he has the privilege of personal chastisement; if life be the forfeit of a larceny above a shilling sterling; these and numerous others equally revolting, are still of rare occurrence in actual practice, and are to be regarded as the expiring relics of the rudeness of by-gone ages, rather than as the recognized and practised law of an enlightened people. These remarks equally apply to many of the Roman laws, for we are not justified in concluding that the Romans were in many things practically cruel and unrefined, because their laws, in many cases, partook of that character. We know that if the Roman parent owned his child as absolute property, with the power of life and death in his hands; if the master held his slave as a mere chattel; and an injury done to him was only recognized as a legal injury to the master; if the wife was subjected to many restrictions wholly unknown at the present day; if divorces *sine causâ* were legally existent, still the Roman parent tenderly loved his offspring; the master was generally kind to his slave, the wife loyal and affectionate to her husband, and he kind and tender to her; and the relation was probably, in every

23

respect, as refined and honourable as we find it at present in the most polished society of any country.

With this general view of the domestic relations alluded to, we now proceed to examine more in detail that of

HUSBAND AND WIFE.

We have no occasion, and indeed it would be out of place at this time, to explain the many nice distinctions as to the several kinds of marriages known to the Roman law; such as *Matrimonium, Nuptiæ, Connubium, Conjugium, Consortium,* and *Contubernium.* We may simply remark that *matrimonium*, or marriage, was a generical term, which embraced every species of that relation, whether between Romans and foreigners, slaves and freemen, &c. or by whatever rite or ceremony the same was contracted; whereas *Nuptiæ* were the only recognized, formal and legal marriages of free Romans with each other. So again, *matrimonium*, or marriage in general was referred solely to the *jus naturæ*; whereas *Nuptia* was wholly a civil and legal contract. In fine, all marriages contracted *jure Romano* were referred to the head of *Nuptiæ*, while all other marriages came under the term *matrimonium*; and were merely respected as valid by the law of nature, and not *invalid* by the Roman law. Legal marriages among the Romans were of three sorts, by *Use, Confarreation,* and *Coemption.* A brief explanation of each is all that our limits will permit.

A marriage *ex usu*, or by prescription, regarded the wife as moveable goods, which by the laws of the xii. tables became property by prescription or use. The time of limitation was a very short one, for if the intended wife lived uninterruptedly for one year with her intended lord, she became his *property* by a species of occupancy; and, like any other *direlict* property, the husband's title to his wife was regarded only as a prescriptive one. Dur-

24

ing the year of probation she had the name of *uxor*, or wife, a word at that time of more limited signification than at present; but after the expiration of that period, the marriage being consummated, she became entitled to the more dignified appellation of *mater-familias*. This prescriptive mode of contracting marriage was the most ancient, and from its very nature must have originated in very primitive times. If the uxor left her lord for only three successive days, the prescription was thereby interrupted, by what was called usurpation, and if she was permitted to return, the marriage *ex usu* could not be consummated but by computing the year from the period of her return. In conclusion of this subject of prescriptive marriage, we have only to remark, that during the year's novitiate it was the lady's privilege to sever the connexion, and return to her home and friends, but that this right was not reciprocal on the part of the intended husband.

The second form of marriage was called *confarreation*, from the Latin word *far*, a peculiarly fine species of meal; because the officiating priest offered to the gods a simple cake, composed of *far*, and the necessary quantity of salt and water. A portion of the same cake was shared between the bride and groom, as an emblem of their union, and this part of the ceremony terminated with the sacrifice of a lamb or a sheep. The wife then became invested, by adoption, with the rights of a daughter, and, as such, entitled to her husband's entire estate, if there were no issue, and shared equally *per capita* if there were children. Marriage by confarreation could be dissolved only by an equivalent one, called *disfarreation*. They both continued in use until about the time of Tiberius.

The third and last rite of marriage to be remarked on was *Coemption*, which consisted of an imaginary reciprocal sale and purchase of each other, effected by the exchange of some pecuniary consideration. The additional ceremonies were very similar to those of confarreation; and its legal effects were the same. In whatever form the marriage was celebrated, the husband possessed over his wife the same right of life and death, as the master over his slave, or a parent over his child. Being placed by the marriage *in loco filiæ*, she *inherited* her husband's estate; and the estate thus acquired, unlike our conception of *Dower*, was held by her, by right of inheritance, under the legal fiction of her being her husband's adopted daughter. On the other hand, the husband, as parent by adoption, inherited his wife's estate.

The marriage rites and attendant circumstances among the Romans, were more striking and pageant than are practised among the moderns. May of the *formulæ* were symbolical, and some rested on the superstitions of the times. The bride appeared clothed in pure white, with a zone or belt; her hair braided, in imitation of a vestal's, with six tresses terminating in a javelin. Over the whole, and covering her entire person, was thrown a yellow gossamer veil; her shoes being of the same colour. Thus attired, she was taken by the bridegroom and his friends from her mother's possession, and carried off with apparent violence; either to denote the reluctance with which she is supposed to leave the parental roof, or in commemoration of the tradition of a very different act committed by the Sabines in the infancy of the Roman state. In consumation of the nuptials, various other ceremonies followed; after which the bride was borne in triumph to her husband's dwelling. The first salutation which met her on this *ductio domi* was apparently an extremely abrupt one. At the threshold she was asked by her husband "*Who are you;*" to which she replied "*I am Caia.*" This name she assumed for the moment, in allusion to Caia, a lady greatly distinguished in the early history of Rome for domestic virtues; and whose distaff, during many

26

ages, was preserved as a valuable relic, and in imitation also of whom the bride bore a distaff and spindle, as an assurance to her husband that, like Caia, she would seek her chief happiness in the discharge of her domestic duties. The bride, however, had the option to make a different reply. On being asked by the groom who she was, she was privileged to reply *"Where thou art Caius, there shall I be Caia,"* a promise of rather ambiguous import, and not so distinctly a vow of *obedience*, as that so commonly in use among the modern nations of christendom.

After this ceremony she seemed to enter the house with reluctance; for she was literally *carried* over the threshold; either to import her attachment to the home she had just left, or, to signify that she would not abandon, or be compelled to leave her new one unless carried over the threshold by compulsion; or lastly because, by an early superstition, all doors being consecrated to Diana, the bride was supposed to be unwilling to *trample* at once on the threshold. Water and fire were then touched by both of the parties, a rite symbolical of their community of property, and that each would willingly endure every peril, even of water and fire, to preserve inviolate the union that had just taken place. Having immediately after sacrificed her dolls to Venus, she was invested with the keys of the house, and the whole ceremony terminated with a splendid entertainment, and an Epithalamium, sung by the guests in honour of the festive occasion.

The Romans were specially careful as to the months, and even the days, in which they married, a portion of which superstition is not without its influence even in the best society of the present day, and, if carefully examined, might be traced, in part, to this Roman source. May was a peculiarly objectionable month, the tradition being that one of the parties, would probably die suddenly, if married in that month. The objection to this month, however,

27

has never reached us, as it is, we believe, a particularly favourite one. June was esteemed by the Romans, the most auspicious; but February was utterly rejected, as it was the anniversary of all funereal rites.

We are to distinguish between *espousals* and *marriage*. The former often took place many months before the nuptials, and was also accompanied by solemn ceremonies. The *sponsalia* or precontracts, were dissoluble by mere dissent, if they had been made before the legal age of assent; and where the parties were affianced, or as it is often called espoused, the marriage contract was then drawn up, and confirmed by the betrothed presenting to his intended bride a ring, usually of iron, to be worn by her on the third finger of the left hand, from a current idea, that an important nerve proceeded directly from that finger to the heart. The parties at their espousals also broke a straw between them, the separate parts of which, each retained, as a species of tally, or strong evidence of the troth which had been pledged. Until the *ductio domi*, which, as we have seen, was the consummation of the nuptials, the lady had the name of *sponsa*, spouse; after which she took that of *uxor*, *wife*.

Marriage among the Romans, was eminently a *consensual* contract. An error *de substantiâ* would vitiate it; as if *Julia* were imposed on *Caius*, instead of *Tullia:* but an error *de qualitate* had not that effect; for, if Tullia were expressly represented by herself, or her parents to Caius, to be extremely wealthy, and yet was portionless; or to be of one age, and she was much older, the contract was still valid. But even to this rule, there were some exceptions; for if a patrician supposed he was marrying one of like condition, or a freeman, by error, married a slave, the contract was wholly null.

As to the degrees of consanguinity, within which marriages were legal, the Roman law varied at different

28

periods. The ascending and descending lines, *in infinitum*, were always excluded; but in the collateral line, marriage between uncle and neice was permitted; and first cousins, who, according to the Civil law mode of computing the degrees, are in the fourth degree, were also competent to intermarry: whereas, under the Canon law, which *pro hac vice*, is the law of England, a marriage between first cousins is invalid, first cousins being in the second degree, and second cousins in the fourth degree. From confounding the two systems, originates the popular and vulgar remark in England, that first cousins may intermarry, and second cousins may not. Marriage within the legal degrees, also required the consent of parents, unless the children had attained their legal age, in males fourteen, in females twelve.

During a short period, marriages between patricians and plebeians were prohibited, but this inhibition, not suiting the growing republican spirit, was repealed. But all marriages between Romans and foreigners, were forbidden, and the offspring of such alliances were denominated hybridous. Foreigners being regarded as barbarians, the prohibition continued, and was only relaxed in favour of the inhabitants of such places as were so fortunate as to obtain the special privilege, called the *Jus Connubii*. The prohibition became virtually abolished in the time of Caracalla, who extended the privilege of *naturalization* to every portion of the Roman empire.

Laws restrictive of celibacy, commenced as early as four centuries prior to the Augustan age. Pecuniary mulcts were first resorted to; subsequently degradation; and, finally, the censors were invested with the power of administering to young men, an oath, that they would marry within a defined period. The well known law called *Papia Poppœa*, from Pappius and Poppœus, consuls in the time of Augustus, enforced against bachelors various

29

severe penalties. These consuls had the arduous office of executing this celebrated law; but what is very remarkable, they were themselves in the state of single blessedness, and though the executors of the law against others, are not known to have enforced it in their own case. Among the penalties of the Lex Papia Poppœa, was the forfeiture to the national Fisc of all legacies and collateral successions; provided the legatee did not marry (being of competent age) within a hundred days after the death of the testator. Having dwelt sufficiently, and, perhaps, too long on the relation of husband and wife, we now proceed to that of

PARENT AND CHILD.

No ancient or modern nation ever legislated so systematically and thoroughly as Rome, on the reciprocal duties of parent and child. If we find absolute power in the parent, and the most undeviating obedience in the child, strongly inculcated and enforced; we also perceive many estimable features of humanity, and numerous wise regulations, eminently productive of harmony, subordination, and happiness. The reciprocal duty of parent and child to support each other, was strictly enjoined. The father was obliged to educate and support his children suitably to their condition; and though he possessed the power to disinherit his offspring, the will was a nullity if he pretermitted his child *sub silentio*. Hence, originated the popular error in England, that a child, in order to be disinherited, *must be cut off with a shilling*. On the other hand, a son, if he had been brought up to some business by his parent, was obliged to sustain his aged or impoverished sires. The obligation was regarded by law, as it is by nature, as a holy one; and when neglected, brought down the curses of the people on the unnatural ingrate; but, if eminently performed, never failed to be rewarded

30

by the best feelings and kindest expressions of all. The story told by *Valerius Maximus* will illustrate this. A Roman lady of eminence had been sentenced to death, but the jailer had neglected to strangle her at the appointed time, and had permitted her daughter to visit her. The mother was then actually perishing with hunger; and all hope of even momentary relief, was banished. The filial piety of the daughter could suggest no other means than to afford her mother nourishment from her own bosom, thus reversing in that trying exigency, the order of nature. This affecting incident was detailed to the Judges, which promptly saved the life of the mother; and transmitted to us, this brilliant example of a daughter's love, and of Roman veneration for the holy tie which binds children to their parents.

A false philosophy as to the origin of parental authority, generated the legal and moral error as to its unlimited extent. That the child is the parent's *property*, is not only erroneous in theory, but essentially calculated to occasion the immoral inferences educed from it, not only by the Romans, but by nearly all the barbarous and demi-civilized nations of every age.

Infanticide was permitted by the Roman law, but was restricted to the *third* year of the child's age. The exposure of children, however, was in practice attended by some evidences of parental affection, as the children were often placed in situations calculated to excite the compassion of others who were either childless or much better able to support them than their parents; and, as a farther evidence of the still lingering effects of parental love, even where the exposure of the child suspended its life upon mere contingences, parents were accustomed in such cases to affix some indelible mark by which it might at a future period be recognized and reclaimed, should it be so fortunate as to escape its peril, and find a parent by adoption.

In addition to the power of actual infanticide, and the exposure of children, which might or might not terminate in their death, parents had an unlimited right of punishment; could imprison them; sell, or emancipate them at pleasure; and, even though *adults*, could, under certain forms, put them to death. This power of life and death, though undeniably a legal one, was not to be wantonly exercised. It was not only to be for some grave cause, but was to be exercised by the father in a solemn and judicial manner, instead of by the civil magistrate. Cases, sometimes, did occur when adult children were put to death without any such protecting forms. For some time prior to the Augustan age, the parental power of life and death had considerably declined; and the Julian law, in the time of Augustus, which permitted a father to kill his daughter, when faithless to her husband, proves that the general power had by that time became questionable. Still the extent of parental authority continued very great, and in fact was not materially mitigated for centuries; and finally became reduced to the point in which it now stands in modern Europe, only after Christianity had subdued both the Romans and their conquerors. Infanticide was recognized as late as the fourth century of the Christian era; but was made a capital offence by Constantine, in the year 374. Another power, which continued to a somewhat later period, was that of subjecting a son or a slave to indemnify, by his personal services, any damages occasioned by him to others. The parent had the option to pay such damages as were judicially awarded against him, (the son or slave not being justiciable in any case) or to subject such son or slave to servitude to the injured person. The actions brought in these cases against the father, were called noxal, and were abolished by Justinian, who,

32

on the compilation of the *Corpus Juris Civilis*, introduced many beneficial changes in all of the domestic relations, as well as in most of the other departments of the science.

We have already intimated, that the theory of Roman law as to parental authority, reposed on the idea that the child was *property*, and *quasi* a slave: hence, the formulæ of emancipations; the acquisition of the son's earnings, and other property, to the father's use. This was the case, with no other exception than the privileges which came under the head of a son's *peculium;* and also, the earnings at the bar, and in the army. The power of the father, so far from being limited to the period of childhood and adolescence, extended throughout life. The father not only possessed the power of selling his son into slavery, in order to satisfy any noxal damages awarded against him, for offences committed by the son against third persons; but the independent power also, which might be thrice repeated; which was not the case, however, even as to slaves: for if a son sold into slavery were emancipated by the purchaser, he reverted to the father, who might again sell him; and if he reverted the third time, he was still not a freeman until emancipated in due form. Hence was it, that if the father really designed effectually to liberate his son, he went through the *formulæ* of three distinct sales, and of as many repurchases, to and from some friend, denominated *pater-fiduciarius*, or father in trust. This ceremony was called a sale by *brass and balance*, because it took place in the presence of a magistrate holding a balance; in one scale of which the son was presumed to be, and in the other, a piece of brass, in primitive times, and subsequently, a brass coin, as the consideration of the purchase. This ceremony, when thrice repeated, made the son *sui juris*, that is, for ever after a freeman. It was abolished by the Emperor Justinian, and emancipation was affected by a simple declaration, before the magistrate, of the father's intention to liberate his son. But notwithstanding emancipation, the father still retained the issues and profits of a moiety of his son's property; and if the son died intestate, the father became his heir, and the protector and guardian of his children, who were also *quasi* slaves to their grandfather, who possessed the same parental authority over them as over his own non-emancipated children. There are three other relations known to the Civil law, which being more immediately connected with that of parent and child, claim some notice from us, at this time. We allude to Adoption, Curation, and Tutelage. By adoption, the relation of parent and child was fully established. The individual, in addition to his own, assumed the name of the family into which he entered. If he were a minor, his adoption was by a fictitious sale, similar to that which took place in the case of emancipation. This species of adoption was called *Simple Affiliation*. There was another called *Arrogation*, which took place when an adult, already *sui juris*, voluntarily subjected himself to the adoption of one who was willing to receive him. This, however, could be effected only through the Public's approbation. The last species of adoption, was by *Testament*. In this, the testator, in his lifetime, had to obtain the Prætor's permission; or, if that had been neglected, the Public were to sanction it after his death, before it could become a valid testamentary adoption. The adopted child was constituted heir, and assumed the testator's name. Adoption became an extensive and curious title in the Roman law, and has left on the jurisprudence of some portions of the continent, many visible impressions.

We have stated that the adopted child added to his own, the name of his adopting parent. The Romans had a mode of naming their children, differing in several respects, from our own. The same individual was often distin-

34

guished by three, and sometimes more names. The four distinct classes of names in use among the Romans, were the *Prenomen, Nomen, Cognomen* and the *Agnomen.* The *prenomen* corresponded with what we call the first, or strictly baptismal name; as, for example, John or Charles. The *nomen* was the *original* family name, and this we have also retained, but denominate it the surname; as, for example, Charles *Hollis.* But what the Romans called the surname, is but seldom known with us; and when used, is merely an addition to the surname, to distingnish a particular person, from one having the same prenomen and nomen; as, for example, Charles Hollis the *red*, to distinguish him from Charles Hollis, the *black;* the one having red, the other black hair. The cognomen, or surname of the Romans, was generally a name of honourable distinction; but occasionally had a different origin, and was then, in fact, what we denominate a nickname. Lastly: The agnomen was a strictly *personal* name, conferred to distinguish, very peculiarly, the individual using it. These classes of Roman names may be illustrated by the name of Publius Cornelius Scipio Africanus, which are named in the order of *prenomen, nomen, cognomen*, and *agnomen:* Africanus being an agnomen, conferred on Scipio by the Roman Senate, for his memorable actions in Africa, as that of Asiaticus was given to his brother Lucius Cornelius Scipio. The agnomen was not optional with parents or others, as the cognomen, etc. were, but was a public testimonial of distinguished merit. So in the name of Marcus Tullius Cicero, *Marcus* was the *prenomen*, or what we call the first christian name. *Tullius* was his own proper family name, which we call the surname, but which differs from the Roman surname, which was their third name: and *Cicero* was a mere addition to his family name, and was a cognomen, or nickname, from *cicer*, a

35

vetch or bean. Cicero never had an agnomen, unless *Pater Patriæ* should be so considered.

In writing their names, the Romans seldom used more than the initial letter of the first, and often of the second name also. As the prenomen of the other sex, generally differed only in its termination in *ia*, instead of *ius*, the initial letter was always inverted, in order to indicate the name to be that of a female; as, for example, *Tullia*, a lady's name, would not be written in full, but merely by the letter T inverted, to distinguish it from Tullius, which would also be indicated by the initial letter only, but *not* inverted.

The *nomen* was not given to males until the ninth, and to females until the eighth day after their birth. The *prenomen* was not added until the male was seventeen, or the female married; and after marriage, the wife did not assume her husband's name, but retained her maiden name. Slaves, if they had any name, almost always bore the *prenomen* and *nomen* of their master; and, in primitive times, if the master had but one slave, he took no name whatever, except the occasional designation demanded by necessity, as we are in the habit of calling a slave, whose name is unknown to us, "Boy," "Man," "Waiter," &c. But when slaves became numerous, as luxury increased, there was no little difficulty in fashioning appropriate names. Females frequently received no prenomen; but if the daughters of a family were numerous, they were designated numerically, with a diminutive termination, which indicated tenderness, as is the case with many other diminutives in other languages. Thus, Secundilla, Tertulla, Quartilla, Quintilla, &c. would indicate, respectively, the second, third, fourth, and fifth daughters.

As promised, we shall now give a very brief account of Tutelage and Curation.

Tutelage, which corresponds in most respects with our

36

guardianship, imposed on the Tutor, the custody of the person and property of the Pupil, and terminated, as to both, when the orphan attained the age of fourteen, at which time, a Curator was appointed, more in reference to the protection of the estate, than of the person of the Minor. Curation lasted until the minor's full majority, which was fixed at the age of twenty-five; but women remained in perpetual tutelage, either to their parents, husbands, or guardians; and this barbarous relic of the jurisprudence of very early ages, continued with but trivial modifications, through every period of the Roman law. Tutelage was either Testamentary, Legal, or Dative, that is constituted by a parent's last Will,—or, in defect of that, by the Law; or, finally, by the Magistrate, where no tutor was provided, either by Will or Law.

The legal tutor was always selected from the Agnati, being the nearest relative *ex parte paterna*, to whom the estate, in case of the pupil's intestacy *would* descend. In this respect the Athenian and English law differ from the Roman, it being considered by the former impolitic and dangerous to entrust the person or estate to any one who by possibility *could* take the succession. The objects of tutelage were infants, idiots, lunatics, women, and prodigals; in respect to the last of which the English as well as our own law (with the exception of a like provision in a few of the states) are unfortunately wholly silent. The law seems to us wise and humane which subjects to an interdict the person and property of confirmed sots and of prodigals of every kind, and which treats them as *quasi* lunatics until they become reformed. The Civil Law, indeed, abounds with salutary provisions for the protection of all who ought to be regarded as *non sui juris*. The offices of Tutor and Curator were not only compulsory on those who were designated, but the due discharge of their trusts was guarded by a legal security or Fide-jussory

37

Caution,—and they were moreover, removeable by the magistrate for just cause, and were also to give additional security, when the persons already given became doubtful, or *lapsi facultatibus*. Here again, the general provision of the Roman is better than the English Law, which gives no adequate remedy for the removal of a *testamentary* guardian.

The *civil*, as well as natural death, of the tutor or pupil, and of the curator or minor, put an end to the respective offices, and however they were terminated, a strict account was to be rendered of the estate. If a controversy arose between the tutor and his pupil, the suit was prosecuted by a curator appointed *pro hac vice* by the Prætor. This curator corresponds with the *prochien ami*, or the minor's next friend, of our law.

In conclusion of this subject we may remark, that the English Law of Guardian and Ward became gradually more assimilated to the Roman, as the Feudal Law and Feudal Institutions declined in England. Feudal Wardships excluded until then the testamentary and legal guardianships, so well known and so salutary in the Roman Law. The former was introduced in England not until the reign of Charles II; and the Chancellor's jurisdiction in the case of Wards cannot be referred to an earlier date than 1696.

The last domestic relation among the Romans which remains for us to notice, is that of

MASTER AND SLAVE.

It resembled in so many particulars that of parent and child, that we shall not dwell on more than its prominent and most interesting features.

As to the origin and right of slavery, the Roman in common with most other nations, recognized four distinct sources of title, in which they supposed slavery might

38

legally arise,—viz. 1. Conquest in a public and just war, 2. Intellectual inferiority. 3. Crime. 4. Paternal power. A very brief examination of each of these alleged sources, will be sufficient to show their fallacy.

As to conquest, the argument was that enemies may be killed and utterly exterminated; and consequently, if their lives be spared, the victor has a perpetual right to their services. That we have a right, in a just war, to kill our enemy is unquestionably true; but it endures only whilst the battle rages, dum fervet opus,—and it ceases the moment the exigency is over. There is, therefore, no right to commute death for slavery; for the very right to take life excludes the existence of such circumstances as would render it proper to save the life of an enemy, with the view to follow it up by his enslavement. The laws of nature and of nations are at this day too well understood, in Christendom at least, for us to be misled by the fallacious reasoning on this point of the Roman jurists. The second supposed source of legitimate slavery, viz. Intellectual inferiority, is still less tenable. Superior minds will necessarily, in every community, and in all states of society, exert a considerable influence over those which are confessedly inferior; but to impute slavery to the legitimate exercise of such mental superiority, is an idle figment, which the notions inculcated by Aristotle do not warrant; but which have been perverted to give a show of authority and reasoning to a wholly untenable position. In the Roman and Greek eye, all *foreign* nations were *barbarians;* they were held to be naturally inferior, and fit subjects for conquest and slavery. But, even if there were any validity in the argument, it did not sustain the slavery which existed among them; for though slaves were never regarded as *citizens*, they were not viewed as *foreigners;* and that they were not considered as essentially inferior, is manifest from the daily practice and experience among the Romans; for slaves enjoyed, and exercised many offices which were peculiarly intellectual. They were often preceptors, physicians, secretaries, stewards, painters, sculptors, and artists of various kinds, and the excellence and the value of their services were well known, and highly appreciated by their masters. Crime, it must be admitted, is, theoretically, a very specious source of legitimate slavery; but is wholly insufficient, in point of fact, and eminently so, even in theory, in regard to the innocent offspring of slaves, made so by the legal necessity of expiating their crimes. As to the last source of the supposed lawfulness of slavery, viz. paternal power, it is in itself based on the most erroneous ideas as to the origin, nature, and extent of parental authority; which under no circumstances, is warranted in reducing children to the state of slavery.

Without further remark, then, we are justified in stating that none of the grounds advanced to sustain Roman slavery, are sufficient in the eye, either of morals or of philosophy. Slavery consequent upon birth, was restricted by the Romans to the offspring of *female* slaves, the state of the *father* having no effect to impress that character on his offspring, where the mother was free. The maxim uniformly was, that *partus sequitur ventrem;* and this was held in connexion with another equally recognised maxim of Roman law, that *Pater est, quem* NUPTIÆ *demonstrant.* In this case, we perceive the distinction between the effects of that species of marriage called *nuptiæ*, and that denominated *contuburnium*, which was confined to slaves, who were deemed incapable of marrying by the legal solemnities of *nuptiæ*. He alone, therefore, was called *pater*, father, who was a freeman, and who had united himself to a free woman by the *nuptial* rites. Hence, the civilians say, that all who are born *extra justas nuptias* have no father, and consequently, must follow the condi-

40

tion, whatever that be, of the mother. The English law of Villenage, now indeed obsolete, but which was a species of slavery, never recognised the Roman maxim of *partus sequitur ventrem:* but in the United States, the rule has always been according to the Roman law, though not for all of the reasons assigned by the civilians; for slaves in this country, are legally capable of contracting the obligations of the only legitimate forms of marriage known to our jurisprudence. The maxim, consequently, applies in all cases; for if the father be a freeman, and the mother be a slave, the offspring are slaves; and if the father be a slave, and the mother free, the children are free.

According to the Roman Constitution, slaves were not citizens: they enjoyed neither political nor civil liberty; they had no political rights. The laws, moreover, subjected them, not only to incapacities of almost every kind, but to degrading *indicia* of their servility. They were often without name, and if they had one, it was generally that of their master: they were not registered as belonging to any tribe; could take nothing by descent, or by purchase, except the small privilege called *peculium;* they, of course, could not make a will, nor constitute heirs, except of that peculium. They could neither plead nor be impleaded. They had no *locus standi in judicio*, except through the name and ministry of their master; and even then, only in cases of gross violence, which was regarded not as an injury to them, but only as a cause of damage to their master: and if maltreated to a limited or small extent, no noxal action could be instituted even by the master. The power of life and death and of sale belonged to the master, with but very trivial limitations. In consequence of the privilege we have mentioned, called *peculium,* a distinct species of slavery arose; for as the *peculium* might consist of slaves, the *servi servorum,* or slaves of slaves, were distinguished in some respects from the slaves held by freemen. The former were called *peculiares*, the latter *ordinarii*. Freemen were either *ingenui*, that is, born free; or *libertini*, viz. those who having been slaves, had been manumitted. Even after manumission, the master retained certain rights; these were called *jura patronatûs*. They conferred on the patron, the right of succession to a moiety of the freedman's estate, provided he died without issue. The patron could also annul all alienations in fraud of these rights, and he was preferred in cases of tutelage and curation over all others: he could, moreover, enforce a species of homage, and could, in case of ingratitude, revoke his manumission, and restore the freedman to his former servile condition, which is contrary to the English and American law, in which the maxim *semel manumissum, semper liberum*, always obtained.

I am conscious of having detained the audience too long; and that some of the topics have been too recondite for the usually expected popular character of a prelection. This I have endeavoured to avoid, and in the brief outline of the four domestic relations, I have been induced to depart occasionally, in some degree, from legal boundaries, into those of the manners and institutions of the Romans. But the student of all laws, must ever bear in mind, that researches into the manners, institutions, and history of a nation are the surest means, and the most faithful lights to guide us into an accurate and philosophical acquaintance with its jurisprudence. With many thanks to the audience for their indulgent attention, I venture, in conclusion, to say to students, and to such of my professional brethren, as have not already done so—

STUDY THE ROMAN CIVIL LAW.

ADVERTISEMENT

October 1837

(Thurgood Marshall Law Library, Special Collections, The University of Maryland School of Law)

ADVERTISEMENT.

From the year 1822 to the year 1823, the author was engaged in delivering an extensive Course of Lectures in the University of Maryland. In 1836, the professorship was resigned into the hands of the *Trustees*, the appointment having been originally received in the year 1817, from the *Regents* of the University, who were superseded by an act of the Legislature of Maryland, in the year 1825. This act which removed the Regents, and appointed Trustees, infringed the charter in several material respects, and laid the foundation for all the misfortunes which have since attended this once very promising institution. No establishment of a similar kind, in this or any other country ever received more of *individual* patronage. From its commencement, during a series of years it was raised by individual exertions, by liberal subscriptions, and by the unwearied toils of its professors, from very humble beginnings to eminence. Its medical class from *twenty* or *thirty*, soon rose to *three hundred and twenty-one*, and its law class from seven, the first year, to forty. The buildings, furniture, apparatus, and the whole *matériel* of the institution were perhaps, unequalled in the country. This is not a fitting occasion to comment on the course taken by the Trustees, from the hour of their *unconstitutional* appointment, to the present day, which led to the resignation of *all of the medical professors*, in a very few months after the *law professor* felt himself compelled to resign!

ADVERTISEMENT.

This little volume is put together merely as some evidence of the exertions of the law professor, whose lectures occupied ten months in the year, often six times a week; and had *they been permitted* to continue, would have been the most extensive series of lectures on *every department* of legal science ever delivered in any University. This volume might have been extended to double the size by inserting other introductory lectures; but the sole object of its publication is, to let our citizens judge, from a small sample, of the exertions made by the law professor, and by all of the medical professors, fully to discharge their respective duties. Applications also, have been frequently made for some of the introductories, as also for the syllabus of lectures, and indeed, for all the materials that entered into the organization of the *Law Faculty* of the University: these, we hope, are sufficiently answered by the little volume now offered at a charge wholly insufficient to defray the expense incurred, as only a few copies remain on hand, the residue having been gratuitously disposed of several years ago. This volume, together with the two editions of the author's COURSE OF LEGAL STUDY, and his LEGAL OUTLINES, as also his MOOT COURT DECISIONS, and abridgment of LORD COKE's REPORTS, with notes (the two last of which will be committed to the press as soon as the author is exempted from expenses incurred in the publication of his other works,) will afford, as he hopes, sufficient evidence, were any needed, that *in breaking up* the law professorship, the Trustees have done the author no little injustice, and themselves no great credit. Whether the state of Maryland will *retrace her steps*, and repeal the *unconstitutional* law; or whether this is to be done through the medium of a *judicial decision*, is yet to be seen; to the author it is one of no personal interest; as, with his resignation of the professorship, he shortly intends also to resign all connection with courts and the practice of his profession, in which he has been so extensively engaged, notwithstanding his arduous occupation as law professor. To students of law and the profession in general, he avails himself of this occasion to express with unaffected sincerity, and a lively interest, his hopes for the *onward march* of all that is '*honourable, laudable and profitable,*' in the science and practice of law; and begs leave to express a hope, that the principles inculcated in the author's views of 'Professional Deportment,' as indicated in some of the following lectures, and especially in his 'Course of Legal Study,' and 'Legal Outlines,' will be followed by the happy results predicted by one of our most distinguished jurists, who says that, 'if its precepts are steadily pursued by the profession, I think it will not be rashness to declare, that the next age will exhibit an American bar, not excelled by any in Europe, and that, high as the profession now stands in our own country, it will attain a higher elevation, an elevation, which shall command the reverence of Europe, and reflect back light and glory upon the land and the law of our forefathers.'

DAVID HOFFMAN.

BALTIMORE, October, 1837.

Part Three

What Books Did David Hoffman Own and Read?

It is impossible to know which law books or cases of the thousands that Hoffman recommended in his various lectures and publications he actually owned and read. We do know that he claimed as early as 1822 to have a "large and valuable library."[1] This library was important enough that it became the source of a law suit for its return after Hoffman left the University of Maryland and took the books and materials with him. The Board of Trustees believed the library belonged to the University of Maryland and the status of the library became the subject of a series of acrimonious letters between the two parties and contributed to Hoffman's final break with the University. We can be more certain that he was familiar with the content of those works of law and history necessary to develop his *Course of legal study* and his *Lectures* for the Law Institute. Hoffman had long felt that an extensive and guided reading experience was essential to becoming a successful lawyer; certainly the materials purchased for his Institute would reflect that need.

As pointed out by Herbert Johnson in the introduction to his bibliography of 18th Century law treatises "law books are generally purchased for utility rather than novelty." We can assume based upon Hoffman's career and the comments he made about law practice in his lectures that this emphasis on utility applies to Hoffman's personal collection of law materials as well. Hoffman's personal law library was not offered for sale at the same time as the other non-legal items presented in the auction catalog below and perhaps were shipped to England along with his household goods.[2] For those items that are non-legal in nature we cannot know with any certainty which of those he read – either in part or *in toto*. Although he urged his students to focus their work and readings on the law, Hoffman also encouraged a wide range of alternative reading. He understood that these other works might not further a lawyers' career in the way that reading the law might, but recognized that such reading would make better use of a student's idle time more so than time spent on other less scholarly pursuits:

> This is not, however, designed to exclude altogether the study of other sciences, or of polite literature, contemporaneously with that of law: the most indefatigable student has either from external circumstances, or from mental exhaustion, many intervals of time, in which he revolts from his immediate pursuit though he would gladly fill them with less laborious avocations. The mind is unwilling to be forever contending with difficulty, or excited to the full measure of its strength: the most diligent require some relaxation of employment, some change to diversify the rugged track of investigation. The sage Ascham, the erudite Erasmus, the deeply thinking Montesquieu, and the sublime Newton, were accustomed to unbend the mind, in the moments stolen from their intellectual toils, by the perusal of the fancies of Dante, or of Tasso, or of some of the voluminous tales and romances of the times.[3]

Adding to our knowledge of what Hoffman may have owned and read are two items in the Thurgood Marshall Law Library of the University of Maryland School of Law that bear Hoffman's personal bookplate. The first is *An Analysis of Coke on Littleton* by George Fisk published in 1824 and is included as part of Hoffman's notes to Title 3 in the 1836 edition of *A course of legal study* attesting again to the utilitarian aspects of Hoffman's personal law library.[4] The second item that we can identify as once being owned by Hoffman was a recent gift to the University of Maryland School of Law: *The identity of Junius with a distinguished living character established, including the supplement, consisting of facsimiles of hand-writing and other illustrations* (1818). The book details evidence used in an attempt to determine the identity of "Junius" – an infamous and psudenonymous political writer and commentator in England. Hoffman, who had his own turn using a pseudonym to

The identity of Junius with a distinguished living character established, including the supplement, consisting of facsimiles of hand-writing and other illustrations (1818)
(Thurgood Marshall Law Library, Special Collections, The University of Maryland School of Law)

disguise his views of life in 19th century America, might have had an interest in what steps were used to unmask "Junius" thus his acquisition of this work as well as a subsequent variation for his personal use. Both versions are present in the auction catalog of 1847. Their presence suggests that the copy now at the University of Maryland had passed out of Hoffman's possession before his departure to England. A third item, also bearing Hoffman's personal bookplate is identified as being in the library of the Maryland Historical Society.[5]

Hoffman assuredly suffered from the *gentle madness* of book collecting. As mentioned in the introduction, Hoffman did not keep any journals or diaries, so we do not have access to his book buying history in the way that we do for some other notable book buyers.[6] That said, we do know from this catalog that he acquired a wide variety of books, books that he used not just in his legal career but throughout his life.[7] Fortunately for historians, when Hoffman left the United States for England in 1847 he left directions with his colleague and friend Henry Wheaton to organize the sale of the unused sheets from his publications along with an auction of his personal library.[8] The catalog for this sale, reproduced here, is preserved in the Library of the Virginia Historical Society and provides a glimpse into the personal book collecting efforts of an important but often overlooked founder of American legal education.[9]

Endnotes

1. [David Hoffman], "Law Institute: To Students of Law." *American and Commercial Daily Advertiser.* May 29, 1822.
2. Herbert A. Johnson. *Imported Eighteenth-Century Law Treatises in American Libraries, 1700-1799.* Knokville, TN: The University of Tennessee Press, 1978. P. ix
3. David Hoffman, *A Lecture Introductory of a Course of Lectures Now Delivering in the University of Maryland.* Baltimore: Printed by John D. Toy, 1823. P. 10.
4. David Hoffman, A *course of legal study: addressed to students and the profession generally.* 2nd ed., rewritten and much enlarged. Baltimore: J. Neal, 1836. P. 230
5. Joseph Butler, *The Analogy of religion, natural and revealed, to the constitution and course of nature: to which are added two brief dissertations; I. Of personal identity; II. Of the nature of virtue.* London, 1736.
6. See for example the detailed and familiar history of Thomas Jefferson's book buying in Douglas Wilson's *Jefferson's Books* published in 1996 by the Thomas Jefferson Memorial Foundation.
7. Schaffer, Thomas. *David Hoffman on the Bible as a Law Book.* "Quarterly: Christian Legal Society." 1981.
8. "Letter to Henry Wheaton," 1847. The Wheaton Papers. The Pierpont Morgan Library.
9. Extensive and valuable miscellaneous library in all departments of knowledge, being a portion of the library of David Hoffman, Esq. – about to depart for Europe. 1847. Reproduced with the permission of the Virginia Historical Society.

Auction Catalogue

Public Sale at Thomas & Sons Auction Store. Extensive and Valuable Miscellaneous Library in all Departments of Knowledge, Being a Portion of the Library of David Hoffman, Esq. June 24, 1847

Pages 453 and 454 show samples from the original auction catalogue. This is followed by a transcription of the text preserving spacing and punctuation and all wording (including some odd wording: "do do do do" (meaning "ditto" in reference to the title above – on some entries), as found in the original. We have left the spelling errors. There are no items 624-632.

—Editor

PUBLIC SALE

AT THOMAS & SON'S AUCTION STORE,

NO. 93 WALNUT STREET, ABOVE THIRD.

EXTENSIVE AND VALUABLE
MISCELLANEOUS LIBRARY

IN ALL DEPARTMENTS OF KNOWLEDGE,

BEING A PORTION OF

THE LIBRARY

OF

DAVID HOFFMAN, Esq.

ABOUT TO DEPART FOR EUROPE.

SALE TO COMMENCE ON

Thursday Evening, June 24, 1847,

AT 7½ O'CLOCK.

The books are generally of the best Editions, and mostly in excellent order.

☞ The books will be arranged for examination several days previous to sale.

Barrett & Jones, Printers, 34 Carter's Alley.

9

ADDENDUM TO HISTORY, TRAVELS, &c.

[624, 625 ☞ Rapin's History of England, with engravings—*fol.*
626 ☞ Thornton's History of London, *as it was*, with very numerous plates; rare and valuable—*folio.*
627 ☞ Life of Cardinal Wolsey, very authentic and curious, *rare—folio.*
628 ☞ ☞ Memoirs of Count De Gramont, a new translation, with splendid English engravings, bound in yellow morocco—*quarto.*
629, 630 *** Maurice's History of Hindostan, London copy, with numerous splendid engravings.
631, 632 Guthrie's Geography, 2 *vols. quarto.*]

No. 3.

RELIGION, MORALS, METAPHYSICS.

334 Holy Bible, Scott's family edition, with notes and concordance.
335 Archbishop Tillotson's Works, complete, *folio.*
336 History of American Missions, with engravings.
337 Bacon's Lives of the Apostles, with engravings.
338, 339 Palmer on the Church, a learned work.
340 341 ☞ Æsop's Fables—a magnificent edition, with several hundred engravings—super royal octavo.
342, 343 Brown's History of the Holy Bible.
344, 345 Magee on Atonement, a *powerful work.*
346 to 349 Prideaux's Connexions with maps, 4 vols. complete.
350 Yahn's History of the Hebrew Commonwealth, translated from the German.
351 ☞ Yahn's Introduction to the Old Testament, *very able.*
352 to 355 Hunter's Sacred Biography, complete in 4 vols.
356 ☞ A superb edition of Gesner's Death of Abel, with beautiful engravings.
357, 358 Brown's Dictionary of the Bible.
359 History of the Old and New Testament, by Reeves, *very good.*
360 Burgh's Dignity of Human Nature—should be in every library.
361 to 365 ☞ Dr. Constantine Pise's History of the Church, complete in 5 vols.
366, 367 The Christian Observer.

PUBLIC SALE

AT THOMAS & SON'S AUCTION STORE

NO. 93 WALNUT STREET, ABOVE THIRD

Extensive and Valuable

MISCELLANEOUS LIBRARY

IN ALL DEPARTMENTS OF KNOWLEDGE,

BEING A PORTION OF

THE LIBRARY

OF

DAVID HOFFMAN, Esq.

ABOUT TO DEPART FOR EUROPE

SALE TO COMMENCE ON

Thursday Evening, June 24, 1847
AT 7 ½ O'CLOCK

The books are generally of the best Editions, and mostly in excellent order

---

☞ The books will be arranged for examination several days prior to the sale

---

Barrett & Jones, Printers, 34 Carter's Alley

No. 1.
HISTORY, BIOGRAPHY, VOYAGES & TRAVELS

No.
1 Kennet's Roman Antiquities.

1, 3 Adam's Flowers of History.

4 Potter's Antiquities of Greece.

5 Bolingbroke on Study of History.

6 Darby's Chronology of all Events.

7 Montague on Ancient Republics.

8 Cecil's Sixty Curious Narratives.

9 Memoir of Felix Neff in the High Alps.

10, 11 Pliny's Letters, by Melmoth.

12 Ferguson on Civil Society.

13 ☞ Nardini's Roma Antiqua. *Quarto*, with numerous plates. Rare and valuable.

14, 15, 16 Cunningham's Lives of Eminent Painters and Sculptors.

17, 18 Turner's Sacred History of the World – complete.

19 Historical Epitome of Europe, from A.D. 800 to 1760.

20 Priestly's Lectures on History. *Octavo*.

21 do do do, a fine copy. *Quarto*.

22 ☞ Baxter's History of England, with numerous engravings – rare and valuable. *Quarto*.

23 to 36 Hume and Smollett's History of England, well bound, 14 vols.

37 State of England under William and Mary.

38 to 41 ☞ Hallam's Middle Ages, 4 vols.

42 to 45 Herodotus, translated by Beloe, with Maps and Notes, 4 vols.

46 to 51 Baker's Translation of Livy's History of Rome – a beautiful copy, 4 vols.

52, 53, 54 Hallam's Constitutional History of England, 3 vols.

55 ☞ Taylor's Manual of History – a great work for its size.

56 History of the Inquisition, Life of D'Aubigne, and of Pope Alexander and his Son, Caesar Borgia.

57 Robertson's History of India.

58, 59 Niebuhr's History of Rome – a powerful work.

60 to 68 Rollin's Ancient History, with Maps and engravings, 9 vols, 2nd to 10th, and last.

69 to 72 Gillie's History of Greece, complete in 4 vols.

73, 74, 75 Life of Lorenzo De Medici, by Roscoe.

76, 77, 78 Robertson's History of Scotland.

79, 80 Robertson's History of America.

81 to 84 Russell's Modern Europe, 4 vols. 3d. wanted.

85, 86, 87 Robertson's History of Emporer Charles V.

88, 89, Smith's translation of Thucydide's History.

90 to 96 Anquetel's Universal History, 7 vols – *good work* – 1 & 2 wanting.

97 to 101 ☞ Bigland's View of the World, 5 vols. *complete*.

102 to 105 ☞ Edwards History of the West Indies, 4 vols., *complete*.

106 to 114 ☞ Gibbons' Decline and Fall of the Roman Empire, 8 vols., *complete*.

115 to 119 Plowden's History of Ireland, 5 vols. *complete*.

120 to 123 Russell's Modern Europe, 4 vols. – the 5th wanting.

124 Lives of Great Men.

125 Lives of Eighteen Illustrious Men, *London* copy.

126 Haily's Life of Milton – a charming work.

Hoffman's Library Auction Catalogue

127 Prior's Life of Edmund Burke.

128 Memoir of the Life of Josiah Quincy.

129 Smith's Biography of Major Andre.

130, 131 Lee's Memoirs of the Southern War.

132, 133 Memoirs of Thomas Jefferson.

133, 134 Ramsay's History of South Carolina, with Maps.

135, 136 Stedman's History of America.

137 Willard's Republic of America.

138 Rush's Narrative of a Residence at the Court of St. James.

139, 140 ☞ Alexander's History of Women.

141 Ramsay's Life of Washington.

142 Knapp's Biography of Eminent Lawyers and Statesment.

143 Life of Washington, by Jared Sparks 8th vol.

144, 145, 146 Sparks' Life of Gouverneur Morris, an admirable work, complete.

147 History of Charles XII., King of Sweden – *Rare*.

148 to 153 ☞ Anderson's History of Commerce, 6 vols. *complete*.

154, 155 American Annals, by Holmes – a very useful work.

156 to 159 ☞ Mayo's Mythology, 4 vols. *complete*, with two hundred superb engravings.

* * * The greatest work extant on Mythology.

160 Gregorie's Inquiry into the Intellect and Literature of Negroes.

161   do   do   do   do   do   do

162 Holland's Life of Martin Van Buren.

163 Crockett's Life of Martin Van Buren.

164 Cowper's Correspondence.

165 ☞ Reminiscences of Dibdin – *a great book* – the best of its kind.

166 Lee's Life of Napoleon – *a powerful work* – Author died before completing the work.

167 Description of Boston.

168 Prisons of Paris in 1793 – Revolutionary Scenes. Authentic.

169, 170 BENVENUTO CELENI, an unequalled piece of autobiography.

171, 172 Memoirs of an American Lady, by Mrs. Grant.

173 Fosse's Journey and Imprisonment in Algiers.

174 Brydone's Tour.

175 New Guide to the City of Florence, with Maps, and Fifty-two Engravings.

176 Tooke's Pantheon, with Engravings.

177 Mrs. Starkie's Directions to Travelers on the Continent.

178 Bulwer's England and the English.

179 Cobbett's Tour in Italy.

180 Cobbett's Tour in France and Holland.

181 An American's Italian Sketch Book.

182 Goldsmith's History of Rome.

183   do   do   of Greece.

184 Carlisle's Heroes in History.

185, 186 The First Cruize of a Green Hand, and Imprisonment in Dartmoor.

187, 188 ☞ American Anecdotes, Original and Selected.

189 Letters from Canada.

190 Madam Campan's Private Journal.

191 Mrs. Ellis' Wives of England.

192, 193 Brown's History of St. Domingo – the most authentic.

194, 195 Neele's Romance of English History.

Hoffman's Library Auction Catalogue 461

196 Griffiths History of Annapolis in Maryland.

197   do   do   do   do

198, 199 Carey's Olive Branch.

200 Letters from the Bahama Islands.

201, 202 Joy Morris' Tour in the Holy Land, &c., &c.

203, 204 Steven's Arabia Petrea, with Maps and Engravings.

205 Carver's Travels.

206, 207 Humboldt's Travels.

208, 209 ☞ Modern Preceptor, with Maps and numerous Engravings – an admirable work for Students.

210 Devernois' History of Geneva.

211 ☞ Letters from the Ægian – very eloquent and authentic.

212 Jackson's Journey from England to the East Indies, with a Map.

213 Rabeau's French Revolution.

214 ☞ Sloane's Rambles in Italy – eloquent and rare.

215 Monler's Jouney Through Persia, with Map and Engravings.

216 Tour in the Island of Jamaica.

217 Staunton's Embassy to China.

218 Tytler's Epitome of Universal History.

219 De Pratt's History of the Congress of Vienna.

220 Graham's Junius Identified.

221 do   do   further Identified.

222 Russell's Tour in Germany – a delightful book.

223 Lectures on American Literature, by Knapp.

224 Borrow's Gipsies in Spain, and his Bible in Spain – most eloquent works.

225, 226 Stephens' Central America, with Numerous Engravings and Maps.

227 Norman's Rambles in Yucatan, with many Engravings.

228 ☞ Maundrell's Travels in the Holy Land, in 1697, with Engravings.

229 Wood's History of Switzerland.

230, 231 Helen Maria Williams' Sketches of Manners and Opinions in the early French Republic.

232 Carr's Travels in Holland.

233 Biographical Dictionary.

234, 235, 236 History of Virginia, by Burke.

237 Notes on Columbia, with plates.

238 Bozman's Maryland.

239, 240 Hutchinson's History of Massachusetts.

243 Sullivan's History of Maine.

244 Williams' History of Vermont.

245 Judge Woodward's Divisions of all Human Knowledge.

☞ A Powerful work. Author died before work ended. *Folio.*

246 ☞ ☞ Conquests of the Counts of Flanders, in French – a *very rare* work, with *several hundred* beautiful engravings of ancient manners, &c., &c. Cost £3ster.

247, 248, 249 Coxe's Travels in Poland, &c., with maps, &c., &c. – *Quarto.*

250, 251, 252 Rollins' Belle Lettres – first vol. missing.

253 ☞ The Ladies Companion.

254, 255 Hopkins Essays.

256, 257 ☞ ☞ *Homer's Iliad Travestied*, with engravings, *extremely rare.* London copy – *out of print – complete.*

258, 259 Hazlett's British Senate.

260 Rights of Women, by Mary Wollstoncraft.

261, 262 Columbian Eloquence.

263 Gerard on the Laws of Taste.
264 Columbian Orator.
265, 266 Smith's Lectures.
267, 268, 269 Lord Kaime's Lectures on Criticism.
270, 271 Ogelvil on Composition, a learned work.
272, 273 J.Q. Adams' Lectures on Belles Lettres.
274, 275 Blair's Lectures on Belles Lettres.
276 Cumberland Observer.
277 The Loiterer.
277 ½ Tooke's Diversions of Purley.

No. 2.
NOVELS, TALES, &c.
☞ *See also No. 799 to 834, and 867 to 890*

278, 279 A Collection of Novels.
289 A Collection of Tales by W. Irving.
280 ½ Wandering Jew.
281 Sanford and Merton.
282 Salmagundi, 2d vol.
283 Moore's Epicurean.
284 Bulwer's Leila, or Siege of Grenada.
285, 286 Schoolcraft's Indian Legends.
287, 288 Croley's Salathiel.
289, 290 Brookes' Fool of Quality, *a great work.*
291, 292 Swallow Bard, by John P. Kennedy.
293, 294 Demetrius.

295, 296 ☞ "*My Uncle Sam*," by Le Brun.

297, 298 Joseph Andrews, by Fielding.

299, 300 Rosamond.

301 The Morals of Pleasure.

302 ☞ The Essays entitled "Elia."

303 A Collection of Novels, "*Rasselas*," "*Vicor of Wakefield*," "*Paul and Virginia*," "*Exiles of Siberia*," Castle of Ofrante," "Gulliver's Travels," Stern's "Sentimental Journey," "*The Sorrows of Werter*," "Theodosius and Constantia."

304, 305 Hyperion.

306 Jack Downing.

307 Ahasuerus, by Robert Tyler.

308 The Harbinger of 53 poems.

309 Lord Byron's English Bards and Scotch Reviewers.

310 Balfredonia, a mock poem.

311 McCulloch's Researches in America.

312 Sartorius, a Tragedy, by D.P. Brown.

313 Lord Byron's Marino Faliero, Doge of Venice.

314 Ximenes, a poem.

315 Terrible Tractoration, a mock poem.

316 Carlisle's Past and Present.

317 Fairfields Poems.

318 Song Book.

319 ☞ Poems occasioned by Pope's Dunciad, 1732.

320 Sommerville's Poem.

321 James Montgomery's Poems.

322 Midas, or Inquiry into Taste and Genius, curious and beautiful.

323 Lindly Murray's English Grammar.

324 Goldsmith's Poetical Works.

325 Chatterton's Poems.

326 Falconer's shipwreck.

326 ½ Byron's Poems, 2 vols.

327 ☞ Motherwell's Poems, full of genius.

327 ½ Campbell's Poems.

328 Pomret's Poems.

328 ½ Beauties of Shakespeare.

329 Bulwer's Pilgrims of the Rhine.

329 ½ The Wreath.

330 A Song Book.

331 History of the late Revolution in Poland.

323, 333 Athenean Letters, Moore's French Revolution, odd vols.

ADDENDUM TO HISTORY, TRAVELS, &C.

624, 625 ☞ Rapin's History of England, with engravings – *fol.*

626 ☞ Thornton's History of London, *as it was*, with very numerous plates; rare and valuable – *folio.*

627 ☞ Life of Cardinal Wolsey, very authentic and curious, *rare- folio.*

628 ☞ ☞ Memoirs of Count De Gramont, a new translation, with splendid English engravings, bound in yellow morocco-*quarto.*

629, 630 *** Maurice's History of Hindostan, London copy, with numerous splendid engravings.

631, 632 Guthrie's Geography, 2 vols. *quarto.*

No. 3.
RELIGION, MORALS, METAPHYSICS

334 Holy Bible, Scott's family edition, with notes and concordance.

335 Archbishop Tillotson's Works, complete, *folio*.

336 History of American Missions, with engravings.

337 Bacon's Lives of the Apostles, with engravings.

338, 339 Palmer on the Church, a learned work.

340, 341 ☞ Aesop's Fables – a magnificent edition, with several hundred engravings – super royal octavo.

342, 343 Brown's History of the Holy Bible.

344, 345 Magee on Atonement, *a powerful work*.

246 [346?- Ed.], 349 Prideaux's Connexions with maps, 4 vols. complete.

350 Yahn's History of the Hebrew Commonwealth, translated from the German.

351 ☞ Yahn's Introduction to the Old Testament, *very able*.

352 to 355 Hunter's Sacred Biography, complete in 4 vols.

356 ☞ A superb edition of Gesner's Death of Abel, with beautiful engravings.

357, 358 Brown's Dictionary of the Bible.

359 History of the Old and New Testament, by Reeves, *very good*.

360 Burgh's dignity of Human Nature – should be in every library.

361 to 365 ☞ Dr. Constantine Pise's History of the Church, complete in 5 vols.

366, 367 The Christian Observer.

368, 369 ☞ The New Testament in French, a fine copy.

370 Dr. Warburton's Alliance of Church and State, *a famous work*.

371, 372, 373 ☞ Newton on the Prophesies.

374 GROTIUS on the Truth of the Christian Religion.

375 The Book of Common Prayer of P.E. Church.

376 Dr. Smith's Sermons.

377, 378 Dr. Hugh Blair's Sermons.

379 ☞ Dr. Horseley's Tracts, of *great note*.

380, 381 The Theological Repertory.

382 Jones' Lectures on the Interpretation of the Scriptures.

383 ☞ ☞ JEBBS' Sacred Literature, a very powerful and learned work, London copy.

384 Campbell's Lectures on Ecclesiastical History.

385, 386 Cobbett's History of the Protestant Reformation – full of curious knowledge and speculations.

387 Pilgrims Progress, with numerous engravings.

388 Simpson's Plea for Religion, a learned book.

389 Dr. Collyer's Lecture on Scripture Facts.

390 Dr. Chalmer's Discourses on Christianity, in connexion with Modern Astronomy, full of eloquence and genius.

391 McCulloh's Evidences of Christianity.

392 Buck's Theological Dictionary.

393 Skinner's Truth and Order.

394 Verplanck's Evidences of Christianity.

395 The Weekly Monitor.

396 The Homilies of the Church.

397, 398, 399 ☞ Whitefield's Letters, *rare and curious*.

400, 401 Dr. Turnbull's Moral Phylosophy [sic].

402 Dr. Smith's Natural and Revealed Religion.

403 to 406 The Theological Repertory.

407 Faber's Difficulties of Romanism–*multum in parvo.*

408 Churchton's Early English church–*conclusive on the subject.*

409 Dick's Christian Philosopher.

410 Bennett's Letter.

411 Brook's Amaranth, with superb engravings.

412 Live of John Calvin, fine likeness and autograph.

413 William Cobbett's 12 Sermons—*curious and instructive.*

414 Lord Brougham's Natural theology.

415 Bayly's Essay on Inspiration.

416 ☞ Baxter's 40 Popish Frauds, Jesuit Juggling, among the most curious books extant of the 17th century, revived in 1835.

417 The Leibnitzian Papers, or Principles of Natural Philosophy and Religion.

418 Carpenter's Natural History of the Bible, with numerous engravings.

419 ☞ Historical Interval between the Old and the New Testament.

420 Botts' Answer to Dr. Warburton's Divine Legation of Moses.

421 ☞ Swedenborg's Angelic Wisdom, 1764, translated 1840.

422 Griesbach's New Version of the New Testament.

423 Shuttleworth's Consistency of Revelation with self and with Reason.

424 Sumner's Evidences of the Christian Religion—a delightful work.

425, 426 Keith's Signs of the Times, quite new—*a golden book.*

427 Dr. Clark's History of the Manners, &c. of the Ancient Jews.

428 Winchesters Inquiry as to the Worth of the THEATRE.

429, 430 Wilson's Evidences of Christianity—a recent work..

431 ☞ Sleigh's *Defensive* Dictionary of Christian Religion.

432 Keith's Evidences of Christianity.

433 Death-bed Confessions of the Countess of Guernsey.

434 ☞ Schmucker on the Revelation of St. John, 1 vol.—all he wrote—a very interesting work.

435 Paley's Horæ Paulinæ—*moral mathematics*.

436 Burton's Views of Man and Providence !!

437 Rome's Right to Withhold the Scriptures from the Laity.

438 Cooper's Family Sermons, translated into *Spanish*.

439 Burnap's Lectures to Young Men.

440 Horne's Manual for the Afflicted.

441 ☞ Schiller's Æsthenic Letters and Essays.

442 ☞ Cooke's Philosophy of the Immortality of the Soul, *quarto*.

443 ☞ the HERO of Baltazar Gratian—an extremely curious and rare work—*quarto*.

444 Dr. Channing's Controversy with Moses Stuart.

445 Rousseau's Social Contract.

446 Carey's Inquiry as to the African Race.

447 Mon. Dupin's *Trial of Jesus*.

448 Carey's Thoughts on Slavery.

449 Mon. De Condorcet on the Human Mind.

450 Historical Questions on the New Testament.

451 An Inquiry into the Doctrine of *Abolition*.

452 Thoughts on Popery, by the late Dr. Nivins.

453 Letter by the leaned Scotch Blacksmith.

454 Domestic Slavery.

455 Beecher on Intemperance.

455 ½ Historia Sacra.

456 Pulpit Eloquence.

458 Collins' Miscellanies.

459, 460 Walsh's Didactics.

461 Aimè Martin Civilization of Mankind by Women.

462 Paley's Philosophy.

463 Same.

464 ☞ Smith's Theory of Moral Sentiments.

465, 456 [465] Dugald Stewart's Philosophical Works—Playfare Brande's.

467 Whately's Rhetoric.

468, 469 Beattie's Elements of Moral Science.

470 Hedge's Logic.

471 *Same.*

472, 473 Lock on Human Understanding—one missing.

474 Madam Chapone—Gregory's Letters, &c.

475, 476, 477 LACONICS.

478 Key to Knowledge.

No. 4.
POLITICAL ECONOMY, POLITICS, &c.

456 ½ Oxford Theology.

457 Thomas á Kempis, 2d vol.

479 Chalmer's Political Annals—*extremely rare*—quarto.

480 Seybert's American Statistics.

481, 482 Hazzard's State Papers.

483, 484 Sir J. Stuart's Political Economy—*rare*, and among the *earliest* British Works on the subject.

485, 486 Smith's Wealth of Nations.

487, 488 ☞ Malthus on Population.

489 Addition to Malthus.

490 Mills' Elements of political Economy.

491 Raymond's Political Economy.

492 Tracy's Political Economy.

493 Carey on Political Economy.

494 Taylor's French Statistics—in English.

495 Cooper's Political Economy.

496 Ganilh's Political Economy.

497 Blodget's statistical Manuel of the United States.

498 Historical Society of Ohio, its Statistics.

499 Inchequin's Letters.

500 Cardozo's P.E., a fine elementary work.

501 Robt. G. Harper's Works.

502 Webster's Political Essays.

503 British Liberties.

504 Sir Isaac Newton's Tables of Annuties, &c, &c.

505 Joyce's Analysis of Smith's Wealth of Nations.

506 Otis' Letters on the Hartford Convention.

507 Essay on Banking System in Philadelphia.

508 ☞ Young's Political Essays.

509 Present System of Banking Exposed, 1841.

510 Working Man's Companion.

511 Moore's Utopia.

512 ☞ Brown on Equality.

513 ☞ Police of London.

514 Renold's Exploring Expedition in the South Sea.

515 Statistics of British Empire.

516 Essay on Human Rights—a late work.

517 American Democracy, by Fennimore Cooper.

518 Defence of the Whigs.

519 Annals of the Poor.

520 Annals of Quodlibet, a mock-political work, supposed to be by John P. Kennedy.

No. 5.
DICTIONARIES.

521 Ludwig's German and English Dictionary. *Quarto.*

522 Marin's French and Holland Dictionary. *Quarto*—rare.

523 Joubert's French and Latin Dictionary—very rare.

524 Ludwig's Dutch and English Dictionary.

525 Ludwig's English, Dutch, and French Dictionary.

526 Eber's German and English Dictionary.

527 Baily's English Dictionary—*rare and valuable.*

528 Kersey's English Dictionary—*very rare.*

529 Walker's Dictionary.

530 Dufief's English and French Dictionary.

531 ☞ The Theatrical Dictionary.

532 ☞ Hoyle's Musical Dictionary.

533 Lampriere's Classical Dictionary.

534, 535 Odd vol. of Dictionary of Philosophical Opinions.

536 Nugent's French Dictionary.

537   do   do   do

538 Johnson's Miniature Dictionary for Ladies' Easy use!

Hoffman's Library Auction Catalogue

539 Dictionary of *Politicts*—curious.

540 Biographical Dictionary.

541, 542 Cubi's English and Spanish Dictionary.

543 Baltimore Directory.

544, 545 ☞ ☞ Dr. Johnson's *Folio* Dictionary—a great work.

546 to 576 Thirty-one copies of KNODLE's Classifying Word Book, for schools—an *original* work, by a *poor*, self taught Genius, now dead, from poverty and excessive toils!!

577 to 623 ☞ ☞ REE's CYCLOPÆDIA—a magnificent work, substantially bound in calf, with six vols. of Splendid Plates and Maps, —in all 47 vols.

No. 6
THE PHYSICAL SCIENCES

633 Bezout on Fluxions.

634 Legendre's Geometry.

635, 636 Cambridge's Mathematics.

637 Young's Algebra.

638 Lacroix's Algebra.

639 Colburn's Algebra.

620 Walsh's Arithmetic.

641 Ship Master's Assistant.

642 Allen's Mathematics, ☞ also new edition of *Euclid*.

643 Pike's Arithmetic.

644 Mair's Arithmetic.

645 Burn's Anatomy, *with Plates*.

646 ☞ Saissy on the Ear, with *Plates*.

647 Cullen's Materia Medica, two vols in one.

648 Sir Humphrey Davy's Agricultural Chemistry.

649 ☞ Dr. Smith's Philosophical Essays.

649 ½ Treatise on Vaccination, by Samuel Scofield, M.D.

650 Muhlenberg on the Grasses.

651 ☞ Martyn's Botanical Dictionary.

652 ☞ Biglow's Flora Bostoniensis.

653 ☞ Muhlenbert's Catlogus Plantarum Americæ.

654 Dr. Johnson on Climate, and change of Air for Health.

655, 656 Heron's Natural History.

657 ☞ ☞ Lawrence on Man, *with Plates*.

658 Cuvier's Theory of the Earth, *with Plates*.

659 to 663 Dr. Rush's Inquiry, complete in 5 vols.

664, 665 Dr. Mason Good's Book of Nature – a charming work.

666, 667 Larrey's Military Surgery.

668 ☞ ☞ Bigelow's Arts, or Technology, with several hundred engravings.

669 Guthrie's Geography.

670 * * Watson's Chemical Essays.

671 Ewell's Chemistry, with Plates.

672 Dr. Davidge's Nosology.

673 Jameson's Domestic Medicine, for the United States.

674 Medical Jurisprudence, ☞ being four Treatises, with Notes, by Dr. Cooper.

675 Dr. Darwin's Phitologia.

676 Dr. Darwin's Temple of Nature.

677 Richerand's Physiology.

678 ☞ ☞ Smillie's Philosophy—should be in *every* Library.

679 Muhlenberg's *Graminum Discriptio*.

680 Browne's Remarks on Darwin's writings.

681 Rose's Botany, with plates.

682,683 Pulteney's Botany.

684 Select Medical Theses.

685 Combe's Phrenology, *with plates.*

686 Hayden's Geology—a *clever work.*

687 Adam's on the Globes—the best treatise.

688 Parke's Chemical Cathechism. [*These books are generally quite new.*]

689, 690 ☞ ☞ Dr. Barton's Medical Botany, with numerous *colored* plates.

691 * * * Peruvian Botany—many plates—*very rate.*

692 Walker's Lectures on Natural Philosophy, with *admirable* Engravings—large quarto—*very rare.*

692 ½ PARKINSON'S HERBAL, 1640, with some thousand Engravings. Pages 1755, folio—very rare, and learned.

693 Millers Animated Nature, *folio,* 600 pages—many hundred *good* engravings—London, 1785.

694 to 698 CURTIS' FLORA *Londinensis,* in 5 royal folio volumes, well bound—Plates to the life—the greatest of all the Botanical works. This work *limited* as to price, but *extremely low.*

699, 700 ☞ Sandivogius' Alchemy—rare and curious.

701 ☞ Foster's Pocket Encyclopædia, a new work—London copy.

702 Vestiges of Creation—universally known.

703 Colburn's Arithmetic.

704 Bard's Compendium of *Obstetrics.*

705 [Italian Exile in England—out of place here.]

706 Mrs. Marcet's Conversations on Chemistry, Jones' edition.

☞ The best student's book extant on Chemistry.

707 Mrs. Marcet's Conversations on Vegetable Physiology, &c.

708   do   do   on Natural Philosophy, with plates.

709 [Cobbett's Ride in France.]

710 Scott's United States Gazetteer.

711 Mrs. Marcet's Conversations on Natural Philosophy, Jones' Edition.

712 Walker's Geometry.

713 Hutin's Manual of Physiology.

714 ☞ Evidence concerning WITCHES and APPARITIONS—rare.

715 Ferguson's Dialogues on Astronomy.

716 Dr. Gibson on the Bones.

717 Dr. Dunglison on Medical Jurisprudence.

718 Dr. Waterhouse's Botany.

719 Hustis on the Diseases of Louisiana.

720 ☞ Mitchell's First Lines of Science, *with plates.*

721, 722 ☞ Berkenhout's Animals, Vegetables, Fossils &c. of Great Britain—a practical work.

723 Linnæus' Sexual System.

724 Synopsis of American Plants.

725 Adams' Geography.

727 Worcester's Geography.

727 Mrs. Marcet's Conversations on Chemistry.

728 [Bigland's Letters on History.]

729 [Godwin's Enquirer.]

730 Beddoes on Consumption.

731 ☞ Knowledge for the People.

732 *Description of All Trades.*

733 McIntire on the Globes.

734 Agricultural Essays, by *Agricola*.

735 Fenning on the Globes.

736 McIntire on the Globes.

737 Natural History, by Burkhard.

738 Botanical Terminology, by Eberle.

739 Harris' Beauties of Nature.

740 Deppuy's Evening Entertainments.

741 ☞ Dreams and Visions.

742 Secrets of Antimony—an *Alchymical* work.

743 Digby's Peripatetical Institution—an *Astrological* work.

744, 745 ☞ ☞ Joyce's Dialogues on Chemistry.

746 [Murray's Grammar Abridged.]

747 Colburn's Intellectual Arithmetic.

748 Tachygraphy, or Short-Hand explained.

749 Hooper's Medical Dictionary—small copy.

750 Questions on History.

751 Inquiry into Sulphurous Fumigation.

752 ☞ ☞ PINNOCK's Catechism, *thirty numbers*—a work of great celebrity, for Youths.

753 Farmer's Library, now publishing by J. S. Skinner, thirteen numbers.

No. 8
MISCELLANEOUS LITERATURE.

764 to 770 SHAKESPEARE's Plays, with Notes by Dr. Johnson and Mr. Stevens, handsomely bound in 17 vols.—complete.

771 to 778 Dr. Johnson's Works, 8 vols.—some missing—but *Lives of the Poets* complete.

779 to 788 ☞ POPE's Works *complete* in 10 vols.

789 to 798 ☞ DR. BEATTIE's Works, *complete* in 10 vols.

799 to 834 ☞ ☞ A series of Novels, severally translated from English into French, in 36 small volumes—*extremely rare* and valuable for beginners in the language—*Robinson Crusoe, Zeluco, Caleb Williams, Mysteries of Udolpho, Don Quixotte,* &c., &c.

835 to 838 The Connoisseur, complete in 4 vols.

839 to 857 ☞ BRITISH ESSAYISTS, in 21 vols. well bound—the 2d and 19th wanting.

858 to 862 ☞ Goldsmith's WORKS, complete in 5 vols. handsomely bound.

863 SENECA's entire works, translated—a superb folio copy, well bound—very rare—London copy, 1620, cost £5 10 0.

864 DRYDEN Comedies, a beautiful *folio* copy, 1701, *limited.*

865 SPENCER's Works, *folio copy,* with Glossary—original copy.

866 SIDNEY on Government—*folio,* worthy of being well bound.

867 to 888 SCOTT'S NOVELS, complete in 22 vols., in calf, with plates.

889 Bulwer's Rienzi.

890 Gaudentia di Lucca, a novel by Godwin.

891 Nott on Intemperance.

892 Veneroni's Italian Grammar.

892½ Lord on Currency and Banking

893 the National Orator.

893½ Bollman on Banking System.

894 Seven books in a lot.

No. 9.
LATIN AND GREEK CLASSICS.

895 Schrevellii Lexicon.

896 Ovid Delphini.

897 Cæsar Delphini.

898 Cicero Delphini.

899 Butmann's Greek Grammar.

900 Neilson's Greek Exercises.

901 Sallustii Delphini.

902 Zumpt's Latin Grammar. ☞ The most approved.

☞ 903 Horace, in Spanish.

904 Bailey's Edition of Ovid –*perhaps the best.*

905 ☞ Gradus ad Parnassum.

906 ☞ Williston's 6 Books of Tacitus, with English Notes.

907 Longinus on the Sublime—Greek and English.

908 to 912 – Gordon's Works of Tacitus translated. Complete in 5 vols.

913 Burnouf and Damphoux's Greeek Grammar.

914 Wilson's Greek Testament.

915 Damphoux's Greek Courses.

916 Anacreontis Carmina, &c. Greek and Latin of Anacreon; of Suppho, &c.

917 Wilson's Greek Prosody.

918 Latin Grammar.

919 Doering's Latin Reader.

920 Maguire's Latin Grammar – very good –*new.*

921 Mair's Latin Syntax.

922 ☞ Gould's Latin Grammar.

923 * * * The second volume of Cæsar, in Latin and French.

924, 925 Excerpta Auctoribus Classics – new—an excellent selection.

926 Excepta ex Ovidio – *very good*.

927 Latin Vocabulary.

928 Selectæ e Profanis.

929 Latin Grammar, for first use.

930 Clark's Corderius – new.

931 Grotius De Veretate Religionis, with English Notes.

932 Latin Reader.

932½ Varley's Latin Proverbs, &c., translated into English.

933 ☞ Smith's *Hebrew* Grammar – very simple for Students.

934 Stricker's Life and Character of CICERO – original and elegant.

935 to 954 ☞ ☞ The Entire Works of CICERO, complete in 20 vols.

955 ☞ The Fregments of Cicero's Republic, *recently* discovered at Rome—*translated* by Featherstonhaugh.

956 Hutchinson's Moral Philosophy, in Latin.

10.
ITALIAN WORKS

957 to 972 "VITE", &c. VASARI's Lives of all the Painter's Sculptors, and Architects. ☞ The most learned of all the works, complete in 16 vols. well bound in Italy.

973, 974, 975, Lanzi's History of the Fine Arts in Italy, " Storia Pittorica," &c., six vols. bound in three.

976, 977 978 Lanzi's Etruscan Language, &c., &c., complete in three vols., well bound.

979 Catalogue of eminent Works appertaining to Italian Sciences and Arts.

980 Denina's Revolutions in Italy, 5 vols. bound in three.

981 Adventures of Telemachus, in Italian.

☞ All these works are of the first class, scarce here, and are *limited low*.

11.
SPANISH WORKS

982 To 985 Spanish Grammars, by Cubi, the best extant; four copies, three nearly new.

986 ☞ Spanish and German Grammar.

987 ☞ Goss' Spanish Grammar and Exercises.

988 ☞ Cubi's Extracts from Spanish Authors – *new*.

989 ☞ Pizarro's Select Dialogues in Spanish and English.

990 Sales' Spanish Extracts.

991 Sales' Selections from the most distinguished Spanish Plays.

992 [Select Comedies, in *Italian*.]

993 [Goldoni's Italian Plays.]

994 Honair's Works, translated from French into Spanish.

995 Lot of Spanish Books.

12.
GERMAN

995½ Beleke's German Grammar – *new*.

996 Bokum's Introduction to the German Language—*excellent*.

997, 998, 999 ☞ Gedichte von Fred. Schiller, 3 vols., complete.

1000 Lot of German Books, 11 vols.
☞ *See German Dictionaries, &c.*

13.
FRENCH

1001, 1002 Richelet's French Dictionary, 2 vols. Complete.

1003 Noel's French Lessons—*selections excellent.*

1004 ☞ Wanostrocht's French Grammar.

1005 Levizac's French Grammar.

1006 Wanostrocht's French Grammar.

1007 Wailey's Principles of the French Language.

1008 Collection of French Lessons.

1009 Bolmar's French Tables, and Key to the Language.

1010 Corney's French Spelling Book – *very good.*

1011   do   do   do   do

1012 Perin's French Grammar.

1013   do   do   do

1014 Lebrun's edition of Telemachus, in French.

1015 (*Calcott's Musical Grammar,* ☞ 3rd edition, *London* – out of place here. *Admirable work.*)

1016 Perin's French Tables.

1017 Bolmar's Colloquial French Phrases.

1018 to 1024 ☞ The Entire Works of ST. Evermond, complete in 7 volumes—extremely rare, and admirable.

1025 to 1030 ☞ New Dictionary of Medicine and Surgery, by a Society of Learned Men, complete in 6 vols.

1031 to 1035 Course of Surgery, adapted to the School of medicine in Paris, by Mons. Vellars, in six volumes, one missing.

Hoffman's Library Auction Catalogue 483

1036 The Art of Dying Wool, &c., by Mons. Wellot, in French.

1037 ☞ Translation of the Works of Horace into French, with the Latin—*rare and curious*.

1038 Vattel's Law of nations, in French.

1039 History of Cardinal Alberoni – *scarce*.

1040 A Treatise on Fortifications, in French.

1041, 1042, 1043 ☞ Hume's England, 4th, 5th, and 6th, vols., in French.

1044 Father Paul Sarpi's Rights of Sovereigns against the Popish Interdicts, &c., in French.

1045, 1046 Mons. Lemoine's *Precis de la Matier Medicale*, 2 vols.

1047, 1048 Cours de Morale, fondee sur le nature, de L'Homme.

1049 ☞ French Plays, translated from the Italian of Senor Manzoni.

1050, 1051 Letters on Agiculture, by a Cultivator, in French.

1052 Dictonary of French Proverbs, explained in Dutch.

1053 ☞ ☞ The Will of Jerome Sharp, a remarkable and curious work – *rare, and well bound*.

1054 ☞ CODICIL to the same, both in French.

1055, 1056 Mons. Dellon's History of Peter the Cruel, in French.

1057 to 1060 Abbé Raynal's Philosophical and Political History of the two Indies, in French.

1061, 1062 St Pier's Studies of Nature, in French, 3d and 4th vols.

1063 ☞ The Lighter Works of the Philosopher of *San Souci*.

1063½ Volaire's Charles XII. of Sweden in French.

1064 Beaunarou.

1065 The French Post Travelling. *"Levre de Poste."*

1066 ☞ Mons. Le Roy's Natural Philosophy in French, with numerous Plates—very rare and curious in the *ancient* physics.

1069 to 1074 *Seven Lots* of French Books.

1075 Lindley Murray's English Grammar.

1076 Poranesi's Italian and English Grammar.

14.
REVIEWS, BRITISH & AMERICAN – Bound

1077 to 1096 Twenty vols. ☞ The English Monthly Review, from 1783 – *scarce and valuable*.

1097 to 1100 The Portico.

1101, 1102, 1103 The Polyanthos.

1104, 1105 The Monthly Magazine.

1106 to 1136 ☞ THE NORTH AMERICAN REVIEW, in 31 vols. well bound.

1137 to 1141 5 vols., *Duplicates*.

☞ See continuation of North American Review, in Nos. 1038, 1039, and 1040—*not bound*.

1142 INDEX to North American Review.

1143 to 1150 American Quarterly, in 8 vols., *well bound*.

1151, 1152 Walsh's American Register.

1153 to 1160 Select Reviews, from *British*, in 8 vols.

1161 to 1165 The American Quarterly, in 5 vols., bound.

1166 to 1167 The Mirror of Taste.

1168 to 1190 Port *Folio*, bound, in 23 vols.

1191 to 1200 ☞ The RETROSPECTIVE REVIEW – very rare and valuable – *limited*—out of print, 10 vols., well bound.

☞ The most learned of all the Reviews.

1201, 1202 The Monthly Anthology.

1203 Analectic Magazine.

1204 Lot of 3 vols.

1205 The Companion.

15.
REVIEWS – Not Bound.

☞ See, also, 1038, 1039, 1040, in a previous division.

1206 The Magnolia.

1207 The Southern Literary Messenger.

1208 Southern Quarterly Review.

1209 The Southern Literary Messenger.

1210 American Quarterly Review, June and September, 1836.

1211 Southern Literary Messenger.

1212 ☞ The American Quarterly Review.

1213 National Industrial Magazine.

1214 American Quarterly Review.

1215 Southern Literary Messenger.

1216 American Themis.

1217 ☞ Edinburg, Westminster, &c., Reviews.

1218 Lorente's Inquisition.

1219 Lot of Novels.

1220 Lot of Select Lives, &c.

1221 Lot of Maps.

1222 Engravings, &c.

1223 ☞ Sixty-three Engravings.

1224 ☞ Fourteen Engravings.

16.
FASHIONABLE MUSIC.

1225 Bollman's Practical Guide to a *Thorough Bass*.

1226 Gilles' Vocal Instructor. An eminent Artist of the Italian Opera.

1227 Labitzky's celebrated Waltzes and Gallopades.

1228 Lemoine's Quadrilles, Gallopades, and Waltzes.

1229 Bolero from *Le Domino Noir*.

1230 Labarre's *Das Redoubl*e.

1231 Kalkbrenner's Theme Favori, from *Norma*, de Bellini.

1232 Rondos, by *Henry Hertz*, for the Piano.

1233 Gallopade from the Opera of Les Diamans, &c.

1234 Music by Jean Strauss.

1235 ☞ King's Illustrations of Fashionable Furniture. London, 1846, thirty-four Plates, colored.

NOTE.

☞ During the progress of the sale of Mr. Hoffman's Law Library, his own legal and literary works will be offered; and those not at *that time* sold, will be continued during the progress of the sale of his *Miscellaneous Library*. The Catalogue of these is as follows:

716 Copies, in sheets, of Hoffman's *Course of Legal Study*," in 2 vols; may be bound in one, continuously, pp. 880. Original selling price, $8.00.

150 Copies ditto, bound in calf and in sheep.

50 Copies of Hoffman's Legal Outlines," complete in one vol.

276 Copies, *bound,* of Hoffman's "*Miscellaneous thoughts on Men, Manners, and Things,*" by Anthony Grumbler, of Grumbleton Hall, Esq.

275 Copies ditto, *in sheets*.

475 Copies of Hoffman's "Viator, or Peep into My Note Book," in sheets.

100 Copies ditto, *bound*.

100 Copies of Hoffman's Introductory Lectures, and of the Syllabus of his entire Course of Lectures, in pamphlet binding, making a volume of about 200 pages.

☞Booksellers are referred to the American, British, French and German Reviews, for extremely favorable notices of these works, some of which are printed at the end of the bound volumes.

www.ingramcontent.com/pod-product-compliance
Lightning Source LLC
Chambersburg PA
CBHW022006300426
44117CB00005B/53